THE CATHOLIC MOVEMENT
in the AMERICAN EPISCOPAL CHURCH

THE CATHOLIC MOVEMENT
in the AMERICAN EPISCOPAL CHURCH

By GEORGE E. DeMILLE, M.A.

PUBLISHERS
Eugene, Oregon

Wipf and Stock Publishers
199 W 8th Ave, Suite 3
Eugene, OR 97401

The Catholic Movement in the American Episcopal Church
By DeMille, George E. and Henery, Charles R.
Copyright © 1950 The Historical Society of the Episcopal Church All rights reserved.
Softcover ISBN-13: 978-1-55635-152-5
eBook ISBN-13: 978-1-7252-1822-2
Publication date 12/26/2006
Previously published by The Church Historical Society, 1950

This edition is a scanned facsimile of the original edition published in 1950.

To Dorothy and the Curates,
Charles, Mac, George,
Jimmie, Dudley, Frank and Ed

PREFACE

The catholic revival in Anglicanism of the nineteenth century often is told as an English story. In fact, the revival owed no little inspiration to the American Episcopal Church across the Atlantic. This was acknowledged by John W. Burgon, the dean of Chichester Cathedral, in his *Lives of Twelve Good Men*, published in 1888. The American Church, he said, had distinguished itself "in preparing the way." In particular, Burgon paid tribute to illustrious bishops like John Henry Hobart of New York, George Washington Doane of New Jersey, and William Rollinson Whittingham of Maryland, observing that "there were in truth many others" this side of the ocean who had borne courageous and steadfast witness to the catholic life of the church.

This American contribution rightly received attention during the centenary of the Oxford Movement in 1933. Most notably, C. P. S. Clarke, canon of Salisbury Cathedral, pointed to the prior and parallel movement of catholic revival in the American Church. In two works, *Bishop Hobart and the Oxford Movement* and *The Oxford Movement and After*, Clarke put forward the claim that Hobart was the forerunner and likely inspirer of the Oxford Movement in England. He made bold to suggest that, in his own use of tracts to teach true church sentiments, the New York prelate prompted the Tractarians to do the same, and that even the emotional fervor of John Henry Newman's preaching may have been modeled after that of Hobart whose famed motto was "Evangelical Truth and Apostolic Order." Clarke also recognized the role of the American Charles Chapman Grafton in the later founding of the religious Society of St. John the Evangelist, a missionary brotherhood in Cowley, England.

The stream of literature related to the anniversary celebration of the Oxford Movement also included a most important volume entitled *Northern Catholicism: Centenary Studies in the Oxford and Parallel Movements,* edited by N. P. Williams of Oxford University and Charles Harris of Hereford Cathedral. The title of the book stemmed from the thesis that there was a northern type of catholicism, neither

Latin nor Byzantine, but clearly western in temper and outlook. This collection of essays primarily centered on British interests, but examined as well other catholic traditions and high church movements in non-papal Christian bodies. Of significance was the admission of an essay by Edward Rochie Hardy, Jr., a tutor and fellow of the General Theological Seminary in New York City, on "The Catholic Revival in the American Church, 1722–1933." It was the first serious summary of the influence of pre-Tractarian high churchmanship in American Episcopalianism, and the subsequent, advanced course of catholic developments in the church.

Then, in 1941, there appeared *The Catholic Movement in the American Episcopal Church* by George E. DeMille. This study had been initiated on the eve of the Oxford Movement commemoration, and its final publication was acclaimed as a landmark in Episcopal Church historiography. The book represented a turning point from an era of general church histories to the stage when monographs on special themes and periods could be anticipated. It not only dealt impressively with a subject long deserving treatment, making use of wide-ranging sources, but it also commended other promising avenues of historical inquiry.

In his account, DeMille detailed the rise of catholic theology and practice from native high church origins, mainly in Connecticut, through the sway of Hobart and his disciples before the advent of the *Tracts for the Times* in America. He illuminated the close connection between high church and evangelical elements in these early years, providing a reminder that the chronicle of one is not unrelated to that of the other. The narrative proceeded to consider how the *Tracts* affected the older high church movement in the American Church, the force they exerted on a younger generation drawn increasingly to ceremonial embellishment, and the conflict this ignited. The last third of the book concentrated on selected episodes in the catholic revival, with informative chapters on topics such as the establishment of religious orders and events in the upper Midwest, a region that came to be dubbed the "biretta belt."

In 1950 a revised and expanded edition of *The Catholic Movement* was brought out due to popular demand. The second edition revealed the author's diligence in taking excellent advantage of recent scholarship in Episcopal Church studies, as well as the documentary material that had emerged in the intervening years, to supplement his earlier exposition. The edition also included a necessary chapter on "Liberal Catholicism" that surveyed the theological endeavor beginning at the end of the nineteenth century to articulate and testify to a progressive Anglo-Catholicism that was both true to tradition and sensitive to modern scientific knowledge and social concerns.

The story told by DeMille is many-sided, full of interest and full, too, of instruction. The prose is lively, vigorous, and lucid. The author demonstrates uncommon deftness in rendering incisive and penetrating character and personality sketches throughout the book. Brief pen-portraits of leaders in the movement are especially rewarding and bring to life many worthy of remembrance. While in entire sympathy with the catholic revival in the American Church, the author is not reluctant to critique sharply his estimation of its weaknesses and excesses.

George Edmed DeMille was born in 1898, in Green Island, New York, and entered upon a career as an educator before seeking holy orders in 1936. He served as a priest in various parochial cures in his beloved diocese of Albany, which comes under review in the epilogue, and was for a time director of diocesan theological education. In the best Anglican tradition, he combined a devoted pastoral ministry with active scholarly pursuit. A prolific writer, he gave new impetus to the enterprise of diocesan and parish histories and raised the norm in this field to a high level. In 1961, he was awarded an honorary Doctorate in Sacred Theology by the General Theological Seminary for his scholarship and dedication in presenting the history of the Episcopal Church to a broad public. In retirement he assisted at the Cathedral of All Saints in Albany, where he had been named a canon in 1951, and he could be found in daily research at the nearby New York State Library, taking delight in the free moment to lending a hand in shelving books and in mining the collection. George DeMille remained the faithful priest, scholar, and teacher until his death in 1983, and there are still many who remember him as a mentor, among them the present writer who is privileged to own his doctoral academic hood.

This reissue of the second edition of *The Catholic Movement in the American Episcopal Church* is very welcome. For more than a half century it has been the standard work on the subject; now it is accessible to a new audience. The general reader will find it an invaluable introduction to the history of a movement that so indelibly influenced the life and thought of the Episcopal Church in America and even of the Anglican Communion. The student of history will find it an essential resource that should not fail to provoke further discussion and study. This classic can be read by all for pleasure and profit.

—Charles R. Henery
Feast of the Transfiguration, 2006

PREFACE TO THE SECOND EDITION

A WORD about the origin of this book may be of some interest to its readers. In 1932, I was a layman of the Church, with a long-standing interest in Church history. As the centenary of the Oxford Movement approached, I noted that while the history of the movement in England had been told and retold, there was no corresponding account of the American developments of Tractarianism. With more courage than discretion, I set out to supply this want. By 1933, I had surveyed the field, and produced an amorphous something that was neither article, pamphlet, nor book. Meanwhile, the same thought had occurred to better scholars than I, and, in the same year, *Northern Catholicism* was published, containing an excellent summary by Dr. Hardy of the movement in America. In 1936, being then a special student at the General Theological Seminary, I had the opportunity of reworking my material under the expert guidance of Dr. Manross.

By 1941, I was ready for publication. But to find a publisher for a work of this sort, with its tenuous prospects of sale, was not easy. Eventually, the Church Historical Society ventured. The result was a pleasant surprise for both author and publisher. The book, in spite of manifest imperfections, was well received and widely reviewed. Above all, it sold. And still more surprising, the sale has continued steadily, until the first edition is exhausted.

Meanwhile, many things have happened. I have continued to explore the field, with considerable results. I have been flooded with letters containing valuable criticism and much additional information. The publication, in 1946, of Dr. Chorley's *Men and Movements in the American Episcopal Church,* has made available a quantity of new matter. Because of all these developments, and because there still seems to be a demand for the work, author and publisher again make their bow to a long-suffering public.

G. E. DeM.

Ascension Day
May 26, 1949

TABLE OF CONTENTS

	PAGE
TITLE PAGE	iii
DEDICATION	v
PREFACE	vi

CHAPTER

I.	A Church in Ruins	1
II.	Pre-Tractarian High Churchmen	9
III.	The Impact of the Tracts	40
IV.	The Beginnings of Ritualism	74
V.	The Fifties—the Storm Subsides	88
VI.	The Second Ritualistic War	108
VII.	The Coming of the Monks	133
VIII.	The Movement in the Mid-West	149
IX.	The McGarvey Secession	163
X.	Liberal Catholicism	171
XI.	The Movement and Prayer Book Revision	191

EPILOGUE: A MODERN AMERICAN DIOCESE	205
CONSOLIDATED BIBLIOGRAPHY	208
GENERAL INDEX	215

CHAPTER ONE

A CHURCH IN RUINS

THE High Church or Catholic movement in the American Episcopal Church, like any other great historic change, can be understood and appreciated only after a survey of the background from which it emerges. In a sense, one cannot properly speak of the Episcopal Church in America before the Revolutionary War. There was no Episcopal Church, but rather a number of scattered Episcopalian congregations, tied together in the loosest possible way by the common and extremely nominal oversight of the bishop of London, and the rather more effective aid and supervision of the Society for the Propagation of the Gospel.[1] With the coming of independence the jurisdiction of the bishop of London was abolished; the S. P. G. withdrew its support; and the fragments were left without a semblance of common organization.

IN VIRGINIA AND THE MIDDLE COLONIES

The history of the Church had been strikingly different in each colony. Virginia, its original home in America, was the colony in which the Anglican Church first began the solution of the problems of extension into a new land and development under the hard conditions of frontier life. The colony was profoundly loyal to king and Church during most of the colonial period. The Anglican Church, by the charter under which the colony was settled, became its established religion, and the colonial legislature acted for the steady extension and establishment of new parishes as population increased. The mild-

[1] Hereinafter called the S.P.G. or the Society.

ness of the laws permitted dissenting denominations to establish and support their own congregations and forms of worship without molestation as long as they obeyed the civil law, but until the Revolution the mother Church held the allegiance of the great majority of the people of the colony. It reached into every community and was given the responsibility for all care of poor and needy people, and, in the lack of a general colonial system of education, the Church, through endowments, through the schools taught by many clergymen, and through its college, was the most wide-spread influence for culture and education in the life of the colony.

By the time of the Revolution the Church had become a native institution, the majority of its clergy being American born. All the great leaders of Virginia's life during the conflict were laymen of the Church, and her clergy, with the exception of a comparatively few Tories, were loyal to the American cause, and rendered large service as members of the county committees of safety, as chaplains and surgeons in the Continental army, and, indeed, in several cases as officers of the line.

But the very fact of establishment became a source of weakness. The civil government legislated for the Church and supported it by taxation; consequently, the Church failed to develop its own leaders and to train its people to give for its support. At the beginning of the Revolution it was generally thought, by both churchmen[2] and dissenters, that the time had come to remove all taxes for church support and to abolish all restrictions which bore upon any body of Christians or any form of religion. This was accomplished completely during the period from 1776 to 1784, and in December, 1784, the Church was formally disestablished and released from every connection with the state. The diocese of Virginia was organized in May, 1785.

Although all religious bodies stood upon an equality of privilege after the disestablishment of the Church in 1784, a movement was now started for the seizure of all property owned by the old mother

---

[2] Throughout this book, the term "churchman" is used in its historic sense, namely, a member of the Church of England or of the Episcopal Church in America.

A CHURCH IN RUINS

Church which had been purchased by tax money, although the state had formally guaranteed to it the quiet possession of all property acquired when it was the Established Church. This movement was started and led by the Baptists, who had come into prominence in Virginia just before the Revolution by their unwillingness to conform to the civil laws. Offering in their form of worship an emotional appeal all too lacking in the rather cold Episcopal Church of that day, they had increased rapidly in numbers, and even after the disestablishment of the Church and the removal of all religious restrictions, they continued their attacks upon the Church with increasing animosity. Their allies in these attacks, strangely enough, were the deists, made strong by the growing disregard for religion which characterized the end of the eighteenth century, and also by the Francophile sentiment which was sweeping the country.

In 1802 a bill was passed by the Virginia state legislature under which the Church lost, not only all property—church buildings excepted—which had originally been purchased with tax-money, but also all its endowments used in the care of the poor and for educational purposes. This blow completed the paralysis of the Church in Virginia. Three-fourths of the parishes were abandoned. Many buildings were torn down or seized by other religious bodies, communion vessels and fonts were desecrated or stolen, records destroyed. In 1812 only thirteen priests from the whole state could be found to meet in convention, and they adjourned with no expectation of ever meeting again. The account given by William Meade, future bishop of the diocese, of his own ordination, serves to illustrate clearly the condition of the Church in Virginia in 1811:

> On arriving at the Church, we found it in a wretched condition, with broken windows and a gloomy, comfortless aspect. The congregation which assembled, consisted of two ladies and about fifteen gentlemen, nearly all of whom were relatives and acquaintances. The morning service being over, the ordination and communion were administered, and then I was put into the pulpit to preach—there being no ordination sermon.

THE CATHOLIC MOVEMENT IN THE EPISCOPAL CHURCH

In the Middle Colonies the condition of the Church was hardly better. During the eighteenth century she had won many converts from the Quakers in Pennsylvania, the Swedes in Delaware, and the Dutch in New York. But at the outbreak of the war the majority of the clergy—with a few conspicuous exceptions—and many of the most influential laity had clung to the mother country, with the result that the Church, thus tainted with Toryism, became odious to the majority of the people. The records of the day abound with melancholy tales of churches closed and priests mobbed, banished, imprisoned. Later the exile of thousands of Tories stripped from the Church many of her strongest supporters. Everywhere was desolation.[3]

IN NEW ENGLAND

The most hopeful corner of the Church was, strangely enough, in that group of colonies where she had been most proscribed and persecuted. Not until 1685 had the worship of the Church been allowed to exist in New England, and then she came in only under the enforced toleration compelled by the royal authority. But once tolerated she began to grow with surprising rapidity. One of the most striking events in the history of the American Church was the conversion in 1722 of President Cutler of Yale and six of his faculty, three of whom became priests of the Episcopal Church. Up to the beginning of the Revolution there was throughout New England a steady stream of converts from Congregationalism; between 1722 and 1775, nineteen of the Episcopal clergy listed in Sprague's *Annals of the American Pulpit* had come from the Congregational body.

[3] Here is Bishop White's testimony, delivered in a charge to his clergy in 1832:

The congregations of our communion throughout the United States were approaching annihilation. Although within this city [Philadelphia] three Episcopal clergymen were resident and officiating, the churches over the rest of the state had become deprived of their clergy during the war, either by death or by departure for England. In the Eastern States, with two or three exceptions, there was a cessation of the exercises of the pulpit, owing to the necessary disuse of the prayers for the former civil rulers. In Maryland and Virginia, where the Church had enjoyed civil establishments, on the ceasing of these, the incumbents of the parishes, almost without exception, ceased to officiate. Farther south the condition of the Church was not better, to say the least.

A CHURCH IN RUINS

In general these converts and their descendants were the strongest churchmen in America. They had read themselves into the Church, coming over in the face of popular odium, accepting often the loss of position as the reward of their faith. They were churchmen, not from habit, but from conviction. Most of them were led to make the change by their historical studies, which had convinced them that Catholicism was essential to Christianity, and that the Church of England was Catholic. They were thus bound to emphasize the peculiar claims of the Church as against the Protestant sects. Indeed, the very fact that they were members of a minority church, living in a society predominantly made up of dissenters, tended to force them into a strong High Church position. They, likewise, had been scattered by the Revolution, but as soon as political circumstances allowed, they were ready to resume their work of propaganda.

The influence of these "Connecticut Churchmen" was by no means confined to Connecticut. Immediately after the Revolution, there was a considerable immigration from Connecticut into New York, flooding Washington County and the "Indian Territory" of central New York. Wherever these immigrants went, they took the Church with them. The result was an astounding growth of the Episcopal Church in New York State between 1790 and 1810—the very period misnamed by Tiffany "the period of suspended animation."[4]

WEAKENED INTERNAL CONDITION

But the external ruin of the Church was less dangerous than her weakened internal condition. In Connecticut and those nearby regions where the influence of the Connecticut converts was strong, churchmen were churchmen indeed. But elsewhere the eighteenth century had done its work only too well. It is a commonplace of history that throughout that century the dogmatic certainty which is the backbone of vital religion was everywhere being gradually weakened. In England Deism was rampant. On the continent of Europe, Voltaire and

[4]DeMille, *History of the Diocese of Albany*, Chapter 2.

the Encyclopedists were the leading intellectual influence. In New England, Congregationalism was fading into the vague religiosity of Unitarianism. And so likewise with the Episcopal Church. Aside from the small band of converts and sons of converts, there seem to have been few churchmen in the whole country with any firm hold on the faith.

There can be no clearer evidence of the doctrinal laxity of the majority of American churchmen at this time than the notorious "Proposed Book" of Common Prayer, accepted by the Philadelphia Convention of 1785. An examination of this strange document reveals an astounding state of mind in the American Church as represented in that convention. From the Book of Common Prayer the Athanasian and Nicene Creeds were torn; the "descent into hell" was extracted from the Apostles' Creed; the use of the Gloria Patri was reduced to a minimum; and a large number of minor changes were made, with the obvious intention of weakening or destroying the Catholic doctrines of baptismal regeneration, priestly absolution, the validity of prayers for the dead, and the Trinity.

This doctrinal vagueness, to call it by the most charitable name, had its natural reflection in the life and worship of the Church. Externally, except for a few Virginian churches erected in the seventeenth century, Episcopal churches were indistinguishable from Congregational meeting-houses. The greater part were white-washed structures of wood. The best, such as Christ Church, Philadelphia, and St. Paul's Chapel, New York, were modified Roman temples in the manner of Wren. Like the churches was the worship carried on within. Chancels were in the main mere alcoves, the central place taken by a massive pulpit, behind which stood the plain wooden table where the Lord's Supper was administered, perhaps once every three months, by a priest who frequently failed to wear even a surplice. Naturally, this infrequent and perfunctory rite was largely disregarded even by people who considered themselves good Episcopalians. Thus, at St. Peter's, Westchester, New York, under the rectorate of Samuel Seabury, who of all pre-Revolutionary churchmen was most likely to teach the Catholic faith and Catholic practice, of two hundred-odd parishioners, only twenty-two were communicants.

After one hundred and fifty years of baffled striving, the American Church at last, in 1784, secured the episcopate. But even this was no unmixed blessing. Of the first four American bishops, two were distinct liabilities. Bishop James Madison (1749-1812), of Virginia, was "an elegant scholar, a good president of a college, and a mild and courteous gentleman," who made one visitation of his diocese, and after that occupied himself entirely with the government of his college. He was popularly charged with being a deist, and while this charge was vigorously repudiated by his friends, the very fact that it could be made seems significant. Bishop Samuel Provoost (1742-1815), of New York, was even worse. He was elected, as far as one can determine, solely because of his politics; he was the only priest of the Episcopal Church in New York City to support the Revolution. Why he accepted the office one wonders; he plainly said that he did not expect the Church in America to survive his generation; and his acts were governed by this opinion. In 1801, after having done his best to cause a schism by refusing to accept the consecration of Bishop Seabury, whom he hated with a rancorous bitterness, he resigned his episcopate, and gave his time to translating Tasso and studying botany. In his retirement he appears to have almost ceased the public practice of his religion. Then, in 1811, like an apparition from the grave, he appeared in public, and announced his intention of resuming his episcopal office. But this move, which was merely an attempt to block the consecration of Hobart, came to nothing.

This, then, was the American Church at the end of the century: barely tolerated in some sections, and distrusted as half-disloyal in all; despoiled of its endowments, with its churches in ruins and its clergy scattered; weakened within by clerical slackness and scarcely veiled Unitarianism; its teaching watery, its rites slovenly, its sacraments almost disused. Within such a body was born the High Church movement.

BIBLIOGRAPHY

Since this chapter is merely introductory, I have not thought it necessary to give references. The following general works I have used for this and all succeeding chapters:

CHORLEY, E. C., *Men and Movements in the American Episcopal Church* (New York, 1946). [Impartial and thoroughly documented. An invaluable companion to Manross.]

MCCONNELL, S. D., *History of the American Episcopal Church* (New York, 1891).

MANROSS, W. W., *History of the American Episcopal Church* (New York, 1935). [Based on sound and original research.]

PERRY, W. S., *History of the American Episcopal Church* (2 vols., Boston, 1885).

WILLIAMS, N. P., editor, *Northern Catholicism* (London and New York, 1933). [Contains an excellent chapter by Dr. E. R. Hardy, Jr., summarizing the history of the movement in America.]

The *Journals of the General Convention* for all the years mentioned in the text.

CHAPTER TWO

PRE-TRACTARIAN HIGH CHURCHMEN

BY THE providence of God, the stream of Catholic teaching and Catholic practice never entirely dried up in the Anglican Church. A broad and full current in the Caroline divines, it had shrunk in the mid-eighteenth century to a mere trickle, found mainly among the nonjurors and the persecuted Scottish Church. But even during that arid era, there are indications of its presence in the colonial Church.

COLONIAL LEADERS

The Rev. John Talbot (1645-1727), the "apostle of New Jersey," has some claims to be called the first of American High Churchmen. His zeal for the establishment of the episcopate in America may be an indication of his views; the fact that he clearly enunciates the dictum, "no bishop, no church," plainly is. It was under his direction that on the feast of the Annunciation, March 25, 1703, the foundation-stone of the church in Burlington was laid. It was certainly appropriate, and it may be significant, that the church was named St. Mary's. Here Talbot ministered faithfully for over twenty years. The nature of his ministry is clearly shown by his report to the S.P.G. in 1724:

> I preach once on Sunday morn & Catechize or homilize in the afternoon, I read the prayers of the Church in the Church decently according to the order of Morning and Evening prayer daily throughout the year & that is more than is done in any Church that I know apud Americanos. . . . I have comonly the

Sacramt administered once a Month & at the great feasts two or 3 daies together.[1]

A priest who recognized the obligation of the daily offices and the value of frequent communion was indeed a *rara avis* in 1724.

The evidence for a distinct High Church position is even clearer when we come to Samuel Johnson (1696-1772), one of the Connecticut converts, first president of King's College, now Columbia University, and the "Father of Episcopacy in Connecticut." According to Dr. Chorley, "his theology was that of the Caroline divines; a staunch defender of the three orders in the ministry; of episcopacy; of the authority of the Church in matters of faith, and one who anticipated the Eucharistic teaching of Seabury by several decades."[2] In one of his sermons we find these clear-cut and striking statements:

> By dwelling in the tabernacle of his body he hath united himself to us, and dwelleth in all mankind, especially in all the faithful who are made members of his body by Baptism and partakers of his blessed Body and Blood in the Holy Eucharist.
>
> As he offered himself a sacrifice and intercedes for us in virtue of it, so he hath ordered a constant commemoration of it to be offered by his ministers and received by his people, in the sacramental bread and wine as symbols of his body and blood, so that the transaction may be represented on earth, while it is performed in heaven.[3]

A direct line leads from Johnson to the High Churchmen of the present day. Johnson's biography was written by the Rev. Thomas Bradbury Chandler (1726-1790), of New Jersey, whose own position is shown by a letter written by him in 1785 to Johnson's son. He comments that the *Journal* of the Virginia diocesan convention is

> a curiosity indeed for it exhibits such a motley mixture of Episcopacy, Presbytery, and Ecclesiastical Republicanism as be-

---

[1] Pennington, *John Talbot*, p. 158.
[2] Chorley, *Men and Movements*, p. 136.
[3] *Ibid*, p. 176.

fore was never brought together and incorporated, and must surprise the whole Christian world. . . . The proceedings of the Convention in Philadelphia, which is to be considered as a kind of Oecumenical Council, were in much the same style, though not so wild and intemperate.[4]

Chandler died before the biography was completed, and it fell to his son-in-law, John Henry Hobart, to see the volume through the press. There can be little doubt that this book was one of the formative influences on the thought of young Hobart, and Hobart has influenced the thought of every American High Churchman since his day.

A careful student of this period finds High Church views cropping up in the most unexpected places. In 1770, the Rev. John Stuart, a convert from Presbyterianism, became missionary to the Mohawk Indians in the province of New York. Driven out with his people during the Revolution, he led them into Canada, where he became the founder of the Anglican Church in Ontario. After the Revolution, William White, not yet a bishop, sent to Stuart a copy of his pamphlet suggesting that in default of bishops, the American Church should elect a convention with power to confer orders. Stuart replied: "I am still clogged with all my old prejudices in regard to the Divine Right and uninterrupted Succession of Episcopacy."[5]

THE FIRST AMERICAN BISHOP

It was the great good fortune of the Episcopal Church in the United States that her first bishop was a man of strong Catholic principles. Samuel Seabury (1729-1796) came from that section of the American Church where such tendencies were most likely to develop. His father was one of the "Connecticut converts," and they were, of all American churchmen, the strongest in dogmatic position and in active churchmanship. This tendency in Seabury was undoubtedly

[4] Beardsley, *Life of Johnson*, p. 370.
[5] G. E. DeMille, *History of the Diocese of Albany*, p. 9.

strengthened by his early visit to Scotland, where he came in contact with the nonjuring Scottish Church—the branch of the Anglican Communion then most conscious of its Catholic lineage. During the war he was one of the most unpopular of all the unpopular Anglican priests because of his active and vigorous advocacy of the loyalist cause. In no other state could such a man, with such a record, have been elected bishop. But the Connecticut clergy evidently considered sound churchmanship of more importance in a bishop than popular political views. Their position is well indicated by the letter written by the Rev. Abraham Jarvis, in the name of the clergy assembled at Woodbury for the election, to the Rev. William White—later Seabury's colleague in the episcopate. In this letter Jarvis dissents strongly from White's opinion, expressed in a pamphlet he had recently published, that Presbyterian ordination was admissible where Episcopal ordination could not be had, and states that "our Church has ever believed bishops to have the sole right of ordination and government, and that this regimen was appointed of Christ himself."[6]

Seabury's influence on the future of the American Church was profound and healthful. As strong in his religious as in his political convictions, he insisted that certain fundamental principles be observed in the organization of the new branch of the Church. It was his firm belief that "the government, sacraments, faith, and doctrines of the Church are fixed and settled."[7] He demanded that, since the government of the Church was divinely committed to her bishops, they must not become, as many churchmen wished, mere agents of the congregations, or honorary figureheads. Thus it was due to his insistence that the bishops were made a separate house in General Convention and given the right of veto.[8] He sharply asserted the Catholicity of the Episcopal Church, and waged unceasing war against

[6]Beardsley, E. E., *Life and Correspondence of the Right Reverend Samuel Seabury, D.D.*, p. 101.
[7]*Ibid.*, p. 274.
[8]*Ibid.*, p. 236.

schismatics from Whitefield on. His sacramental views were remarkable for a priest brought up in the deistical eighteenth century. In his first charge to the clergy of his diocese, he states clearly the sacramental nature of Confirmation, which he held to imply "the actual communication of the Holy Spirit to those who worthily receive it."[9] Unlike his brother bishops, who were little disposed to bother about the lesser sacraments, Seabury was indefatigable in his administration of Confirmation. His last charge, a truly Catholic document in its entirety, is an equally clear statement of his position with regard to Baptism and the Holy Communion, so pronounced in its language as to be worth quoting:

> Some writers on this subject under the idea of making it plain to ordinary capacities, have I fear banished from it all *spiritual meaning*—making it a mere empty remembrance of Christ's death ... We have therefore a right to believe and say that in the Holy Communion, the faithful receiver does, in a mystical and spiritual manner, eat and drink the Body and Blood of Christ.[10]

In the same charge Seabury refers to the Eucharist as a "true and proper sacrifice," speaks of the necessity of supporting the Holy Catholic faith (these are his exact words), attacks the exclusion from Baptism of the idea of regeneration, and exhorts his priests to "hold fast, and contend earnestly for, the faith as it was once delivered to the saints."[11] This is the very language of the *Tracts for the Times,* and this was spoken in 1796.

It is worth noting that he occasionally wore the mitre—probably the only bishop in the Anglican Church to do so at the time.[12] This is perhaps a trifle, but a significant trifle. Of the utmost importance, however, was his successful struggle for the incorporation in the new American Prayer Book of the canon of the Eucharist which he had

[9]*Ibid.,* p. 221.
[10]*Ibid.,* pp. 278-80.
[11]*Ibid.,* p. 282.
[12]Seabury, W. J., *Memoir of Bishop Seabury,* p. 362.

obtained from Scotland, and which, through the English nonjurors, was derived from the first Prayer Book of Edward VI, and the Eastern liturgies. Thus the attempt at revision of the Prayer Book, which so nearly resulted in the semi-Arian "Proposed Book," ended by giving to the Church a Book of Comomn Prayer decidedly more complete and Catholic in its canon than the English Book. This achievement of Seabury's practically committed the American Church from the beginning to a strongly Catholic teaching in regard to the sacrament of the altar. It is clear, then, that before 1800 the first American bishop had taken up a definitely High Church position, and was teaching, with all the authority of his office, many of the things advocated as startling novelties by the Tractarians after 1833.

The suspicion with which Seabury's Toryism during the Revolution was regarded—a suspicion which to some extent hung about him to the end of his days—tended to restrict his personal influence to his own diocese. But in an indirect way he, and the strong Churchmen who had preceded him in Connecticut, affected the whole theological color of the Church in the North. Even before the end of the Revolution, Connecticut emigrants were pushing up the Connecticut River into the present state of Vermont. Many of them were churchmen, and they took the Church with them. The present churchmanship of the diocese of Vermont is a direct inheritance from these settlers. When, after the Revolution, the Indian country in central and western New York was thrown open to settlement, again we find settlers from Connecticut moving in, and wherever they settle, Connecticut churchmanship goes with them.

Both the nature and the pervasive influence of this Connecticut churchmanship on the Church at large are clearly shown in the American Book of Common Prayer. The American form of the prayer of consecration, comes to us, through Connecticut, from the Scottish Church, the nonjurors, and ultimately from the first Prayer Book of Edward VI (1549). Still more indicative is the office for the Institution of Ministers. This office was drawn up in Connecticut in 1799. It was added to the Book of Common Prayer in 1804. This is important. The slowness with which the Church makes changes in her book of worship, the care with which she undertakes such alterations, insure that when she has placed something in her Prayer Book, that something is a deliberate setting forth of her mind. Now the office of Institution is High Church to the core. The office opens with an episcopal letter, setting forth the source of the priest's authority and his accountability to the bishop. The term "priest" is used consistently, and the priest is empowered "to perform every act of sacerdotal function." We are informed that God "has promised to be with the Ministers of Apostolic Succession to the end of the world," and that he has "built his Church upon the foundation of the Apostles and Prophets." We pray that the congregation may desire "the prosperity of the Holy Apostolic Church, and may profess the faith once delivered to the saints." We ask to be delivered from "the sins of heresy and schism." The mind of the Church which composed and authorized this office was decidedly a Catholic mind.

But it was left to a far more remarkable man than Seabury to become the nation-wide leader of the High Church movement in America.

THE GREATEST OF THEM ALL

The double consecration, in 1811, of Alexander Viets Griswold (1766-1843) and John Henry Hobart (1775-1830) might well be called the Pentecost of the American Church. These two men, so different in personality and belief, became the leaders of the two chief schools of thought in the Church. Griswold, quiet, unassertive, genuinely humble, deeply pious, filled with missionary spirit, was one of the finest fruits of the Evangelical movement.

Here it is necessary that we should pause and note one of the chief differences between the relation of the Evangelical and High Church movements in England and in America. In England the Evangelical revival preceded by some thirty years the beginning of the Oxford

Movement. During these years Evangelicalism was almost the only living force in the English Church. The Oxford Movement, therefore, found its rival strongly entrenched; most of the opposition to the *Tracts* came from Evangelical bishops. In America, on the other hand, the two streams of Church revival rose at almost the same time, and were in many respects interdependent. Thus Griswold, a Connecticut churchman, had far more of definite Church principle than most Evangelical English bishops of the day. Devereux Jarratt (1733-1801), the founder of Evangelicalism in Virginia, believed firmly in the apostolic succession. On the other hand, many of the contemporary American High Churchmen were strongly affected by Evangelical piety and enthusiasm.

Hobart, in so many ways the opposite of Griswold, I consider the greatest religious leader the American Church has produced. He was the sort of man who makes his mark wherever fate drops him. One of his bitterest theological opponents remarked of him, "If I had to trust the destinies of the country to one man, that man would be John Henry Hobart."[13] His portrait is that of no stained glass saint, but of a living and intensely interesting personality. Short, broad, muscular, with eyes that snapped behind thick-lensed glasses, with a firm mouth, a square and obstinate chin, but a high and candid forehead, he was of the stuff from which born leaders are made.[14] Ardent, impulsive, filled with a consuming zeal, tremendously energetic, delighting in a fight, yet honest enough to admit with disarming frankness his occasional hasty injustice, he drew people to him. No one who had once come within the circle of his followers ever quite succeeded in freeing himself from the impress of that dynamic nature.

He had, naturally, the faults that usually accompany his type of genius. He was so convinced of the rightness of his aims, so sure of the wisdom of his measures, that he not only dominated but domineered.

[13] McVickar, J., *Professional Years of Bishop Hobart*, p. 135.
[14] *Ibid.*, p. 35.

PRE-TRACTARIAN HIGH CHURCHMEN

"He had a quick temper; did not take kindly to opposition; and the few Evangelical clergy of the diocese were made to feel the iron hand. Nor did he shrink from sharp rebuke of the laity."[15]

He sometimes failed to do justice to other men who were working for the same aims but by different methods. His effort to block Bishop Chase's collections in England for the building of Kenyon College is the extreme example of this trait, and the worst blot on Hobart's record. While, then, the circle of his devoted followers was very large, there was also a considerable group who regarded him with all the hatred of which clerics are capable, who looked upon him as the most dangerous man in the Church, a very Machiavelli, whose machinations were to be resisted at all costs.

From the day of his ordination to the diaconate, in 1798, Hobart was a marked man. His rise was swift: in two years he had become assistant minister at Trinity Church, New York; thirteen years later, at the age of thirty-six, he was elected assistant bishop of the diocese, and immediately assumed the leadership of the High Church party.[16]

The genesis of Hobart's strong Church principles is interesting. They were in part a product of reaction. He was brought up in the diocese of Pennsylvania, by no means a center of strong churchmanship in those days, and he was the favorite pupil of Bishop White, of whom Wilberforce says, with some truth and more unfairness, that "he always inclined to those counsels which bore most faintly the stamp of his own communion." His college training he received at Presbyterian Princeton. And yet even while he was an undergraduate we find in his letters this significant statement: "God communicates his grace through the channel of appointed means."[17] Like the Connecticut churchman, whose successor he was, he learned

---

[15] Chorley, *Men and Movements*, p. 152.
[16] Of all American Church leaders, Hobart seems pre-eminently a good subject for biographical writing. That there is no decent biography of him is one of the mysteries of historical scholarship.
[17] *Posthumous Works of J. H. Hobart*, p. 27.

theology in opposition, and "his experience of debates on episcopacy with his Presbyterian associates not only served to deepen his own conviction, but stood him in good stead when he was called to defend the polity of the Church against such formidable antagonists as Dr. Mason and Dr. Linn, Presbyterian giants of those days."[18]

"God communicates his grace through the channel of appointed means." This early sentence might well be called the motto of Hobart's religious thought. He was a born ecclesiastic—a lover of order and discipline. This natural authoritarian bent was strengthened both by his contacts and his studies. He married a daughter of the Rev. Thomas Bradbury Chandler, an eighteenth century High Churchman, who had fought side by side with Seabury for the integrity of the Prayer Book and the doctrine of the apostolic succession. Hobart's pastorate at Hempstead, Long Island, where Seabury's father had once been rector, brought him again into contact with the High Church tradition. At Trinity he was under the orders of Bishop Moore, a decided High Churchman of an old-fashioned type. Finally, he studied deeply in the Caroline divines, particularly Hooker and Andrewes, and in such seventeenth and eighteenth century writers as Stillingfleet, Bull, Waterland, Wilson, and Jones of Nayland.

The basis of Hobart's theological position was his belief in the visible Catholic Church. He held firmly to "the ordinances of the Church, administered by a priesthood who derive their authority, by regular transmission, from Christ, the divine head of the Church, and the source of all government."[19] Even more roundly he maintained, in the vigorous series of controversial letters published in 1807 under the title, *An Apology for Apostolic Order,* that

> "Episcopacy is unchangeable, because it is the originally constituted mode of conveying that commission, without which there can be no visible ministry, no visible sacraments, no visible church."

[18] Chorley, *Men and Movements,* p. 142.
[19] McVickar, *op. cit,* p. 59.

Like his English teachers, he leaned heavily on the primitive Church. Holding such views, he was inevitably outspoken in his opposition to Protestantism. He insisted that "the separation of the Church from the word of God, of the sacred volume from the ministry, the worship, and the ordinances which it enjoins, is wrong."[20] With such opinions, backed by such a temperament, he was naturally engaged in continuous controversy—with dissenters, with lax churchmen of his own communion. We find him repeatedly charging his clergy against midweek prayer meetings, against cooperating with Protestant Bible and tract societies, against anything which seemed to compromise in any way the unique character and position of the Church.

A prolific, though not a particularly beautiful writer, year after year there poured forth from his pen tracts, defenses, vindications, charges—upholding the cause of the Church against all comers. It has been suggested that the notion of the use of tracts by the leaders of the Catholic revival in England came from the experience of Hobart. He was quick to see the importance of the periodical press to the Church. In 1808 he became editor and proprietor of the *Churchman's Magazine,* which had been started in 1804 by a group of Connecticut clergy, and which was the first regular periodical of the Episcopal Church in this country. Thus with Hobart the Episcopal Church in America ceased to be downtrodden and apologetic, and became in the highest degree militant.

In all this, of course, Hobart's basic position, though not his expression of it, corresponded closely with that of the contemporary High Churchmen of England. But he was at the opposite pole from a High-and-dry. The famous admonition of the English Bishop, "Preach the Gospel and keep down enthusiasm," would never have proceeded from his mouth. To the definite and uncompromising Church principles we have noted, Hobart added a profound devotion, a fiery missionary spirit, such as were to be found in no English High Churchman of his day. Archdeacon Strachan, who visited America in 1816, remarked of his preaching:

[20] *Ibid.,* p. 314.

> "It was impossible to hear him without becoming sensible of the infinite importance of the Gospel. He warned, counseled, entreated, and comforted, with intense and powerful energy ... He appeared in the pulpit as a father anxious for the eternal happiness of his children ... a man of God preparing them for their Christian warfare—a herald from the other world."[21]

In this, of course, we see the influence of the Evangelical movement; indeed, Hobart's chosen watchword was "Evangelical Truth and Apostolic Order." Thus he kept the proportion of the faith; thus in him those two essential characters, the prophet and the priest, were united.

In the long run his most useful and effective writings were not his controversial pamphlets, but his manuals of devotion, *The Companion for the Festivals and Fasts, The Companion to the Altar,* and *The Clergyman's Companion,* partly original, partly revisions of older English works, which Hobart issued between 1804 and 1807. In all three are notable anticipations of ideas which we commonly ascribe to the next generation. In the first named work, we find emphasis on the Church's power to remit sins, on the right use of the Christian Year, on the duty of fasting.

The second volume, which has much more of Hobart in it, is even more significant. Its warmly devotional tone contrasts pleasantly with the sacramental laxity of the colonial Church. It uses the terms Eucharist and altar. It insists on the necessity of frequent communion and of proper preparation for receiving. In its actual Eucharistic theology it holds closely to the Prayer Book; the elements are "symbols" or "emblems"; the Body and Blood of Christ are spiritually received. But the tone is what really matters. A quotation from one of the prayers will give that tone better than pages of description and analysis:

> Prepare my heart, by the powerful influence of thy grace,

[21]Chorley, *Men and Movements,* p. 148. It has been suggested, with considerable probability, that the union of doctrinal certainty with a real passion for souls, which made Newman's preaching so novel in its day, was one of the things he learned from Hobart.

PRE-TRACTARIAN HIGH CHURCHMEN

for worthily receiving the crucified body and blood of my blessed Lord. Awaken my contrition, quicken my faith, enliven my love, confirm my resolutions of obedience, that going to the altar, relying on my Redeemer's merits and his righteousness, I may obtain reconciliation with thee, my God—may receive supplies of that quickening grace, which will conduct me through the sorrows and temptations of this mortal pilgrimage, to the blissful fruition in the heavenly Zion, of the everlasting glories of the Godhead; to whom, Father, Son, and Holy Ghost, my almighty Creator, my merciful Redeemer, my eternal Sanctifier, be ascribed all power and might, majesty and dominion, henceforth and for ever."[22]

This sounds old-fashioned and a bit strained to modern ears, but to the man who could write that sort of prayer, the Church and its sacraments were no mere subjects of theological speculation: they were a way of life, based solidly on the Prayer Book, but finding in the Prayer Book what few men had found for a hundred and fifty years previous.

In one respect, indeed, Hobart definitely went beyond the Prayer Book as it then was. In his funeral sermon for Bishop Moore, he boldly advocated prayers for the dead, and declared his belief in an intermediate future state. But this intermediate state, Hobart goes on to say, is not to be confused with the Roman notion of Purgatory. Indeed, he is always careful to distinguish between his positions and Roman teaching. He is suspicious of the term sacrifice applied to the Eucharist. The bread and wine are more than memorials, they are symbols of our Lord's body and blood. But the bread and wine are not changed into Christ's Body and Blood, though the Body and Blood of Christ are spiritually taken and received. He is strongly opposed to anything savoring of Mariolatry, or to the invocation of the saints. Admitting to the full the priestly power of absolution, Hobart does not advocate auricular confession, holding that the confession and absolution in the offices and the Communion service have all that is necessary for sacramental validity.[23]

[22] Hobart, *Companion to the Altar*, p. 35.
[23] Hobart, *State of the Dead*, pp. 6, 35, 96.

[21]

But Hobart's writings, important though they were, did far less for the Church than his life. One of his chief works as bishop was the quickening of religious education. In charge after charge, he dinned into the ears of his clergy the need for frequent catechizing, the value of Sunday Schools. He threw himself with customary energy into the founding of Hobart College. But the crown of his educational work was the General Theological Seminary. In the founding of this, both the strength and the weakness of Hobart are clearly illustrated. In 1813, only two years after he became bishop, we find him addressing the diocesan convention on the necessity of a seminary, and year after year he repeats the statement. But what he planned was a diocesan seminary, *his* seminary, teaching his views of the Church, sheltered under his wing. And so he steadily refused to cooperate in the movement for a general Church seminary until he had made sure that he could control such an institution; then he became its strongest backer.[24]

After three years of vicissitudes, the seminary was finally, in 1822, located in New York. Hobart acted for a time as professor of pastoral theology, and until his death was mainly responsible for its government. His magnetic personality and positive views were admirably calculated to attract young men to the institution, and once within its walls, where the impact of his dominating mind could be felt, they were never quite the same again. Thus there grew up around him a striking group of young men, imbued with his principles, and filled with something of his fire. The elder Doane and the younger Samuel Seabury, Whittingham, Kemper, Ives, the Onderdonk brothers—the list of his pupils is almost the roster of High Church leaders from 1820 to 1850. Moreover, the distinctively High Church tone which he gave to the seminary has persisted to this day, and that, year after year for more than a century, she has poured into the life stream of the Church priests strong in Catholicism is primarily due to Hobart.

It is important to bear in mind, however, that in Hobart's mind

---

[24] Hobart's unfortunate attempt to prevent the founding of Kenyon College was really due to his fear that this would prove a successful rival to his seminary.

High Churchmanship, Catholicism, had nothing to do with what is so unfortunately called "ritualism." He was, indeed, a ritualist in the strict sense of the term. Devotedly attached to the Prayer Book, believing in discipline as an essential characteristic of Catholicism, he insisted on a literal obedience to the rubrics. He had no patience with extemporaneous devotions, or with relaxations of the rubrical requirements. He insisted on the importance, the obligation, of the daily offices; he desired that chancels might be built so that the people might see the priest at the altar; it was largely due to his insistence that the General Convention of 1826 passed the canon making compulsory the use of the so-called antecommunion service every Sunday. It is rather ironical, in the light of later history, that the primary liturgical object of Hobart—an object which sprang directly from his Catholic principles, his belief in order and discipline—was absolute uniformity in the performance of the services of the Church. No one, I suspect, would have been more infuriated by the anarchic individualism of the later "ritualists."

In one other respect Hobart gave direction to the High Church movement. Faced with what was perhaps the greatest missionary field of the world in that day, the Episcopal Church in America had been unbelievably slow in taking up her responsibilities. Hobart, in spite of his love of centralization, in spite of having passed all his life on the Atlantic seaboard, saw early the need for active missionary effort in the West. He visited constantly the far corners of his diocese, which included the whole of New York State, much of it wild and unchurched country. His labors to establish the Church among the Indians in central and western New York bore fruit, not only in his own diocese, but even in the distant territory of Wisconsin. Both in his diocese and in his seminary he started a tradition of missionary effort that was to affect the future of the whole High Church movement in America. His influence was also felt in a negative direction. He had little interest in foreign missions; thus for decades the foreign field remained a Low Church preserve. It is a significant fact that

Hobart died in 1830, on a missionary tour of the western part of his diocese, literally burnt out by the energy of his restless spirit.

SOME OF HOBART'S PUPILS

Hobart's early death was a great loss to the movement, but his work was carried on by his pupils. He was succeeded in the see of New York by Benjamin Tredwell Onderdonk (1791-1861). Onderdonk was inevitably somewhat of an anticlimax after Hobart. He was a devoted pastor and a hard-working bishop, as the record of his visitations testifies. In his ideas he re-echoed, almost *ad nauseam*, Hobart's teaching on the apostolic succession. He was particularly interested in the decent and orderly performance of the services of the Church, welcoming the erection of Gothic churches, which were just beginning to come in, advising the better arrangement of chancels, and approving the use of crosses on steeples. A wise contemporary has thus estimated him:

> He was far from being brilliant or eloquent; not specially attractive as a preacher, so far as I can learn or remember; nor of much depth or originality. But he was a man of extraordinary executive ability and unwearied industry, of excellent judgment, and thorough devotion to the work which the Church laid upon him, whether as Priest, Doctor, or Bishop.[25]

A more influential and much more colorful man than Onderdonk was George Washington Doane (1799-1859), the poet of the movement in America. Like his teacher, he was a personality, strong in his opinions, scholarly, with a notable aesthetic and literary flair. He was a respectable poet, sufficiently blessed with humor to be able to translate Horace. Three of his hymns, *Softly Now the Light of Day, Thou Art the Way*, and *Fling Out the Banner*, have achieved permanent popularity, and attest his deep personal religion. He was far-reaching in his plans, sanguine at times beyond the limits of good judgment, with a cleverness at repartee that deserves comparison with Sydney

---
[25]Hayes, *Diocese of Western New York*, p. 84.

PRE-TRACTARIAN HIGH CHURCHMEN

Smith's. On the debit side he was an inveterate wire-puller, and dramatic to the edge of insincerity. His career from the time of his ordination in 1821 was like Hobart's in its meteoric brilliancy. In 1825 he was made professor at Washington (now Trinity) College, Hartford. In 1830 he became rector of Trinity Church, Boston, then as now, one of the outstanding parishes in the country. He at once set out on a campaign with two objectives— to make his parish the center of High Churchmanship in Massachusetts, and to capture control of the diocese for his party. Initially somewhat successful, both of these attempts ultimately failed.[26] Doane, like Hobart, had the faculty of arousing intense opposition, and this opposition was on the point of defeating him seriously when his election as bishop of New Jersey gave him the chance to withdraw gracefully from Boston and to make a fresh start. The reaction set up by his unfortunate political moves threw Trinity Church and the diocese of Massachusetts into the Low Church camp.

Doane's churchmanship before 1840 was largely a copy of Hobart's. Indeed, he was in no sense an originator. As insistent as his teacher on the vital connection between the Church and the school, one of his chief labors, and the source of his chief difficulty as bishop, was the founding at Burlington, New Jersey, his ecclesiastical capital, of St. Mary's School for girls and Burlington College for boys. He planned, but was never able to carry out, a diocesan system of parochial schools. A sacramentalist, he advocated daily services and a weekly Eucharist, and established both at Burlington. He enforced, with amusing difficulty, the use of the surplice by his clergy; on his first visitation of his diocese he carried around with him a suitcase full of surplices to clothe the unfrocked. He opposed strongly the then universal system of renting and selling pews. He was the first churchman in this country to see the advantage and desirability of the cathedral system. He and Hopkins were the first American High Churchmen to look back with sympathy to the Middle Ages. It is noteworthy in

[26]Doane, W. C., *Life and Writings of George Washington Doane*, pp. 152 ff.

this connection that among his poetical works are translations of a
a number of office hymns from the breviary. He was, wherever he
went, actively engaged in carrying on Church publications, lending
to the movement the strength of a rather brilliant and always
fluent pen.

William Rollinson Whittingham (1805-1879), another of Hobart's pupils, was a person of a far different type, perhaps more solid, but decidedly less attractive. A precocious child—he was ready for ordination at twenty— ascetic, stern, uncompromising, witty but absolutely humorless, a profound linguist and an insatiable student, he was the first great scholar of the movement in America. His researches early led him to an almost complete anticipation of the ideas of the early Tractarians; so much so that it was said of him by an English priest, "If the whole Catholic Church was buried save only your Whittingham, I believe out of that one man the whole Catholic Church might rise up again like our Lord in living glory." His biting sarcasm and total lack of aesthetic appreciation are well illustrated by his comment on a festal service at St. Paul's, Baltimore:

> The fortnight ended yesterday with a great splurge at St. Paul's. Such musical doings, the veracious chroniclers in the newspapers say, as have never been seen in Baltimore before—a terrible feather out of the cap of the Romanists, who have claimed hitherto the undisputed and indisputable pre-eminence in that line. Think of one hundred and fifty singers! and six trumpets! and the two best violins in Baltimore! and trombones, and bass-viols, and what not. I rather wonder that I survive it.[27]

In 1831 Whittingham became editor of *The Churchman,* which had been established in that year as the semi-official organ of the High Church party. In 1836 he was made professor of ecclesiastical history at the General Seminary, and during his four years' tenure of that office was an important influence in the formation of Catholic ideas in the minds of the seminarians. In many ways, these four years were the most useful of his life, and it was perhaps a pity that

[27]Brand W., *Life of Bishop Whittingham,* Vol. II., p. 122.

he was drawn away from a work for which his combination of sound scholarship and strongly Catholic ideas so supremely fitted him. But there was a hardness, a lack of flexibility in his mind, that growing harder with age, greatly reduced his possibilities as a leader in the Church. Thus he early became, and always remained, a bitter and bigoted anti-Romanist. It is interesting to note in the letters he wrote from Europe during his travels in 1835 his constant expressions of abhorrence for Roman ceremonial, coupled with a surprising admiration for Roman sermons.[28]

His election in 1840 as bishop of Maryland gave to the border states a focal point of High Church teaching.[29] He never became a ceremonialist, insisting always on rigid obedience to the letter of the Prayer Book, and disapproving, with a conservatism that seems to have increased year by year, any change or enrichment.

Scarcely less important than these men, though he never became a bishop, was Samuel Seabury (1801-1872), grandson of the first American prelate.

> "A scholar and logical, he was always strong in whatever position he assumed. With keen wit, imperturbable temper, a great master of sarcasm, and unsparing in dealing with the foibles of others, he was the most provoking of controversialists. He could be very grave and earnest in upholding important truths, but, as it seemed, he would often sacrifice the benefit of convincing for the pleasure of discomfiting an opponent. He was too independent to be a man of a party, but he was not afraid of the name partisan."

In 1833 Seabury succeeded Whittingham as editor of *The Churchman,* a position for which he was eminently fitted. This position he held until 1850, combining it after 1838 with the rectorship of the Church of the Annunciation, New York, which he founded to put into practice the principles of Hobartian High Churchmanship.

[28]Brand, *op. cit.,* Vol. I, p. 148.
[29]This does not mean that he was the beginner of High Churchmanship in Maryland. Bishops Claggett and Stone were both old-fashioned High Churchmen, while Wyatt, long rector of St. Paul's, in many respects went beyond him.

THE CATHOLIC MOVEMENT IN THE EPISCOPAL CHURCH

HOPKINS THE ARTIST

Meanwhile, in what was then the far West, another churchman was, quite independently of the Hobartian influence, arriving at highly Catholic views. That John Henry Hopkins (1792-1868) so early became a High Churchman is an excellent reason for inferring, apart from all other evidence, that in the early nineteenth century Catholicism was in the air. In 1823 Hopkins was one of the most successful lawyers in Pittsburgh. Trinity Church, of which he was a member, was in extremely low water. The vestry, looking about for a life-saver, took the extraordinary step of offering the rectorate to Hopkins if he would take orders.[80] He accepted, gave up his lucrative practice, and was ordained deacon by Bishop White. Unsatisfied with his necessarily scant preparation, he then began to read in the Church Fathers, commencing with those of the apostolic age. But unlike most of his contemporaries, especially in America, he did not stop at the apostolic age, but kept on reading, coming eventually down to St. Bernard.[81] He was thus the first of American churchmen to look into the period of history stretching between 400 and 1500. From this study he emerged a full-fledged High Churchman.

But it was not in scholarship that Hopkins was to make his chief contribution to the High Church movement. As Hobart was the executive, Doane the poet and politician, and Whittingham the scholar, of pre-Tractarian High Churchmanship in America, so Hopkins was the artist. He was a thorough musician, and enough of a composer to write a setting for the Communion service. When, in 1824, a new church building was needed for his parish, he proceeded to design one, which was neither a meeting-house nor a pseudo-Roman temple, but at least an attempt at Gothic. A little later we find him writing a treatise on Gothic for priests about to build, giving sample designs. He maintained a school in his own house, and in the room which served for a chapel, his artistic soul found its opportunity.

[80]Hopkins, J. H., *Life of Bishop Hopkins*, p. 66.
[81]*Ibid.*, p. 114.

PRE-TRACTARIAN HIGH CHURCHMEN

The music was of his own arrangement; the furnishings of his own design; and among the pictures on the wall was the copy made by him of the *Madonna of the Chair*. Moved thus by temperament and by study, Hopkins was the first of American High Churchmen to revolt against the bareness of contemporary churches and contemporary ceremonial, to look sympathetically on the Middle Ages, and to attempt to reclaim from that disused storeroom something of value for the Church in his own day. Where Hobart and his followers were authoritarians, Hopkins was a romanticist.

In 1825, as a result of his patristic studies, he had reached the conclusion that the Eucharist should be celebrated with the mixed chalice and with unleavened bread.[32] Less sure of his position than Whittingham, but far more receptive to ideas, he pursued a strikingly independent course of his own, now going along with the general tendency of the High Church movement, now in the van, and occasionally in direct opposition to it. One of the leading qualities of his mind was an uncompromising honesty that kept him from being a good party man and led him at times into exceedingly uncomfortable positions. Thus his removal to Boston in 1830, where he served as assistant to Doane at Trinity, brought him into direct contact with the High Church movement in the East. But he soon turned back indignantly from following Doane in his attempt to capture the diocese by sharp politics, and had much to do with Doane's defeat.[33] Hopkins' election in 1832 as first bishop of Vermont placed another diocese in High Church hands.

SOUTHERN CHURCHMANSHIP

Uninformed northern High Churchmen of the present day are apt to think of the South as being, and as always having been, a sort of religious Death Valley—dry, below sea level. This is both unfair and unhistorical. One of the striking things about the Virginia Evangel-

[32]Hopkins, *Life of Bishop Hopkins*, p. 115.
[33]*Ibid.*, p. 149.

icals was their strong hold on certain doctrines which are basic to the Catholic faith. Devereux Jarratt (1733-1801) is rightly considered the father of American Evangelicalism. Reacting against Latitudinarianism and Low Church teaching, with their emphasis on a sort of secular morality, he stressed the ancient teaching of original sin and the necessity of grace—the two cornerstones of sacramentalism. He attached great importance to the Lord's Supper. When the Methodists began to ordain their own clergy, he attacked these "self-created priests," and asserted that the Methodists had "embraced a new faith." And he affirmed his loyalty to the Church in terms which might have come from Hobart or Seabury:

> "I dearly love the Church. I love her on many accounts—particularly for the three following: I love her because her mode of worship is so beautiful and decent. . . . I love her, because of the soundness of her doctrines, creeds, articles, etc. I love her because all her officers, and the modes of ordaining them are, if I mistake not, truly primitive and apostolic. Bishops, priests, and deacons were, in my opinion, distinct orders in the church in her earliest and purest ages. These three *particulars,* a regular clergy, sound doctrine, and a decent, comprehensive worship, contain the essentials, I think, of a Christian church."[84]

Richard Channing Moore (1762-1841), who in 1814 became the second bishop of Virginia after having been rector of a New York parish, had a considerable leaven of High Church principles. He believed in the divine origin and perpetual obligation of the Christian ministry under the episcopal form. He was strongly attached to the liturgy of the Church, and insisted on strict conformity to the Book of Common Prayer. He held *ex animo* the doctrines taught in the Creeds, Articles, and Homilies. He had no sympathy with the "novel inventions of heresy and schism."[85] Even after the lapse of more than one hundred years, the influence of such men as Jarratt and Moore is discernable in the Southern Church. Within the past few years, when

---
[84] Quoted in Chorley, *Men and Movements,* p. 23.
[85] Henshaw, *Life of Moore,* p. 290.

issues have arisen in General Convention involving basic principles in the Church, Fond du Lac and Virginia have been found standing side by side.

John Stark Ravenscroft (1772-1830), first bishop of North Carolina (1823-1830), beginning as a lay preacher in a sect called Republican Methodists, concluded that something more than an inward call was needed to give one authority to preach the Gospel, and finally, in his own words, "had to turn his attention to the Protestant Episcopal Church for that deposit of apostolic succession, in which alone verifiable power to minister in sacred things was to be found in these United States."[88] He became a definite Hobartian, gloried in the name of High Churchman, and refused his consent to the consecration of Bishop Meade, feeling that Meade was weak in distinctive Church principles. It was in all probability the personality of Ravenscroft that made the Church in North Carolina a sort of island of High Churchmanship in a sea of Evangelicalism. He was followed as bishop by Levi Silliman Ives, the most extreme of early High Church bishops. These men gave to the Church in North Carolina a character that has endured to this day.

Theodore Dehon (1776-1817), who became second bishop of South Carolina in 1812, was no controversialist, but a saintly priest, whose particular contribution was the application of Catholic teaching to parochial life. "Rating public prayer and the sacraments above preaching, he would at any time curtail his sermon, or altogether omit it, rather than any part of worship." He was one of the first to observe weekday holy days; he kept a strict Lent; he cultivated a special reverence for and observance of Holy Week. His sacramental practice was admirable, and far in advance of his time. He insisted that baptisms be performed in public. He held that the Eucharist was the proper act of Christian worship, that it should be administered every Sunday, and that it should be approached only after careful

---

[88] Quoted in Chorley, *Men and Movements*, p. 162.

preparation. He delighted in administering the Communion to the sick."[87] One wonders whether in the long run, such patient and truly evangelical labor did not make more practicing Catholics than the noisier work of more famous men.

THE WINNING OF THE WEST

The movement for the evangelization of the West, first begun by Philander Chase, a great missionary and generally classed as an Evangelical,[88] was quickly taken up by High Churchmen. We have mentioned Hobart's lead in this direction. Doane was equally enthusiastic in the cause of Western missions, and shortly after 1830 the leadership in this work tended to pass largely into High Church hands. The first missionary bishop to cross the southern Appalachians, Bishop Otey of Tennessee, gave instructions that on his tomb should be inscribed "Bishop of the Holy Catholic Church in Tennessee." Even more predominant was High Church influence in the Northwest. While the Evangelical tendency remained strong in Ohio, farther west the story was quite different. In 1835 Jackson Kemper, one of Hobart's pupils, was elected to a missionary diocese which at different times included all of what are now the states of Indiana, Missouri, Wisconsin, Kansas, Iowa, and Minnesota. Under his vigorous leadership, High Churchmanship was firmly established at many points in this vast territory.

[87] Chorley, *op. cit.*, p. 157.
[88] But Chase, like many of the early Evangelicals, held some decidedly High Church views. Speaking of his first meeting with Father Nash, the great missionary of central New York, he says:

"It was a meeting of two persons deeply convinced of the primitive and apostolic foundation of the Church to which, on account of its purity of doctrine and the divine right of its ministry, they had fled from a chaos of confusion of other sects." [Chase, *Reminiscences*, Vol. I, p. 32.]

Morever, the late George Franklin Smythe, who made a thorough study of Chase, and whose *History of the Diocese of Ohio* (Cleveland, 1931) is one of the best regional histories extant, calls Chase a "High Churchman of the old-fashioned Connecticut type" (p. 229), and states that in 1825 all the Ohio clergy were of this type. After Charles P. McIlvaine became bishop of Ohio in 1832, the Evangelicals quickly gained the ascendency.

PRE-TRACTARIAN HIGH CHURCHMEN

OPPOSITION AND PARTY CONFLICT

The High Church movement had not proceeded thus far without opposition. By 1830 the old, stagnant Low Churchmanship of Provoost and William Smith had pretty well died out, crushed between the millstones of revived Evangelicalism and Hobartian High Churchmanship. But because of its very vigor, Evangelicalism, in its more militant and partisan moods, was a more dangerous adversary than the do-nothingism of the older Low Churchmen. The inevitable conflict between the parties came to a head most frequently in episcopal elections. Thus in 1811 the Low Churchmen dragged Provoost from his retirement, and attempted to set him up again in office as the only way of preventing the election of Hobart.

Maryland had as its first bishop, Thomas John Claggett, a High Churchman of the old school, who followed Seabury in wearing the mitre. The election of James Kemp as his suffragan in 1814 came after a bitter contest, and protests were made against Kemp's consecration by members of the Evangelical party. His chief opponent, the Rev. George Dashiell of Baltimore, later left the Church and started a short-lived schism.

In 1826, when Bishop White of Pennsylvania asked for an assistant, so fiercely contested was the election that the first convention called to elect was forced to adjourn without making a choice. It is interesting to note that one of the main motives behind the Low Church opposition was fear and hatred of Hobart, whom one of the delegates stigmatized as "the Talleyrand, the would-be archbishop." Eventually, exactly what the Low Churchmen feared came to pass. Henry Ustick Onderdonk, one of Hobart's pupils and close followers, was elected.[89]

We have already noted the attempt of Doane to capture the standing committee of Massachusetts, and thus to rule the diocese over the head of Bishop Griswold. An aftermath of this quarrel was the deter-

---

[89] Hopkins, *Life of Bishop Hopkins*, Chapter V, *passim*.

mined effort made by the Low Churchmen to block the confirmation by the standing committees of the election of Doane as bishop of New Jersey. In 1829 there was a similar attempt on the part of the High Churchmen to prevent the consecration of Meade as assistant bishop of Virginia. This attempt, which was led by Bishop Ravenscroft, was made on the floor of General Convention

In all these contests, honors were fairly evenly divided; and in all fairness it must be admitted that in general the High Church party was the more aggressive. The worst of these contests was that they could hardly be called contests of principle. No vital theological points were involved; they tended rather to degenerate into wars of personalities, party wire-pulling combats. Cries of "heresy" and "treason" were deferred until the next decade.

GROWTH AND PROGRESS OF THE MOVEMENT

The American Episcopal Church in 1840 presented a far different picture from that which we drew in our last chapter. The scattered, despoiled, broken-down, and semi-heretical body which sent its representatives to the General Convention of 1785 had come to life. In communicants she had grown from a possible ten thousand to an actual fifty-five thousand, many of them converts from the Protestant sects. Her missionaries had crossed the Appalachians, swept through the central states and bridged the Mississippi. She had even found energy to send her ambassadors to China, the Near East, and Africa.[40] In every settled part of the continent dioceses were being erected, churches were rising. To claim all the credit of this for any one party would be the height of unfairness. The calm statesmanship of White, the Evangelical fervor of Chase and Griswold and Meade, had played their part in the great work. But there is, I think, considerable evidence to support the opinion that in 1840 the native High Church

[40] This in spite of the fact that many High Churchmen did not approve of foreign missions.

movement, the movement stemming from Seabury and Hobart, was well on its way to a quiet conquest of the whole Church.

In 1840 nineteen men sat in the House of Bishops. Seven of these—H. U. Onderdonk, B. T. Onderdonk, Ives, Doane, Kemper, Whittingham, and Hopkins—were thoroughly and unquestionably strong High Churchmen, and of the seven, six were pupils of Hobart. Seven more—Brownell, Moore, Otey, McCoskry, Polk, DeLancey, and Gadsden,—were High Churchmen of various shades and colors. Five only—Griswold, Chase, Meade, Smith, and McIlvaine—were definitely Low Churchmen. This composition of the House of Bishops is very significant. We have already noted the geographical range of High Churchmanship. But still more significant, and more promising for the future, was its pervasiveness. Bishop White, whose long episcopate spanned most of the period we have been considering, was a fairly good barometer of the prevailing religious tone and feeling. In 1785 he was Low Churchman enough to be willing to accept the meager and truncated doctrines of the *Proposed Book;* in 1826, having been subject for twenty years to the influence of Hobart and the Hobartians, he was indignantly exclaiming to his diocesan convention: "I had as lief be called an atheist or infidel as a Low Churchman."[41] By the middle Thirties, we find such notable Evangelicals as Bishop Griswold and McIlvaine defending the apostolic succession in terms worthy of the *Tracts.* Even in such a generally Low Church diocese as Ohio, there were indications of the trend of the times. The Rev. John Hall, grandfather of the leading theologian[42] of the American Church, and one of the numerous band of self-made converts who have read themselves into the Church, was before 1840 using the daily offices and the weekly communion, and even hearing confessions. All the evidence at hand leads me to believe that by 1840 the native High Church movement

[41] Ward, *Life of Bishop White,* p. 127.
[42] The late Rev. Francis J. Hall (Dec. 24, 1857-March 12, 1932).

had captured most of the strategic points, and was well on its way to becoming the norm of belief and practice of the whole American Church.[48]

There is no better way of ascertaining the tone, the belief, the practices of the movement at this stage than a perusal of the pages of *The Churchman* from 1830 to 1840. This periodical was during most of the decade edited by Samuel Seabury, who perhaps best represented the pure milk of the Hobartian word. In the pages of *The Churchman* we have the constant stressing of the apostolic succession, the same stress that runs through all the sermons of all the High Churchmen, the constant emphasis on the visible Church—an emphasis and a stress that do become a bit tiresome. There is the same insistence on the value of the sacraments. One of the great theological controversies of the decade was waged over the knotty point of baptismal regeneration, *The Churchman,* of course, standing for a real change effected by the sacrament. In 1836 Seabury was asserting, in more exact language than was ever used by Hobart, that "our standards affirm the doctrine of the Real Presence of Christ in the Eucharist," and supporting the statement by quotations from the classic English divines.

Until 1830 the chief adversaries of the Church in America had been the Protestants—notably the Congregationalists in New England and the Presbyterians in New York. Against them the most vigorous polemics of Hobart were directed, and Rome was apt to be dismissed with a rather contemptuous aside. But after 1830 the influx of Irish immigrants, and the resulting rapid growth of the

---

[48]The testimony of the Rev. Stephen H. Tyng, one of the leading Evangelical priests of the century, bears out this opinion. Speaking of the period before 1840, he says:

"At this time there were three schools or parties in the Episcopal Church. I can only describe them as they appeared to my mind. First, was the Moderate party, with Bishop White as the leader; then, the extreme High Church party, led by Bishop Hobart; and last, the decided Evangelical party, with such men as Griswold and Moore . . . The first two schools were about equal in number; the latter was very feeble, except in Virginia. The old men were followers of Bishop White, the young and ambitious clergy followed Bishop Hobart. Of the five hundred ministers then in the Episcopal Church, there were about fifty who were willing to take a stand with Bishop Griswold." [C. R. Tyng, *Life of Stephen H. Tyng,* p. 508.]

PRE-TRACTARIAN HIGH CHURCHMEN

Roman Catholic Church, brought about a sharp change in the conditions of theological warfare. And thus after that date, *The Churchman* becomes more and more vigorously anti-Roman. Rome, and not Geneva, is now the enemy. Anti-Roman tracts proceed from the pens of other leading High Churchmen—notably Hopkins. There were even occasional conversions to Rome during the period—not many, but enough to keep the anti-Roman feeling stirred up. This fact is very important; the growing menace of Roman strength had a great effect on party relations within the Church during the next decade.

In the mattter of rite and ceremony High Churchmanship still stood for rigid uniformity, for strict construction of the rubrics. And in this direction much progress had been made. The slovenly performance of the services, which had almost been the rule before 1800, had by 1830 largely come to an end. The increasing emphasis on the sacraments was affecting, inevitably, the outward form of church buildings. The chancel was more and more frequently raised several steps above the body of the church. The altar was usually set altarwise against the east wall, with lectern and pulpit pushed aside so as to make the altar plainly visible. The enormous colonial pulpit was disappearing. The use of Gothic—too often carpenter's Gothic—while not directly connected with High Church views, was quickly taken over by High Churchmen. The cross on the steeple was beginning to replace the weather-cock as the outward emblem of the Church. But as yet there was no apparent tendency to move beyond into the strange regions of "liturgical enrichment."

FAULTS OF EARLY HIGH CHURCHMANSHIP

Admirable as this early High Church movement was, it had its faults. There was about it a certain smugness. It said, in effect: "We, the Protestant Episcopal Church in the United States of America, are a part of the Holy Catholic Church; that part, indeed, which represents the Church in its most primitive and best form.

We have all the essential Catholic doctrines and practices. Our liturgy is perfect. Let us but use what we have, and the world is ours." Now the danger with this sort of attitude is that it leads directly into Pharisaism. When people hold such a view, there is no room for progress, no room for self-questioning, no room for healthy humility. The contrast between this attitude and that of the English Tractarians is very striking. To Newman and Pusey, the English Church was in a bad way, maimed and deformed by the Reformation, half apostate, needing to be recalled to her true Catholicity. The English reformers were consciously and courageously setting their faces against the current. But in America the current was running, and running swiftly, in the High Church direction. There are times when one is inclined to wonder if the progress of American High Churchmanship would not have been far smoother, and its success far more general, if Keble had never preached his Assize sermon. But there was the danger that assurance might turn into mere complacency; the American movement, left to itself, might have ended in dry rot.

BIBLIOGRAPHY

BEARDSLEY, E. E., *Life and Correspondence of the Rt. Rev. Samuel Seabury* (Boston, 1881).

BRAND, W. F., *Life of William Rollinson Whittingham* (New York, 1886). [Invaluable for the period 1830-80. Contains many letters.]

DOANE, W. C., *Memoir of the Life of George Washington Doane* (New York and London, 1860). [To be used with caution.]

HALL, F. J., *Life of the Rev. John Hall*, MSS. in library of General Theological Seminary; printed in *Historical Magazine of the Episcopal Church*, IV (1935) pp. 308-313.

HENSHAW, J. P. K. *Memoir of the Life of the Rt. Rev. Richard Channing Moore, D.D.* (Philadelphia, 1843).

HOBART, J. H., *Apology for Apostolic Order*, in *The Churchman Armed* (New York, 1844).
— *Companion for the Altar* (New York, 1843).
— *The State of the Departed* (New York, 1825).

PRE-TRACTARIAN HIGH CHURCHMEN

HOPKINS, J. H., JR., *The Life of Bishop Hopkins* (New York, 1873). [Brilliantly written. Excellent for the early career of its subject, but not quite dependable for the period 1840-50.]

McVICKAR, J., *Early Years of the Late Bishop Hobart* (New York, 1834). — *Professional Years of Bishop Hobart* (New York, 1836).

NORTON, J. N., *The Life of Bishop Ravenscroft* (New York, 1859).

PENNINGTON, E. L., *Apostle of New Jersey, John Talbot* (Philadelphia, 1938).

SCHROEDER, J. F., *Memorial of Bishop Hobart* (New York, 1859).

SEABURY, W. J., *Memoir of Bishop Seabury* (New York and London, 1908).

SMYTHE, GEORGE F., *A History of the Diocese of Ohio until the Year* 1918 (Cleveland, 1931).

TYNG, C. R., *Life of Stephen H. Tyng* (New York, 1890).

CHAPTER THREE

THE IMPACT OF THE TRACTS

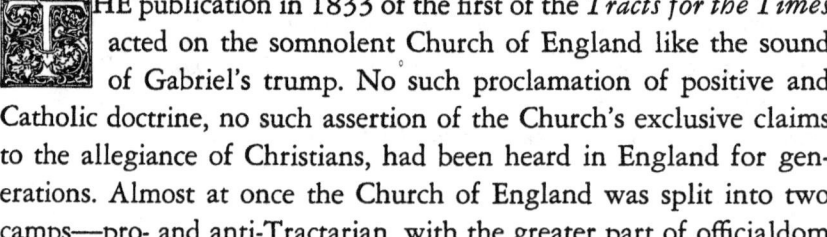HE publication in 1833 of the first of the *Tracts for the Times* acted on the somnolent Church of England like the sound of Gabriel's trump. No such proclamation of positive and Catholic doctrine, no such assertion of the Church's exclusive claims to the allegiance of Christians, had been heard in England for generations. Almost at once the Church of England was split into two camps—pro- and anti-Tractarian, with the greater part of officialdom decidedly anti.

There used to be, and still is in uninformed quarters, a notion that the High Church movement in the United States was an imported affair—a mere offshoot of the Oxford Movement.[1] As the last chapter has, I hope, clearly demonstrated, in 1830 the American Church was far more Catholic in feeling and in teaching than her elder sister. Indeed, Hobart, the father of American High Churchmanship as a vigorous force, was in some sense the foster father of the Oxford Movement. His *Tract on Episcopacy,* published in 1807, in which the full doctrine of the apostolic succession was stated with Hobartian vigor, was read and commended highly by Hugh James Rose, one of the leaders of the earliest stage of the movement in England. In 1823 Hobart made a prolonged visit to England, where he met several of the later Tractarians. In March, 1824, he dined

---

[1] As recently as 1945, the Rev. Alexander Cummins, editor of *The Chronicle,* restated this theory in its most absolute form in an article in *The Churchman.* His thesis is that in 1833 the Episcopal Church in this country was "Protestant and Evangelical; . . . it was young and lusty; it was growing; it had wealth." and then, "a blight settled upon our Church. The Oxford Movement, slowly spreading, became that rebellious sect, the Anglo-Catholic party." To talk like this is simply to ignore the whole body of facts presented in the previous chapter of this book.

with Newman at Oxford.[2] At this time, Newman was a young man, his ideas still unformed; Hobart was the outstanding American churchman, a great talker, a magnetic personality, and probably the most Catholic-minded bishop in the Anglican Communion. There can be little doubt that this dinner was an event in Newman's life. And in 1839 he acknowledged this indebtedness and in part repaid it in his article in the *British Critic* entitled "The Church Principles of Bishop Hobart"—a glowing tribute from a great man to his great predecessor.

THE RECEPTION OF THE TRACTS IN AMERICA

I think it fair to say that the *Tracts* were far more favorably received in America than in England. The reason for this is obvious. There was little, if anything, in the earlier *Tracts* which had not long been taught in the American Church, and by men of the highest authority. Seabury, Hobart, Doane, Hopkins, had nothing new to learn from Keble and Newman about the apostolic succession, or the sin of schism, or the value of the sacraments, or the authority of the Fathers. The *Tracts* were well received, not because they taught new doctrine, but because they fell in with one of the prevailing currents of thought in the American Church. It is not surprising, therefore, to find Bishop Stewart of Quebec remarking that he had heard more about the *Tracts* in a three days' sojourn in New York than in a year's residence in London.

The Churchman, at this time under the editorship of the younger Samuel Seabury, is an excellent measure of American High Church reaction to the *Tracts*. The first mention of them in its columns occurs in 1835, when they are quoted on primitive episcopacy.[3] In 1836 the tract, *Richard Nelson,* is reprinted in full.[4] In 1837 we strike the first controversial note. Seabury, obviously replying to some one else's criticism, declares that the devotional practices introduced by

[2]Clarke, C. K. L., *Bishop Hobart and the Oxford Movement*, p. 6.
[3]*The Churchman*, Vol. IV, p. 793.
[4]*Ibid.*, Vol. IV, p. 1105.

Newman at Littlemore are not superstitious, but needless. In 1838 Newman is first mentioned by name; in the following year there is a rather cautious commendation of the *Tracts,* approving of their general tendency, while not giving unqualified endorsement to their every word. *Tract 75,* on the Breviary, is given limited approval. Even *Tract 90,* which appeared in 1841, was not too much for Seabury. Concerning it he observes:

> "We do not deny that there are some views advanced in the Tract, both doctrinal and historical, which are not in accordance with our own; but we mean to say, that the principles of interpretation adopted in the Tract are, in our opinion, neither evasive nor slippery, but honest, manly, and straightforward."[5]

In general Seabury is too sure of his own position, too certain of American High Churchmanship in general, to feel any "apprehension that the republication of the *Tracts* among us will make converts to what are deemed their peculiar views."

The reception given to the *Tracts* was so favorable that, in 1839, Mr. Charles S. Henry, one of the publishers of the *New York Mirror,* thought it worth while to bring out the first American edition of them. This was no mere commercial speculation. Mr. Henry was a churchman of the true Hobartian stamp, who gave the enterprise his financial backing in the hope that the *Tracts* might prove effective against the contrasting errors of Rome and rationalism. In his preface to this edition, Mr. Henry shows himself a man keenly aware of the history of Church parties in America, asserting that "in the bosom of the Episcopal Church in this country, from influences derived from the non-juring period of English Church History, and from our Church having no connection with the State, it has resulted that some of the leading doctrines of the Oxford divines, relating to the constitution of the Church, and to the Ministry, have been better preserved than in the English Establishment."[6] Among the clergy

[5]*Ibid.,* Vol X, p. 28.
[6]*Tracts for the Times* (New York, 1839) p. 4.

who sponsored this publication was Dr. Jonathan M. Wainwright, later provisional bishop of New York.

THEIR EFFECT IN THE GENERAL THEOLOGICAL SEMINARY

Seabury's attitude represents fairly well that of the Hobartian group. They approved, but with reserve. But the chief effect of the *Tracts* was felt, naturally, by the younger men, particularly by the students at the General Theological Seminary. Here was no different basic doctrine, indeed, than their own teachers and bishops had delivered to them, but the old doctrine, which had tended to settle into a smug conservatism, was now clothed with a new splendor. The intense piety of Pusey, the daring iconoclasm of Froude, above all the literary genius of Newman, acted like a tonic on the new generation. They had been placed in a receptive mood by the teachings of Hobart, Whittingham, and Onderdonk. The ground was seeded, and the *Tracts* were like the summer sun. Furthermore, the general tone of the *Tracts,* the *Athanasius contra mundum* attitude, was just the thing to appeal to the latent chivalry and the inborn revolutionary spirit of men in their twenties. And so, between 1835 and 1845, a notable ferment was going on within the walls of the institution on Chelsea Square. Everyone was reading Newman, and most were falling under the spell of his magic pen. Coxe, Tucker, Carey, Wadhams, Walworth, Adams, Breck—the list of the Newmanites is very nearly the roll call of the notable men of the seminary during this decade.

In certain important respects these men differed widely in their attitude toward the Church from the older High Churchmen. The Hobartians were conservatives, whose doctrine was that the Anglican Church had all things needful to salvation. But to these younger men, as to the writers of the *Tracts,* much was wrong with the Church. She was indeed Catholic, but she had largely forgotten and disused her Catholic heritage. To them the Reformation was no great deliverance, but in great part a deformation, behind which it was necessary to go if the Church was to recover her Catholic faith and practice.

An amusing manifestation of this revolutionary spirit is recounted by Doctor Samuel Turner, who in 1843 was acting dean of the seminary:

> The day before Christmas, 1843, I happened to go into the long-room, which was used as a chapel, to see how it was dressed. My attention was arrested by a wooden cross about two feet high, placed on the front railing of the chancel, ornamented partly by evergreens, and partly by artificial flowers. As rumors of certain practices accordant with those of the Church of Rome being in use by some students, had already been considerably circulated, and in very exaggerated forms; and as one student, who in all probability entered with Romanist tendencies, had lately left the Seminary and joined that Church, I thought it highly inexpedient to suffer a novelty like this to pass unnoticed. ... The same night, Christmas-eve, the Seminary bell was rung at twelve o'clock, to the surprise and annoyance of the neighborhood; and some of the students, without asking permission of the Dean or Faculty, held a midnight service in the chapel.[7]

In this sort of manifestation there is obviously as much of high spirits as of High Churchmanship, but it had a certain significance. As a consequence of this breach of discipline, two students were expelled. It is interesting to note that neither of them joined in the exodus to Rome the next year.[8]

But the *Tracts* had a much more important reaction on the student body than this sort of horseplay. We have noted that domestic mission work was already a tradition among High Churchmen. When, therefore, in 1841, Bishop Kemper visited the seminary in search of volunteers to help cultivate his enormous field, he met with a surprisingly ready response. Three men, all pupils of Whittingham and devout readers of the *Tracts,* offered themselves to him. They were

[7] Turner, S., *Autobiography*, p. 198.
[8] For a very full treatment of the Seminary and the Tracts, see the admirable article by Dr. E. Clowes Chorley in the *Historical Magazine of the Episcopal Church* for September, 1936 (Vol. V, 177-201).

THE IMPACT OF THE TRACTS

William Adams, James Lloyd Breck, and John Henry Hobart, son of the bishop.

Breck was the foremost of the three. A born missionary because he was a born pioneer, he had the restlessness, the impatience with settled communities, the longing to be out on the edge of things, that characterized such men as Boone and Harrod. His aim, which he later ascribed to the teachings of Whittingham, but in which we can trace more clearly the innovating spirit of the *Tracts,* was to be a missionary of a new sort, a missionary such as the Anglican Church had not seen since the Reformation. He planned to found a missionary order, combining military discipline, asceticism in life, and apostolic zeal.[9]

Encouraged by Kemper, whose own training under Hobart had made him receptive to such an idea, the three founded at Nashotah, in the wilds of Wisconsin, the first monastic institution in the American Church. This was to be at once a missionary center, a seminary, and a monastery. The community rose at five, recited the canonical hours, received the Holy Communion once a week, supported itself in part by manual labor, and evangelized the country for miles around.[10] In 1844, Breck attempted to have a daily Eucharist, but this lasted for a year only.

The results of this experiment were far-reaching. For years the community barely managed to keep itself alive. The poverty and physical hardships of the life were trying in the extreme. Hobart, after a few years, returned East. Three other men who had joined the pioneers left to enter the Church of Rome. Furthermore, there was a sharp difference in ideals between Breck and Adams. Breck was Tractarian; Adams was Hobartian. Breck's ideal was missionary and monastic; that of Adams was scholastic. Even Breck eventually pushed on farther west into Minnesota, and ended by marrying and

---

[9] It was originally planned that they should work under the Rev. Richard Cadle, an experienced missionary and an old Hobartian. But Cadle, to whom was given the title of "superior" or "prior," was more than a little uncomfortable with his eager young associates. He remarks, "The imposition of celibacy I candidly confess I do not like, not being in the slightest degree oxfordized." Cadle soon left for other fields. [Greene, Howard, *Reverend Richard Fish Cadle,* p. 134.]

[10] Breck, Charles, *Life of James Lloyd Breck,* p. 37.

moving to California. But though the monastic idea had to be dropped, Nashotah struggled on, becoming eventually firmly established as the center of High Churchmanship in the Northwest, representing in its life and teaching the Catholicism of the Oxford Movement, as General Seminary stood for the native High Churchmanship of Seabury and Hobart.

ATTACKS ON THE TRACTS

The controversy between High and Low Church, a controversy that is in its nature eternal, had been going on in this country ever since the consecration of Bishop Seabury. But it had been conducted on lines very foreign to modern thought. The practical questions at issue between the parties had been such matters as the use of the ante-communion service, the desirability of prayer meetings and revivals, and the legality of union services with Protestant congregations. The controversy over the apostolic succession had settled into a sort of compromise, both sides accepting the succession as a fact, and a valuable fact, the question at issue being the necessity of such succession for the existence of a Christian Church. The quarrel over baptismal regeneration, which had drawn a tract from Hobart, and had disturbed the Thirties, had also died out. Beyond these matters there had been, as we have noticed, a good deal of political bickering and manoeuvering of a personal and rather nasty sort. But in general the opposition between the parties had greatly died down during the decade before the appearance of the *Tracts*.

Then came the *Tracts,* and as they grew more radical, as their followers moved farther and farther away from the position of the older High Churchmen, the latent differences between the parties reappeared, and the character of the partisan warfare was completely changed. There could be in this country nothing like the almost universal condemnation from the episcopal bench which greeted the later *Tracts* in England. Not until 1839 did the Low Churchmen begin to be alive to the menace of the new ideas. The first bit of

THE IMPACT OF THE TRACTS

episcopal hostility to Tractarianism which I have been able to find is contained in a letter of Bishop Moore of Virginia, in which he speaks of "the disposition manifested by some of our brethren, both in England and this country, to unsettle the religious opinions of the members of this Church."[11] This comment well illustrates the earliest objections raised against the *Tracts* on this side of the Atlantic. They were suspect, not because they were wrong, but because they were upsetting. But this attitude soon passed into one of more definite opposition. In the same year, Bishop Moore, in his convention address, is doubting whether the Tractarians are sound on the doctrine of justification.

The first real contest directly traceable to the *Tracts* came in the Maryland election of 1840. Maryland was a border state, ecclesiastically as well as politically. To the south lay Virginia, rapidly becoming the headquarters of the Evangelicals, with its distinctively Evangelical seminary at Alexandria. To the north was New Jersey, under the High Church rule of Bishop Doane. The diocese itself was divided. Within the city of Baltimore, the strongest parish, St. Paul's was, under the long rectorate of Dr. William E. Wyatt, a center of High Churchmanship.[12] The next largest parish, Christ Church, was aggressively Evangelical. And so the two factions joined battle for the control of the diocese. When it became evident that Whittingham, the High Church professor of ecclesiastical history at the General Seminary, was the strongest candidate, an attempt was made to force him, as a preliminary to his election, to disavow the *Tracts*. That, after his refusal to do this, his election was still carried through without much of a struggle is evidence that the conflict was not yet at its bitterest.[13]

Through the year 1840 the storm grew momentarily fiercer. The

---
[11]Henshaw, J. P. K., *Life of Bishop R. C. Moore*, p. 287.
[12]Wyatt, for years the leading priest of the diocese of Maryland, and eight times president of the House of Deputies of the General Convention, was another of the numerous pupils of Bishop Hobart. During his fifty-year connection with St. Paul's Parish, he established a boys' school, and introduced the weekly Eucharist and the use of linen eucharistic vestments.
[13]Brand, W., *Life of Bishop Whittingham*, Vol. I, pp. 197 ff.

Evangelicals were rapidly realizing the fundamental difference between their theological position and that of the Tractarians. Furthermore, the Romeward tendency of some of the Tractarians began to be apparent; and that, combined with the rapid increase of the Roman Church in America, gave a new impulse to the anti-Tractarians. In 1840, therefore, Bishop Charles P. McIlvaine (1799-1873), of Ohio, one of the great preachers of the day, a notable public figure, and probably the ablest of the Evangelical bishops, began the attack. The first gun was fired in a sermon on justification, delivered to his diocesan convention. This was followed later in the year by a whole broadside from the volume entitled *Oxford Divinity*. This able, well-written, and slashing work was the first serious attempt in this country to controvert the basic position of the Oxford divines. Complete and whole-hearted in his denunciation, McIlvaine maintained that they—and by implication their American predecessors and followers—had lost hold of the basic Protestant doctrine of justification by faith. He maintained that the Oxford theology was "an essential departure from the great and precious truths of the Gospel . . . thoroughly unscriptural, thoroughly contradictory to the doctrines of our Articles and Homilies and great standard Divines, thoroughly Popish in principle." With this beginning the bishop could see all the corruptions of Rome approaching: "The seminal principle of Invocation of Saints; the partially developed duty of praying for the dead; the half-way step to image-worship . . . the approach to a disuse of preaching, and to a service in an unknown tongue . . . the almost doctrine of Transubstantiation"—these had already appeared. The only logical thing for the Tractarians to do, McIlvaine concluded, was to move in a body into the Roman camp.[14]

In 1841, as if to justify the bishop's conclusion, *Tract 90* appeared, and the storm broke in full fury. Bishop after bishop condemned the *Tracts* in episcopal charges. Even so moderate and saintly a prelate as Griswold of Massachusetts spoke his mind in no uncer-

[14] McIlvaine, C., *Oxford Divinity*, p. 538.

tain terms. After attacking, in his convention address, the furnishings of Trinity Church, Nantucket, as "corresponding with the idolatrous conceits of Christians in those corrupt ages of the Church which some affect to call primitive,"[15] he thus characterized in a letter to the vestry of the same parish the aims of the Oxford reformers:

> I am well aware that there is a new sect lately sprung up among us, called Puseyites, or Low Papists, who have, chiefly in England, written and preached, and published much against the Reformation, and are endeavoring to bring back into the Church of England many of those superstitious mummeries, and idolatrous practices, for protesting against which so many of her pious Bishops and other ministers have been burnt at the stake.[16]

A far more violent enemy of the Tractarians was William Meade (1789-1862), assistant bishop of Virginia. A careful scrutiny of all the evidence available leaves me convinced that he was an able administrator, a heroic missionary, a devout priest, and a most unpleasant person. Of North of Ireland ancestry, he was a Puritan to the core, Calvinistic in his theology, intolerant of anything bordering on worldliness, censorious in his moral judgments, bitter in his enmities, with a tormenting conscience that made him a perpetual inquisitor. In all the theological and personal quarrels of two decades, he was a leading figure. In 1842, when the gentler voice of Bishop Moore had been stilled by death, Meade blasted forth against the *Tracts* as full of "those erroneous and strange doctrines which, from time to time, in all ages, have assailed the peace of the Christian Church, and which the Bishops are solemnly sworn to banish and drive away."[17] We shall meet him again in the near future, carrying his attack from the diocese into General Convention.

But before that Convention met, Bishop Meade had an excellent opportunity to demonstrate his hostility to Catholic-minded churchmen of any variety. In May, 1842, the convention of the diocese of

---
[15]Stone, J. S., *Life of Bishop Griswold*, p. 425.
[16]*Ibid.*, p. 442.
[17]Johns, J., *Life of William Meade*, p. 263.

Virginia met to choose an assistant bishop. One of the most lovable and valuable priests in the diocese was Nicholas Hamner Cobbs. A pupil of the early Evangelicals, he had absorbed from them definitely Catholic principles. He accepted cordially the doctrine of the apostolic succession, believed firmly in baptismal regeneration, used the term Eucharist, kept holy days, and worst of all, "he was convinced that the Oxford movement, all things being considered, was doing more good than harm; he did not subscribe to all the tracts by any means, but he sympathized with the movement as a whole, believing that its insistence on ecclesiological principles was greatly needed."[18] He was therefore anathema to Bishop Meade. What took place at the convention is thus related by one of its members:

> "The most important business of that Convention was the election of Dr. Johns of Baltimore, to be the Assistant Bishop of this Diocese. There was another candidate more beloved by the Society, Rev. N. Cobbs of Petersburg, but Bishop Meade threw his patronage in the scale of Dr. Johns, and after much unpleasantness, and I must add, unfair, management, the election of Dr. Johns was secured."[19]

This election was but a part of what seems to have been a systematic campaign on the part of Meade to root out of Virginia anything savoring of Tractarianism—a campaign which resulted in the departure from the diocese of Cobbs and Thomas Atkinson, both of whom became eminent bishops later in the day.[20]

---

[18] White, G., *A Saint of the Southern Church*, p. 77.

[19] *MSS Journal of the Rev. William T. Leavell*, in the Virginia Diocesan Library.

[20] In a MSS of Bishop Meade's, preserved in the library of the General Theological Seminary, is the following record of a conversation between himself and a a Mr. Christian in 1844:

> "He spoke of the parties *High* and *Low* existing in the Church & of the disposition of the Low Church party in V———a to persecute the other. He alluded to the election of Bishop Johns two years since, & how improperly it was forced on the Church, that it was my act, & how much it was condemned by himself, & the great body of the clergy and laity who would certainly have chosen Mr. Cobbs but for my interference.
>
> "He spoke of the course now pursued by the Bishops of V———a towards those who differed somewhat from them, that it had the effect of driving Mr. Cobbs & ——————— [illegible, probably Atkinson] out of their native state . . . He spoke of the different conduct of Bishop Moore (whom he called a High Churchman) toward the Low Churchmen."

THE IMPACT OF THE TRACTS

But Meade was far exceeded in verbal violence by McIlvaine, who returned to the anti-Tractarian attack in a charge delivered to his clergy in 1843. In this attack there is no compromise. Tractarian doctrine is characterized as "this evil doctrine," an "awful perversion of the Gospel," and "an impudent grasping at priestly domination." But McIlvaine was no mere caller of names. His position was consistent and logical. He views Tractarianism as an attempt to unprotestantize the Church of England.[21] It is, then, a reversion to "the apostate Church against which she—the Church of England—protests."[22] Modern Romanism, which McIlvaine considers a far more dangerous adversary than the Church of the Middle Ages, is to him "a revival of anti-Christian heresy."[23] Any attempt to go back of the Reformation is to him an unmixed evil, since at the Reformation the "preaching of justification had raised from the dead the whole testimony of the Gospel."[24] He has no patience with the claim, common to Tractarians and old High Churchmen, that the tradition of the Church is to be used in the interpretation of Scripture. He is a consistent biblicist; to him the doctrine of the Episcopal Church is wholly based on the "single authority and entire sufficiency of scripture."[25] His final conclusion as to the value of the *Tracts* is clear enough: "I know of no good these writings have done."[26]

DEFENDERS OF THE TRACTS

These were the extremists, and complete condemnation of the Tractarians was confined to them. A fair representative of the moderate High Churchmen was Bishop Thomas Church Brownell (1779-1865), of Connecticut, a diocese so proud of its ancient standing that a "Connecticut churchman" was a proverbial expression, certifying its bearer as orthodox. Brownell stated that while he did not appre-

[21] McIlvaine, *Charge to the Clergy*, p. 6.
[22] *Ibid.*, p. 7.
[23] *Ibid.*, p. 8
[24] *Ibid.*, p. 5.
[25] *Ibid.*, p. 9.
[26] *Ibid.*, p. 28.

hend any material change in the doctrine, discipline, or usages of the Church would come from the influence of the *Tracts,* yet he welcomed them as tending to the ultimate elucidation and establishment of Catholic truth.[27]

Similar was the attitude of Bishop William H. DeLancey (1797-1865), of Western New York. In 1841 he tells his convention that he "entertains no fears of injurious effects to the Church amongst us from these writings";[28] the intelligence of the clergy and laity who read them will sift the wheat from the chaff, repudiating whatever is found inconsistent with the Bible and the Prayer Book. Writing in 1843 an article for the *Gospel Messenger* entitled "What is NOT Puseyism?," DeLancey lists carefully the Catholic truths held by American High Churchmen before Pusey was born. Among them are episcopacy, the apostolic succession, the inward grace of the sacraments, the real and spiritual presence of Christ in the Eucharist, the value of the liturgy, the use of the cross, bowing at the name of Jesus, the observance of saints' days, litany days, and the daily offices, the refusal to canonize Henry VIII and Luther, and the view that Laud was a martyr.[29]

Somewhat less favorable was Whittingham, whose conservative temperament and intense anti-Romanism were undoubtedly shocked by the extreme tendencies of many of his own former pupils, but whose basic principles were too well established and in too close agreement with the general Tractarian position to be readily altered by the popular outcry.

Outspoken in defence of the *Tracts* were Seabury and Onderdonk. Onderdonk, in his address to the New York convention of 1841, advised the laymen of his diocese to read the *Tracts,* and attributed to their influence the evidences he had noted of greater reverence in the use of the Prayer Book and greater care in the ornamentation of churches.[30] Seabury, in *The Churchman,* persistently counterattacked

[27] Beardsley, E. E., *Diocese of Connecticut,* Vol. II, p. 328.
[28] Hayes, C., *Diocese of Western New York,* p. 146.
[29] *Ibid.,* p. 167.
[30] *New York Convention Journal,* 1841, pp. 81-85.

THE IMPACT OF THE TRACTS

against McIlvaine; in this attack he was joined by Bishop Otey of Tennessee. McIlvaine deeply resented this attack, and a warfare of "open letters" ensued, in which Bishop Onderdonk, as sponsor for *The Churchman,* was involved. Thus began McIlvaine's hostility to Onderdonk, a hostility which was to have serious results in the days of the Onderdonk trial.[81]

Doane, whose connection with the Tractarians was longest and most intimate of any American bishop, dating from 1834, when he brought out the first American edition of Keble's *The Christian Year,* was, of course, an unqualified defender of the *Tracts.* For years he maintained a correspondence with the English leaders. In 1841 he visited England, talked with Keble and Pusey, deplored Newman's dangerous tendencies, and returned home with renewed determination to carry on the defence of Anglican Catholicism.[82]

Hopkins, as usual, struck off his own course. In 1838 he had visited England, met Pusey and Newman, with whom he had previously corresponded, and returned to America enthusiastic about their work. In 1842, in his formal charge to his clergy, he takes up the case of the *Tracts.* He begins by expressing his admiration for them:

> I hold the Oxford Tracts in high estimation, as writings of a most useful tendency in some respects, particularly adapted to the present circumstances of our venerated mother Church of England. With some of the distinguished authors I have held a personal intercourse, marked on their part with the kindest liberality and most friendly attention. And I have never doubted, for a moment, the purity of their motives, their attachment to the Church, the ardour of their piety, their deep reverence for sacred things, their exalted standard of Christian effort, their learning, and their spirit of rare meekness and humility.[83]

But then, with characteristic Hopkinsian independence, the bishop goes on to enumerate those points on which he did not agree with

---

[81] It was also credibly reported that Bishop Onderdonk asked all candidates for orders if they had read the *Tracts,* and if they had not, exhorted them to do so.
[82] Doane, W. C., *Life of Bishop Doane,* p. 271.
[83] Hopkins, J. H., *Life of Bishop Hopkins,* p. 215.

the writers whom he had just commended in such terms. He does not consider episcopacy essential to the very being of a Church; he does not accept the infallibility or inerrancy of the Church in interpreting scripture; he considers that the Tractarian views of the Real Presence approach the heresy of Transubstantiation; and he holds that the method of interpreting the Articles of Religion advocated in *Tract 90* utterly destroys the object for which those articles were framed. But after thus establishing his own independence, Hopkins ends on a note of praise:

> Clearer notions of Church principles and a far higher estimate of their value, a more elevated standard of clerical character, a humbler temper, a more zealous effort to do good, a more sacred regard to divine services, and a plainer line of ecclesiastical subordination, may be traced, under divine Providence, to their influence.[34]

Hopkins followed this charge, in 1843 and 1844, by a series of four open letters entitled, *The Novelties which Disturb our Peace*. The title of these letters is really the severest thing about them. They are a fair and temperate discussion of four alleged errors of the Tractarians. Against the writers of the *Tracts*, Hopkins asserts the validity of lay baptism—thus proving himself the better Catholic. He maintains again that episcopacy is valuable, but not essential to the very being of a Church, and that the Protestant sects are not, therefore, to be unchurched. He holds that Pusey's view of the Real Presence is wrong, and that the true view is the receptionist. Finally, he is sure that the attempt of *Tract 90* to reconcile England with Rome is utterly opposed to the truth, the Church of England being in fact reformed and Protestant.

In these letters Hopkins was, it seems to me, led by his fears of Romanism to something like a denial of his normal theological position. It was not characteristic of Hopkins to defend justification by faith only, in terms worthy of McIlvaine, or to assert that the Church

[34]Hopkins, J. H., *Life of Bishop Hopkins*, p. 216.

is not a corporation, but an aggregation. But in the letters there is nothing of the rant which characterized so much of the anti-Tractarian writings; and one feels throughout Hopkins' genuine respect for Newman and Pusey, and his genuine discomfort at having to disagree with them.

When, in 1842, Francis P. Kenrick, the Roman Catholic bishop of Philadelphia, issued a pamphlet welcoming the Tractarians to Rome, Hopkins was instant in replying that the Catholic position was still, as it always had been, tenable within the limits of the Anglican Communion, and that Catholic and Roman were far from synonymous terms. This reply by so definite an anti-Romanist as Hopkins was of extreme value to the High Church cause, reassuring the plain man within the Church of the loyalty of the older group of High Church bishops.

THE CAREY ORDINATION

But the opponents of Tractarianism did not rest content with theological dissertations and episcopal thunderings. It was the apparent determination of the extreme Evangelicals to make the Church too hot to hold a follower of the Tractarians. Their first target was Arthur Carey. Carey, the first man of his particular type to be produced by the Anglican Church in America, was in some respects a gentler Richard Hurrell Froude. Thoughtful and reserved, even as a boy, precocious in his studies, ascetic in his life, brilliant in his writings, daring in his thinking, gifted with a singular purity and sweetness of character, he had first imbibed High Church principles in the schools maintained by Bishop Hopkins at Burlington, Vermont. Coming to the General Seminary in 1839, when the influence of the *Tracts* was at its height, he at once fell under the spell of Newman, whom he followed to an extent deplored by more cautious seminarians. Suspected of concealed Romanism by conservative members of the faculty, he had rendered himself doubly suspect by his unfortunate friendship for B. B. J. McMaster. McMaster was one of those irritating young men who delight in defending the extremest positions with the sharpest of tongues.[35] He was at this time on the edge of seceding to Rome, and Carey was thought to be completely under his influence.

When, in 1843, Carey presented himself to Bishop Onderdonk for ordination as a deacon, it was felt that the case needed investigation. Two leading Low Church priests of the city, Doctors Hugh Smith and Henry Anthon, therefore, accused him of heresy. The bishop appears to have acted fairly and wisely. Although Carey had passed his canonical examinations, and his testimonials were in perfect order, the bishop called together eight assessors, and with them subjected Carey to a most searching examination.

It ought not to be difficult to discover just what opinions Carey held, for never was an inquisition given fuller publicity. Doctors Smith and Anthon published a pamphlet containing what purported to be a full account of the examination, with questions and answers quoted verbatim. This was reviewed *in extenso* by Seabury, who was one of the assessors, and who claimed that the Smith-Anthon account was full of omissions and distortions. Finally, Carey himself supplemented his original answers by fuller explanations. It is on the last statement, not on the pleadings of the prosecutor or the counsel for the defense, that I have based my conclusions. It is evident, first of all, that whatever else Carey held, he believed in Newman. The balanced attitude, the refusal to join in a sweeping condemnation of all things Roman, or to endorse as perfect all things Anglican, the realization that the Anglican Reformation had its evil side—these came straight from Littlemore. He held—and claimed the support of Bishop White for his position—that the Thirty-nine Articles have not the binding force in this country that they had in England at that period. All these were enough to make a man suspect in that day of clash and conflict.

But on basic issues, Carey seems to have been sound enough. He

---

[35]After his secession, McMaster quarreled with Archbishop Hughes and with Orestes Brownson, was jailed for disloyalty during the Civil War, and died an utterly discredited old man.

believed in the Real Presence, but not in Transubstantiation, refusing, with Anglican theologians in general, to define the manner of the Presence. He believed, and backed his belief with the great name of Hobart, in an intermediate future state and in the efficacy of prayers for the departed, but not in purgatorial punishment or expiation. He denounced indulgences and masses for the dead as gross errors, condemned the invocation of saints as currently practiced by the Church of Rome, and categorically stated that with his present principles he could not subscribe to the creed of Pius IV, nor take orders in the Roman Church.[86]

Most of these views are now held by multitudes of Anglican priests, and apparently Bishop Onderdonk and the majority of the attending priests considered that they contained no serious heresy, since they declared that there was no obstacle to his ordination. The accusers, dissatisfied, attended the ordination, and when the bishop, as the office prescribes, demanded if there were any impediment to the ordination, the two priests, robed in surplice and scarf, rose in their places and solemnly protested. The bishop refused to entertain their protest; whereupon they paraded out of the church.[87]

This scene was followed by a perfect hurricane of pamphlets from both sides. Most of the older High Churchmen took up Carey's cause; Seabury at once made him assistant at the Church of the Annunciation, where he remained until his death in 1844 took from the movement one of its most attractive figures. Thus he escaped further trouble. Not so his right reverend consecrator. Bishops Chase, McIlvaine, and Hopkins protested in print against his action in ordaining Carey; an anti-Onderdonk party was formed in the diocese of New York; and the feeling thus aroused led directly to the tragedy of the Onderdonk trial.

[86]A sizeable bookshelf might be filled with materials on the Carey ordination. The chief sources are: Smith-Anthon, *The True Issue of the True Churchman* (New York, 1843); the review of the above in the July 22, 1843, issue of *The Churchman*, presumably by Seabury; Carey's own answers, in *The Churchman*, August 26, 1843.

In the first edition of this work, I based my conclusions on the Smith-Anthon pamphlet, and completely mis-stated Carey's position. *Mea culpa*. However, Bishop Whittingham had the same experience.

[87]Walworth, C. A., *Oxford Movement in America*, Chaps. V and VI, *passim*.

A recent discovery has just demonstrated the close connection between the two events—the ordination of Carey and the suspension of Onderdonk. On July 31, 1843, Presiding Bishop Chase sent a circular letter to all the bishops, asking for their opinion about the ordination of Carey. His letter, with replies from all the bishops except four, has been recently found among the Chase papers, and was published by Professor Richard G. Salomon of Bexley Hall, Kenyon College.[38] The correspondence between these replies and the votes of the writers at the trial of Bishop Onderdonk is amazing.

THE BATTLE IN THE GENERAL CONVENTION OF 1844

When the next General Convention met in Philadelphia, on October 2, 1844, everyone in the Church knew that there was to be a grand trial of party strength. Early in the year the Rev. Stephen H. Tyng, one of the strongest of the Evangelicals, and the editor of *The Episcopal Recorder,* the organ of the most militant section of that party, had thus avowed his intention:

> Not a delegate should be elected, either to a State or to a General Convention, whose views and actions are not known. Not a Trustee should be appointed over the Seminaries of the Church whose mind is not thoroughly understood. Not an officer should be appointed, of any kind in the Church, who is not clear of the errors which are so seen and known in our midst.

Bishop Meade came to the Convention with a set of resolutions all prepared which completely denounced Tractarianism, but apparently they were never acted on.[39] In the House of Deputies, however, several such sets of resolutions were offered, the most striking being those of the Rev. Adam Empie of Virginia. After a preamble, in which *Tract 90,* the *British Critic,* Palmer's *Narrative,* and the Carey ordination, are mentioned, the resolutions read as follows:

[38]Richard G. Salomon, "The Episcopate on the Carey Case," *Historical Magazine of the Episcopal Church,* Vol. XVIII (September, 1949), 240-281.
[39]Johns, J., *Life of Bishop Meade,* pp. 264, 274.

THE IMPACT OF THE TRACTS

> *Resolved,* That we do therefore solemnly protest against the errors and abuses of Tractarianism as inconsistent with the Gospel and with the principles of our Protestant Episcopal Church. For Tractarianism teaches that there is no material difference between the doctrines of our Church and those of Popery . . .
>
> *Resolved,* That we do most earnestly caution both our clergy and laity to guard against this Popish poison that is gradually and rapidly diffusing itself over the Church.[40]

These resolutions were too bitter even for Evangelical consumption. The actual contest came over a more moderate, or at least a more equivocal, set:

> Whereas, in the estimation of many Ministers and Members of the Protestant Episcopal Church in the United States, serious errors of doctrine have, within a few years, been introduced and extensively promulgated, by means of Tracts, through the periodical Press, and from the Pulpit: and whereas it is important, for the preservation of the peace and purity of the Church, that such errors, if existing, should be met, and as far as practicable removed, by the action of the Convention.
>
> *Be it therefore Resolved,* if the House of Bishops concur, That it is desirable to prepare and promulgate a clear and distinct expression of the opinions entertained by this Convention respecting the Rule of Faith, the Justification of Man, the nature, design, and efficacy of the Sacraments, and such other matters as, in view of the foregoing circumstances, may be deemed expedient by the House of Bishops.
>
> *Be it further Resolved,* that it is desirable that such expression of opinion should originate in the House of Bishops, and receive the concurrent action of this House, and that the House of Bishops be requested to take action accordingly.[41]

The ultimate object of these resolutions, vaguely worded though they were, was to secure from the most authoritative source possible in the American Church a distinct condemnation of Tractarianism, and thereby of the whole High Church party—to place High Church-

---
[40] *The Churchman,* Vol. XIV, p. 139.
[41] *Journal* of the General Convention, 1844, pp. 30-31.

men in this country in an even worse position than they held in England. The debates were, as one would expect, long and bitter, degenerating occasionally into personalities, as in Ogilby's attack on Tyng. The discussion began on the eighth day of the session, and was continued on the tenth, the eleventh, and the thirteenth—this session going far into the night.[42] When the vote was finally taken, the party opposed to the *Tracts*—perhaps one had better say the party desiring a flat condemnation of the *Tracts*—had decisively lost. The vote stood as follows:

Clergy, affirmative, eight. Negative, fifteen. Divided, four. Laity, affirmative, eleven. Negative, eleven. Divided, one.

This vote was, of course, by dioceses. It is interesting, and gives one some notion of the state of parties within the Church, to analyze the result. Vermont, Connecticut, New York, Western New York, New Jersey, Delaware, Maryland, North Carolina, Florida, Alabama, and Tennessee were all unanimous in opposing the attack on the Oxford Movement. Maine, Virginia, Georgia, and Ohio were the only dioceses unanimous in support of the resolutions.[43]

Elated by this victory, the High Church deputies then offered this substitute:

Resolved, That the House of Clerical and Lay Deputies consider the Liturgy, Offices, and Articles of the Church sufficient exponents of her sense of the essential doctrines of Holy Scripture; and that the Canons of the Church afford ample means of discipline and correction for all who depart from her standards.

And further that the General Convention is not a suitable tribunal for the trial and censure of, and that the Church is not responsible for, the errors of individuals, whether they are members of this Church or otherwise.

This resolution was passed almost without opposition.[44]

The result of these memorable proceedings was to commit the Church to a policy of toleration. Although many, perhaps a majority

---

[42] Full account of the debate in *The Churchman,* Vol. XIV, pp. 126-39.
[43] *Journal* of the General Convention, 1844, p. 63.
[44] *Ibid.,* pp. 64-65.

of the deputies at the Convention were opposed to Tractarianism, Catholic doctrine had been too long accepted, and by too powerful a section of the American Church, to allow any such sweeping condemnation. The Low Church party had made its bitterest attack and failed.

One thing, however, the opponents of Tractarianism could do. Bishop Henry U. Onderdonk, of Pennsylvania, who had been elected after one of the bitterest of the early clashes between High and Low Church, had fallen into the use of intoxicating liquors as a relief from the pain of a long continued illness. Threatened with trial, he came before the Convention, acknowledged his fault, and submitted to suspension from his office. The net result was the complete triumph of the Low Church party in Pennsylvania. For decades only a Low Churchman could be elected bishop of that important diocese.

THE INVESTIGATION OF THE GENERAL SEMINARY

But now the attack shifted. The General Seminary had been from its inception, as we have noted, the home of High Churchmanship. Her students had, more than any other group within the Church, responded to the call of the *Tracts.* The burlesque proceedings of the previous Christmas had been noised abroad, and Bishop McIlvaine had secured complete information about the matter. Most of the extremists of this date, the high-flyers, who made the hair of good Protestants stand on end, were students within her walls. One student had actually been converted to Romanism during the previous year. Above all, the Carey ordination had forced the state of the seminary upon the attention of every churchman. When, therefore, the Board of Trustees of the seminary prepared its triennial report for the General Convention, a dispute arose, and a minority of the board, among whom was Bishop Hopkins, refused to sign the report, which declared, in effect, that all was well with the lads. The question was thus thrown into the House of Bishops, and that House resolved, after the adjournment of the Convention, to proceed to the seminary, and there look into things for themselves. This investigation was, of course, precipitated by the Low Churchmen, but the High Church leaders, with keen political sense, immediately fell into line. The actual resolution authorizing the investigation was moved by Bishop Doane, and seconded by Bishop Ives.

The Low Church bishops, of whom McIlvaine was the most active, submitted a series of question to be asked the faculty, of which the following are fair samples:

12. Are the works of the Rev. Dr. Pusey, Messrs. Newman, Keble, Palmer, Ward, and Massingberd, or any of them, used as text books, or publicly or privately recommended in the Seminary?

29. Are the Oxford Tracts publicly or privately recommended to the students in the Seminary?

35. Are the doctrinal and other errors of the Roman Church, as referred to in the 39 Articles, duly exposed in the instructions of the Seminary?[45]

To balance these there was a number of questions submitted, one would think almost with humorous intent, by High Church bishops, professing anxiety lest the students were being led into the errors of Calvinism, private judgment, and German rationalistic criticism.

These questions, totalling 43 in number, the professors were required to answer in writing, and Professor Ogilby, Whittingham's successor in the chair of Church history, who was suspect as being a close friend of Bishop Doane, and who had made rather an exhibition of himself in the Convention by his attack on Dr. Tyng, was given a special grilling. But no apparent heresy or treason was uncovered, and the whole affair ended in a coat of whitewash being applied to the institution.[46]

Before the House of Bishops adjourned, they drew up a pastoral letter, obviously written in large part by the Low Church bishops. The letter emphasizes the doctrine of justification by faith only (dur-

[45] *Journal* of the General Convention, 1844, pp. 232-233.
[46] The record of the investigation in the *Journal* of the General Convention, 1844, covers 24 pages (pp. 227-250) of fine print.

ing this period, whenever you hear much about justification, you may be sure that a veiled attack on Tractarianism is in progress). It condemns, in terms reassuring to sound Protestants, "the blasphemous doctrine of Transubstantiation, and the abominable idolatries of the Mass." It ends, significantly, by admonishing professors at theological seminaries to be especially careful that candidates for the ministry are grounded in sound doctrine.[47]

THE ONDERDONK TRIAL

The Convention ended in toleration; the investigation of the seminary in something approaching farce; but the next attack on Tractarianism resulted in stark tragedy. Foiled in their attempt to secure an authoritative condemnation of the principles of the Tractarians and their American sympathizers, some of the most active leaders of the opposition shifted their forces to the personal front. In many ways the bishop of New York, Benjamin T. Onderdonk, had made himself the most obnoxious of the High Church leaders. He had been outspoken and uncompromising in his defense of the *Tracts*. He had protected Tractarianism in the seminary. Above all, he had ordained Arthur Carey, and during the pamphleteering war which followed that ordination, had virtually dared his critics to bring him to trial. While the Convention was still sitting, sinister rumors about his morals had been heard, and one abortive attempt had been made to bring up his personal character as a subject of discussion in the House of Bishops. As a result of this, Bishops Ives, Kemper, and DeLancey went to New York immediately at the close of the session and made personal investigation of these rumors. They found no ground for action. But the charges were taken up by Bishops Otey, Elliott, and Meade, who, after their investigation, presented Bishop Onderdonk for trial on the grounds of immorality and impurity.

This trial, the most notorious in our ecclesiastical annals, was for years so obscured by party spirit that to find the truth of the matter

[47]*The Churchman,* Vol. XIV, p. 141.

seemed hopeless. However, all the evidence which was produced at the trial is still in existence, and a careful perusal of it leads, I think, to certain very definite conclusions. In the first place, the overt acts alleged seem to us today ridiculous. No actual adultery was charged; the assertion was that the bishop in his conversations with women had indulged in certain pettings and pattings with evil intent. The most serious of the allegations was completely disproved, the woman in question denying in court that the bishop had ever acted as represented. The opinion of Bishop DeLancey, one of the coolest and sanest heads in the House of Bishops, was that Onderdonk had been merely unfortunate in his freedom of manner. However, this was during the Victorian era, when the sexual taboo was at its height. Furthermore, the bishop's case was sadly mishandled by himself and his advisors. And, above all, in the fevered atmosphere of that year fair judgment was practically impossible. The votes of the court were distinctly partisan.

Three scrutinies were taken. On the first, eight bishops voted for deposition—Chase, McIlvaine, Polk, Lee, Johns, Eastburn, Henshaw, and Hopkins. Six of these were strong Evangelicals; Polk was a moderate; and Hopkins, as we have noted, was temporarily anti-Tractarian. Six voted for admonition, which was to say, "We acquit you of any evil intent, but please be more careful." They were Ives, Doane, DeLancey, Gadsden, Whittingham, and Kemper. All were High Churchmen. Smith and Freeman, Evangelicals, and Brownell, moderate High Churchman, voted for suspension. Eventually, since the majority of the court had pronounced him guilty, the High Churchmen agreed to suspension, but simply in order to ward off deposition. The suspension was never repealed. Regarded by his fellow High Churchmen, and by the larger part of his diocese, as a martyr, Onderdonk lived in retirement until his death in 1861, always asserting his innocence, and several times vainly petitioning the House of Bishops for restoration. He is buried in Trinity Church, New York, where his recumbent effigy, robed in cope and mitre, with the serpent

THE IMPACT OF THE TRACTS

of slander writhing under his feet, testifies to the steadfast faith of his friends.[48]

The Onderdonk trial, like all such personal assaults, proved nothing. It did not even prove a serious setback to High Churchmanship in the diocese of New York. The continued loyalty of the diocese to its accused diocesan, and the principles for which he stood, was repeatedly demonstrated. In 1845, the diocesan convention refused to pass a resolution stating that Bishop Onderdonk, even if restored to office, could never be a useful bishop of New York. In 1846, it resolved to pay him a part of his salary, the remainder of the income of the episcopal fund being used to pay for the services of supplying bishops. In 1849, it refused to ask for the bishop's resignation, and petitioned General Convention to put into operation its own canon forbidding indefinite suspension.

When, in 1851, a canon had been passed by General Convention permitting the election of a provisional bishop, the diocesan convention again showed its loyalty to High Church principles. On the first ballot, Seabury, one of the most conspicuous defenders of the *Tracts* and of Bishop Onderdonk, received a plurality in both orders. His name was withdrawn on the second ballot, whereupon the Rev. John Williams and the Rt. Rev. Horatio Southgate, both decided High Churchmen, became the leading candidates. Eventually, in 1852, the Rev. Jonathan M. Wainwright, who had likewise stood out as a supporter of Onderdonk, was elected to the semi-vacant see.

SECESSIONS TO ROME

But if the suspension of Bishop Onderdonk was no great setback to High Churchmanship in the diocese of New York, the case was far otherwise in the General Seminary. Immediately after the trial the seminary authorities themselves instituted a sort of inquisition.

---

[48] The best summaries of the case are by Manross, "*History of the American Episcopal Church*" pp. 280-81; and by E. C. Chorley, "Benjamin Tredwell Onderdonk, Fourth Bishop of New York," in *Historical Magazine of the Episcopal Church*, Vol. IX (1940), pp. 1-51.

They were thoroughly justified, for by this time a considerable number of the student body had ceased to feel any loyalty to the Protestant Episcopal Church.

One of these students, Clarence Walworth, has written two small volumes, entertaining in the extreme, which show how far his group had gone from the position of the Hobartians. To the old High Churchman the American Church was not only Catholic, but the best modern exemplar of Catholicism. But James A. McMaster, speaking of the Church, refers to "her poor remnant of Catholicism."[49] He thus expostulated with another student who had just tipped his hat to an Episcopal Church:

> "What are you taking your hat off to, Wadhams? To that old meeting-house? There's nothing inside of that but a communion table, where the vestrymen put their hats. Wait till you come to a real church with a real altar and a sacrifice."[50]

While the Hobartians were strongly anti-Roman, the seminary group definitely copied such Roman usages as the daily reading of the Breviary. They practiced devotion to the Blessed Virgin: Walworth ends one of his letters, "May God and Our Lady prosper us."[51] They had a strong belief in celibacy. Wadhams spoke his mind in regard to a married priesthood in good round terms:

> "My view of a priest is, that he is a man so long as he remains unmarried, and as soon as he has married he is an old granny."[52]

They advocated and used private confession. Some of these things have since that time become commonplace in the American Church, but in 1845 there was little room for men who talked like this within her borders.

The determined effort of the faculty to root out disloyalists resulted in a series of conversions. There had already been one or two to leave the Episcopal Church for Rome. In 1841, James Roosevelt

---

[49] Walworth, *Reminiscences*, p. 56.
[50] *Ibid.*, p. 50.
[51] *Ibid.*, p. 86.
[52] *Ibid.*, p. 27.

THE IMPACT OF THE TRACTS

Bayley, the young rector of St. Peter's, Harlem, had gone; a decided loss, no doubt, since he subsequently became archbishop of Baltimore. In 1844, Edward Putnam left the seminary a convert. But in 1845 the conversions came thick and fast—Clarence Walworth, McMaster the firebrand, Benjamin Whicher, and Edgar Wadhams, who became the first Roman Catholic bishop of Ogdensburg. They were followed by Nathaniel A. Hewit and Dwight E. Lyman from Maryland, and William H. Hoit from Vermont. Six men left Nashotah. Francis Asbury Baker went from Maryland to join Hewit in founding the Paulist Fathers, and one went even from ultra-Low Church Ohio, Henry Richards.

But there were no such losses as the movement experienced in England. The seceders were all, with one exception to be hereafter noted, young men, without established position within the Church, most of whom had been converts to the Episcopal Church from various Protestant bodies.[53] Several were young men of great promise, but no outstanding leaders, no men of the calibre and position of Newman or Manning, were lost. This was largely due to the fact that the old High Church party, strongly entrenched, holding many of the chief sees, was able to prevent anything like the systematic persecution of Tractarians which went on in England. Doane, Kemper, and, above all, Whittingham, distinguished themselves by making their dioceses refuges for young priests driven from other sees.

The case of John Murray Forbes deserves separate mention. Like Newman and Manning, Forbes has the distinction of having been eminent in two branches of the Catholic Church. He was a man marked out for fame, of superb presence, a little above medium height, of handsome features and florid complexion. On leaving the General Seminary, he became in 1834 rector of St. Luke's Church, New York, where he followed the Hobartian tradition of Whittingham and Ives. In 1841, influenced by his reading of the *Tracts,* he

---

[53]Wadhams, for example, was baptized four times: first by a Presbyterian minister; then by a Baptist minister; next by a priest of the Episcopal Church; last by a Roman Catholic priest.

[67]

instituted daily services and a weekly communion. He was a close friend of his predecessor, Bishop Ives, and it was in St. Luke's that the bishop received the professions of Oliver S. Prescott and William Glenny French, the first members of Ives' new monastic community at Valle Crucis, North Carolina. The events of the Forties led Forbes to re-examine his position as a priest in the Episcopal Church, and in February, 1848, he resigned his rectorate. But, like Newman, and unlike the Walworth-McMaster group, he left the Anglican fold slowly, regretfully, painfully. His reasons for leaving are clearly suggested by a sermon preached by him in 1847, in which he speaks of "the mournful and manacled state of our Mother Church of England, with a Queen's Privy Council for its virtual head," and "the divided and distracted state of our Church at home, with two living voices and two energizing systems."[54] Although there was little doubt as to his destination, so great was the affection of his parish for him that his resignation was not accepted until October, 1849, when he actually entered the Roman Church, accompanied by his curate, Thomas S. Preston. He became pastor of St. Ann's Roman Catholic Church, New York. That he was highly regarded by that Communion and rose to some eminence in it, is shown by his being awarded the degree of Doctor of Sacred Theology by Pope Pius IX, and by being sent by Archbishop Hughes of New York to organize the American College for Priests in Rome.

But he found the Roman yoke unendurable. In 1859, in a brief and dignified letter to Archbishop Hughes, he announced his intention of returning to his former allegiance:

> When I came to you it was, as I stated, with a deep and conscientious conviction that it was necessary to be in communion with the See of Rome; but this conviction I have not been able to sustain, in face of the fact that by it the natural rights of man and all individual liberty must be sacrificed—and not only so, but the private conscience often violated, and one forced, by

[54]Tuttle, Mrs. H. C., *History of St. Luke's Church*, p. 512.

THE IMPACT OF THE TRACTS

silence at least, to acquiesce in what is opposed to moral truth and justice.[55]

This was his only *Apologia,* and in view of the countless explanatory volumes in which countless converts have laid bare the turmoil of their souls, one is inclined to respect the reticence of Forbes. His deposition reversed, he became in 1869 dean of the General Seminary.

TOTAL EFFECTS OF THE TRACTS IN AMERICA

To sum up in a word the total effects of the *Tracts* in America is no easy matter. Their most obvious result was to sharpen the dying hostility between High and Low Church, to make plain the cleavage in fundamental doctrine. They precipitated conflicts that ran through the decade, conflicts waged with varying fortunes, but resulting, on the whole, in securing for the High Churchmen, even of the extreme Tractarian school, an assured toleration within the Church.

On the other hand, they tended to make a great many plain people, especially among the laity, link together Tractarianism and Romanism, to make them suspicious of any person or party bearing the High Church label. This suspicion is clearly reflected in the episcopal elections of the period. Thus, between 1830 and 1840, fourteen bishops were elected. Of these, eleven were High Churchmen, though in varying intensity. But of the fifteen elected between 1841 and 1850, only five could by any stretch of the imagination be termed High Church, and not one of these was an outstanding leader of the party. The *Tracts,* then, definitely stopped for a time the slow, peaceful penetration of the Church by Catholic principles, a penetration which had been going forward so decidedly in 1840.

More disastrous than this, far more disastrous than the secessions to Rome, which were more startling than dangerous, was the rift opened by the *Tracts* within the High Church movement itself, a rift so wide and deep that an advanced High Churchman of the next

---

[55]He later remarked, "I had to come back to retain my regard for truth. I saw so much that was false." (Riley, *Life of Hoffman,* p. 594.)

decade[56] asserted that the great enemy of true Catholicism within the American Church was not the Low or the Broad Church, but the old High Church party. As late as 1935 an extremist who had seceded to Rome stated that "strange as it may seem, the greatest obstacle to the spread of the Oxford Movement in America was the existence of a well-established and powerful High Church tradition." This is undoubtedly an exaggeration, but an exaggeration which has some truth in it. Thus the *Tracts,* or rather the outcry against the *Tracts,* drove Hopkins for a time into the arms of the Evangelicals; they made Whittingham, as we shall see, a persecutor of ritualists; they led Kemper to attack party spirit and "the blasphemies of Rome." Younger men, less certain of themselves, like Coxe, DeLancey's successor as bishop of Western New York, who had once been an avowed Newmanite, ran in their terror to the opposite extreme, and became bitter enemies of anything which savored of Tractarianism. From 1840 on, then, we find in the American Church not one, but two High Church movements: the one, native, conservative, centering largely in the East, with the General Seminary as its nursery; the other, imported, advanced, finding its strongest support in Nashotah and the Mid-Western dioceses. The difference persists to this day.

On the credit side, the *Tracts* undoubtedly accomplished much good. In 1855, when the tumult and the shouting had in part died away, and it was possible to view the whole matter of Tractarianism in a clearer light, Bishop Horatio Potter of New York, one of the coolest and most statesmanlike men who ever sat in the American House of Bishops, attempted to sum up the results of the movement:

> All this may serve to explain the philosophy of what has been taking place during the last twenty years in the Anglican Church and in the Church in this country. It must, I think, be confessed by every enlightened observer, that the *movement* which has occurred in the Anglican Church within twenty years, is the most energetic and the most important of any which has been witnessed in that branch of the Church, since the period of the

[56]John Henry Hopkins, Jr.

THE IMPACT OF THE TRACTS

Reformation. Outward pressure and other causes constrained her to appeal to higher evidence and authority than the accident of a state establishment. She dug down to her foundations. She pointed to Scripture and to the records of the first Christian ages, to prove that her origin was from God, and her power divine ... The Church set herself to resuscitate and reclaim those old Catholic elements, which had ever been a real and essential part of her system; but which, for a long period, had been too much in abeyance, and too much overlooked ... The ethos of the ancient Church was revived and renewed in the modern. The old Catholic symbolism grew again into favor; and the purest branch of the Church of God, on earth, refused any longer to ignore or eschew the most affecting sign of the Christian Faith, merely because it had been abused and dishonored by one of the most corrupt.

Coincident with this revival of Catholic truth and the primitive ethos, was a wonderful revival of spiritual life and energy. Noble churches went up by hundreds in quarters where before not five had been added in a century. Colonial Bishoprics established and endowed all round the globe, and served by Catholic-minded men of the true Apostolic spirit—new life infused into the whole parochial system at home—a spirit of earnest devotion taking possession of the great schools and universities, in which the youth of the land are trained—unwonted devices and efforts to reach and reclaim the children of vice and misery—more abundant prayers and alms—*these* are some of the abundant tokens ... that the Church as a whole has arisen and shaken herself from the dust.

And the fact that the recent movement in the Church tends, like other movements, to excess, and that the excess is in the direction of Romanism, no more proves that the movement itself is essentially Romanish, than the fact, that the movement at the Reformation tended to excess; the excess in that case, being in the direction of rationalism and infidelity, proved that the Reformation was essentially infidel.[57]

In summary, it may be said, then, that the *Tracts* gave the High Church party a clearer view of its own principles and of the logical

---
[57] *New York Convention Journal*, 1855, p. 108.

conclusions of those principles; they inspired its younger adherents with new life and zeal; they broke up the old High Church complacency; they had their part in inspiring the missionary movement led by Kemper and Breck; they gave to High Churchmanship a warmth, a color, an intensity of devotion that had been sometimes—though not always—lacking in the more intellectual Catholicism of the older High Churchman. Hobartian Catholicism tended to degenerate in a mere Catholicism of theory; the *Tracts* showed the way to a Catholicism of worship and life.

BIBLIOGRAPHY

(The *Lives* of Hopkins and Whittingham continue to be valuable.)

BEARDSLEY, E. E., *History of the Episcopal Church in Connecticut*, 2 vols., New York and London, 1868.

BRECK, C., *Life of the Rev. James Lloyd Breck*, New York, 1886.

CHORLEY, E. C., "The Oxford Movement in the Seminary," in *Historical Magazine of the Protestant Episcopal Church*, Vol. V, pp. 177-201.
—"Bishop Benjamin Tredwell Onderdonk," in *ibid.*, Vol. IX, pp. 1-51.

CLARKE, C. K. L., *Bishop Hobart and the Oxford Movement*, Milwaukee, 1933.

DOANE, G. W., *A Brief Examination*, Burlington, 1841. (Reply to McIlvaine.)

HAYES, C. W., *The Diocese of Western New York*, Rochester, 1904.

HENSHAW, J. P. K., *Memoir of the Life of the Rt. Rev. Richard Channing Moore*, Philadelphia, 1842.

HEWIT, A. F., *Life of the Rev. Francis A. Baker*, New York, 1868.

HOLCOMBE, J., *An Apostle of the Wilderness*, New York, 1903. [Breck.]

HOPKINS, J. H., *The Novelties Which Disturb Our Peace*, Philadelphia, 1844.

JOHNS, J., *Memoir of the Life of the Rt. Rev. William Meade*, Baltimore, 1867.

McILVAINE, C. P., *Oxford Divinity*, London, 1841.
—*Charge to the Clergy of the Diocese of Ohio* (New York, 1843).

THE IMPACT OF THE TRACTS

PROTESTANT EPISCOPAL CHURCH, *Proceedings of the Court Convened for the Trial of the Rt. Rev. Benjamin T. Onderdonk, D.D.*, New York, 1845.

—*Pamphlets Concerning Bishop Onderdonk*, New York, 1844 (in G. T. S. library). See also, extensive bibliography, *Historical Magazine of the Protestant Episcopal Church*, Vol. IX., pp. 45-51.

SALOMON, RICHARD G., "The Episcopate on the Carey Case," *Historical Magazine of the Episcopal Church*, Vol. XVIII (Sept. 1949), 240-281.

STONE, J. S., *Memoir of the Life of the Rt. Rev. Alexander Viets Griswold*, Philadelphia, 1844.

TURNER, S., *Autobiography*, New York, 1863.

TUTTLE, MRS. H. C., *History of St. Luke's Church, New York*, New York, 1926.

WALWORTH, C. A., *The Oxford Movement in America*, New York, 1895.
—*Reminiscences of Edgar P. Wadhams*, New York, 1893.

WILSON, J. G., *The Centennial History of the Protestant Episcopal Church in the Diocese of New York*, New York, 1886.

Volume 14 of *The Churchman* gives a full account of the debates of the General Convention of 1844.

CHAPTER FOUR

THE BEGINNINGS OF RITUALISM

RITUALISM, or, to give it the more correct name, ceremonialism, is a very comparative thing. Legally speaking, there is in the American Church almost no standard of ceremonial. Neither the Ornaments Rubric nor the Canons of 1603 have in this country any binding force, and the enactments of General Convention on the score of ceremonial have been very few and simple. Such elementary matters as the use of the surplice or the furnishings of the chancel are determined only by custom, and the custom of the American Church has differed widely in different ages and different localities. One might almost define a ritualist—we bow to popular usage—as one who employs a more elaborate ceremonial than the priest who preceded him.

Thus, in 1800, a priest who wore the surplice was a ritualist. And, as late as 1840, the use of even this simple vestment was far from universal. It is estimated that in 1837 there were not half a dozen surplices in the whole diocese of Ohio. An extract from one of Bishop Whittingham's letters, written about this time, indicates clearly what one of the leading High Churchmen of the day considered not merely adequate, but laudable and remarkable in the way of ceremonial:

> Six clergymen in surplices, and a bishop in his robes, kneeling in a chancel defaced by no gigantic deformities called pulpit and desk, round an altar-shaped communion table, and joining a well-trained choir in the chants of the Church . . . must be admitted to be a cheering exhibition of the decent pomp of our holy mother.[1]

[1]Brand, W. F., *Life of Bishop Whittingham*, Vol. I, p. 260.

THE BEGINNINGS OF RITUALISM

In the North things were a bit more advanced. Thus, by 1820, a ritualist was one who used the ante-communion service every Sunday. Extraordinary efforts were made by the High Churchmen of the Hobartian school to enforce this stupid usage. These men knew so little of the history of liturgics that they conceived the provision of collects, epistles, and gospels for every Sunday to be an implied command that the ante-communion service should follow matins every Sunday. To the same men, and at the same time, was due the extensive adoption of that ridiculous monstrosity, the Hobart chancel. Strangely enough, this has been laughed at as a Low Church innovation. As a matter of fact, it was advocated by Hobart, and for the laudable purpose of bringing the communion service out from the concealment of the chancel—where the communion table was practically invisible behind the high central pulpit—and performing the main service of the Church in the sight of the congregation.

CHANGES IN THE CHURCH BUILDING

But before much could be done in the improvement of worship, there had to be a considerable change in the church building itself. The meeting-house, so characteristic of the Church in the North, with its great central pulpit and its half-concealed altar, was obviously planned for Morning Prayer and sermon, and not much else could be done in it. I am perfectly aware that there is no necessary and logical connection between Catholicity and Gothicism. The Church had developed a rich and full ceremonial seven centuries before Gothic was born. The Eastern Church has managed to worship with considerable elaboration without ever constructing a pointed arch. And a ride in a Fifth Avenue bus will demonstrate to anyone that today a rich Gothic building does not always house a rich mediaeval ceremonial. But historically, in the nineteenth century, Catholic revival and Gothic revival often went hand in hand.

THE CATHOLIC MOVEMENT IN THE EPISCOPAL CHURCH

We have already noticed how Hopkins, in Pittsburgh in the late Twenties, was slowly feeling his way towards bringing all the arts, architecture among them, once more into the service of the sanctuary. A lack of trained architects had forced him to design his own church, and frequent requests for plans and suggestions led him to publish, in 1836, his *Essay on Gothic Architecture,* a book of specimen plans. It was not a very successful piece of work. Hopkins had never seen a Gothic building. With all his cleverness and aesthetic feeling, he was not an architect.

> "Nowhere in these drawings do we find a deep chancel; galleries are still retained; the altar cowers below the pulpit; the patterned ceiling gives a strange impression of the Adam style gone Gothic."[2]

But in spite of all this, the work was symptomatic.

England had its Pugin, the United States its Upjohn. In the work of Richard Upjohn, the first man to design intelligently in Gothic in this country, the connection between theology and architecture is intimate. Upjohn was a High Churchman and a lover of Gothic. When, in 1839, he was called upon to submit plans for the repair of Trinity Church, New York, he found his opportunity. With considerable difficulty, he persuaded the vestry that a new building was necessary; he fought for his own notion of what that building should be; and the completed structure, with its elevated altar and chancel of unprecedented depth and majesty, clearly expresses his own churchmanship, and was planned as the theatre of a developed Catholic ceremonial.[3]

Enrichment of ceremonial is, of course, the almost inevitable concomitant of Catholic doctrine. When you have been proclaiming loudly in words the apostolic succession of your bishop, you are bound at length to want to show it forth symbolically by dressing him in cope and mitre. When you have been asserting in sermons and

[2] Upjohn, Everard M., *Richard Upjohn, Architect and Churchman* (New York, 1939) p. 13.
[3] *Ibid.,* Chapter 4.

controversial pamphlets the immense gulf between the Catholic Church and the Protestant sects, you naturally emphasize the fact by trying to make your church building look different from the neighboring meeting-house. And, above all, when you are teaching the full Catholic doctrine of the sacraments, you are inevitably led to demonstrate that doctrine in action and in dress. Ceremonial, rightly understood, is only the translation of Catholic doctrine into visible symbols; and with the increased teaching of Catholic doctrine in the 1840's, there was sure to come an enrichment of ceremonial.

THE FATHER OF RITUALISM IN AMERICA

And yet, curiously enough, the real father of ritualism in America was a man not commonly classed among High Churchmen at all. In 1827, William Augustus Muhlenberg founded at Flushing, Long Island, a Church school for boys. From it came such leaders in the Church as Breck, Coxe, Tucker, Odenheimer, and Kerfoot. Muhlenberg was a poet, a thorough musician, and a liturgical artist. In the chapel of this school, he made the first attempt, aside from the little noticed work of Hopkins in the West, to surround the services of the Church with increased symbolic suggestiveness. Flowers on the altar—then so ritualistic a practice that a decade later we find bishops charging against it—Christmas greens and Christmas carols, a vested choir of men and boys, acolytes even—these were among his "advanced" practices.

> "The chapel was brilliant on the great feasts with candles and emblems. At the Christmas services a picture of the Virgin and Holy Child was placed above the altar, wreathed with holly. On Good Friday a picture of the Crucifixion, draped in black. On Easter . . . there were the bright lights and the fragrant flowers."[4]

In these practices, Muhlenberg preceded the *Tracts;* indeed, the origin of his ceremonial tastes was one which no thoroughgoing

[4] Knauff, Christopher W., *Doctor Tucker, Priest-Musician* (New York, 1897) p. 18.

Tractarian would have approved. Muhlenberg came of a Lutheran family, had early belonged to the Lutheran Church, and brought over from it an aesthetic feeling for color and music in worship, to which he gave full play in the Flushing chapel.

His churchmanship is in fact impossible to label. His theological training had been directed by Bishop White; but from some source he had learned to place a higher value than White on the apostolic succession, holding that "as to the validity of ordination . . . non-Episcopalians may be right, but Episcopalians cannot, by common consent, be wrong." This was not the Hobartian position, but it was far from Latitudinarian. When *The Tracts* appeared, he was captivated by them, and still more by Newman's sermons. But as time went on, he began to feel that the logical conclusion of Tractarianism was Romanism, and he escaped from it to a position all his own. Eirenic in temper, broad in his sympathies, calling himself an Evangelical Catholic—a title reminiscent of Hobart—and refusing to be bound by the platform of any party, he was perhaps for this reason a more effective worker in the advance of Church art than many who flaunted the party flag. In 1845 he continued and expanded his work by founding the Church of the Holy Communion, New York, where the practices of the Flushing chapel were continued, but in an environment that gave them much greater influence on the Church at large. This was the first church in New York to have free pews, and one of the first to have weekly communions.

In 1844 John Ireland Tucker, like his teacher Muhlenberg an accomplished musician, and a seminarian during the period when the influence of the *Tracts* was at its height, founded the Church of the Holy Cross, Troy. Here, for the first time in America, the choral service was performed, and the use of Gregorian chants was introduced. The church building was Early English, with a stone altar raised high above the level of the nave, and backed with a picture of the Crucifixion.⁵ So impressive was the building for those days that Francis Baker, later one of the founders of the Paulist order, declared that it was his ideal church.⁶ Tucker's influence on Church music in America was far-reaching; the Tucker Service Book, with its Victorian Gregorians, its Merbeck, and its Plainsong Prefaces, opened up a new world to American Church musicians.⁷

All the indications of ritualism we have so far noted took place in the diocese of New York, and though even these modest beginnings aroused the inevitable cry of "popery," there was, under the episcopate of Onderdonk, no possibility of official opposition. Indeed, Onderdonk's consistent policy, and a contributing cause of his downfall, was a steady encouragement of ceremonial advance.

In the diocese of Massachusetts, where the troubles of 1832 had left bad tastes in many mouths, the case was far different. In 1843, the Rev. Frederick Pollard, a priest just out of General Seminary, where he had drunk deeply of Tractarian ideas, came to Trinity Church, Nantucket. Here he pulled down the three-decker pulpit, built an altar, raised above the level of the church floor and backed by a reredos, and put on it two candlesticks and a picture of the Madonna and Child. He read the gospel and epistle from the now customary stations at each end of the altar. The daily offices were read from a fald-stool, facing the altar. There was a credence; wafer bread was used; and the priest was assisted by a server, who was not vested.⁸ These things, so utterly normal today, were sufficient to draw down the wrath of Bishop Griswold, and the result was the explosion of episcopal ire chronicled in our last chapter.

THE CHURCH OF THE ADVENT, BOSTON

But this was only the beginning of troubles in Massachusetts. In 1844, a group of prominent Boston laymen, the most distinguished

---
⁵Knauff, C. W., *Dr. Tucker*, pp. 113-43.
⁶Hewitt, A., *Life of Baker*, p. 79. A few years later, the church was made more impressive by the addition of a deep chancel designed by Upjohn.
⁷It is very easy to sneer at Tucker. The Service Book was bad, the Hymnal very bad, but they were valuable for their day.
⁸*The Living Church*, Vol. 71, p. 463.

of whom was Richard Henry Dana, determined to found a parish with the definite object of putting into practice in parochial life the principles of the Oxford Movement. They called as rector of this new Church of the Advent, the Rev. William Croswell, a pupil of Hobart, and, therefore, an avowed High Churchman, and a bosom friend of Bishop Doane. Pollard came from Nantucket to be his assistant. Begun under such auspices, the parish had from its foundation certain distinctive and, to that generation, startling characteristics. The pews were free—an innovation almost insulting to that type of upper-class respectability so often identified with the Episcopal Church. Daily services were held, and the Holy Communion was celebrated every Sunday in a manner calculated to inspire deeper reverence and devotion. Men as divergent in opinion and as far themselves from anything like Tractarianism as Phillips Brooks and Oliver Wendell Holmes, bore testimony to the profound effect the parish had on the religious life of Boston. Thus does Holmes—a man not disposed to admire obscurantism or ultra-conservatism in any form—witness to the essential Christianity of the Church of the Advent:

> For this was a church with open doors, with seats for all classes and all colours alike—a church of zealous worshippers after their faith, of charitable and serviceable men and women; one that took care of its children and never forgot its poor, and whose people were much more occupied in looking out for their own souls than in attacking the faith of their neighbors. In its mode of worship there was a union of two qualities—the taste and refinement which the educated require just as much in their churches as elsewhere, and the air of stateliness, almost of pomp, which impresses the common worshipper, and is often not without its effect upon those who think they hold outward form as of little value.

But, to the bishop of the diocese, these things were only shocking. In 1843, the saintly and generally moderate Griswold had been succeeded by Manton Eastburn—a Low Churchman as violent as

McIlvaine, and without McIlvaine's impressiveness of personality and undoubted intellectual power. Even the most favorable accounts of him leave the impression of a person, harsh and dictatorial in manner, immovable in his prejudices, without the slightest tact or ability to see another's point of view. On his first visit to the Church of the Advent, there was a scene. Immediately at the close of the service, he broke into a storm of protest against the manner in which the service had been conducted. The extreme practices to which he objected were kneeling toward the altar, instead of facing one's chair; chanting the psalter in the Prayer Book version, instead of in metre; preaching in the surplice; and, worst of all, the arrangement of the chancel, which contained a wooden altar, covered with a plain crimson cloth. On the altar was a low retable, holding four candles, which, however, were burned only at night; behind it was a window ornamented with that popish symbol, the cross.[9]

The bishop followed up this scene by writing an open letter, which was published in *The Christian Witness,* his official organ, upbraiding the vestry for permitting these novel and childish usages, pointing, as they did, straight to the superstitions of Rome.[10] The vestry, however, contained men too eminent in position and too strong in their beliefs to be upset by this sort of intimidation; and they replied by publishing a respectful protest against the bishop's actions. Croswell also answered, in a pamphlet as notable for its sanity, moderation, and good manners as the bishop's open letter was for its scolding.[11] So great was the wrath of the bishop at this continued contumacy, that he even refused to allow a priest who had been temporarily officiating under Croswell, to carry out an engagement to preach at Trinity Church, Boston, of which the bishop was rector—a step that called forth a remonstrance from the vestry of Trinity.[12]

[9]Croswell, H., *Memoir of the Rev. William Croswell,* p. 353. Some malicious person pointed out that while Bishop Eastburn was rector of the Church of the Ascension, New York, that church had been rebuilt by the High Church architect, Upjohn. There was a cross on the altar, another on the spire.
[10]*Ibid.,* p. 357.
[11]*Ibid.,* pp. 362-74.
[12]*Ibid.,* p. 380.

Furthermore, he flatly refused to visit the Church of the Advent until the services were reformed. Year after year, until 1854, the clergy of the parish were forced to go through the farce of notifying the bishop that they had candidates to present for confirmation, receiving his refusal to visit them, and then conducting their candidates to some safe and sane Low Church, where the bishop condescended to confirm them.[13]

This queer sort of excommunication continued as long as Croswell lived. At his death, in 1851, the Rt. Rev. Horatio Southgate, an old and staunch High Churchman who had once been sent as missionary bishop to Constantinople, was called as rector. He at once set about remedying this impossible state of things. The whole matter was laid before the General Convention of 1856, which enacted a canon requiring each bishop to visit every parish in his diocese at least once in three years.

OTHER EARLY LEADERS

In spite of episcopal opposition—and such opposition was not confined to Bishop Eastburn—the tendency to enrich the services went on. St. Stephen's, Boston, was soon following in the lead of the Advent, and here the bishop appears to have raised no objection. In 1849, the Rev. Henry Waterman became rector of St. Stephen's, Providence, Rhode Island, where he built up a center of Catholic practice that still remains notable. In 1850 the experiment of the Church of the Advent was repeated in New York, when the Church of the Transfiguration was organized, under the rectorship of the Rev. George B. Houghton, who had learned Tractarian doctrine as a student at the General Seminary, and, as assistant to Muhlenberg at the Church of the Holy Communion, had discovered how to translate that doctrine into appropriate ceremonial. Free pews, a church open all day for private prayer, daily Eucharists, and a staff of priests always at call—these features marked the life of the Trans-

[13] *Ibid.*, pp. 388-93.

figuration. On Ascension Day, 1846, the noble Gothic structure which Upjohn had designed for Trinity, New York, was consecrated, and in the same year daily services were instituted in it. Old St. Peter's, Philadelphia, under Odenheimer, later to succeed Doane as bishop of New Jersey, followed in the same steps. In 1848, St. Mark's, Philadelphia, was built from designs furnished by the Ecclesiological Society of London, and here in 1849 the daily service was established.

The formation, in 1848, of the New York Ecclesiological Society marked the beginning of a real effort to study the science of liturgics. The president of this society was the Rev. John Murray Forbes, rector of St. Luke's; the secretary, his assistant, the Rev. Thomas S. Preston; their patron, Bishop Ives of North Carolina. As will be seen in the next chapter, the choice of officers was unfortunate. Under their auspices, Bishop Ives attempted, at his abortive monastery in Valle Crucis, to set up and ornament a model chapel. The altar was furnished with two candles, and superfrontals in the five-color sequence—the first instance I know of in this country. The Holy Communion was reserved in a pyx on the altar. In the publications of this society, one finds such strange new terms as piscina, super-altar, funeral pall, altar stone—enough to send the shudders down the spine of every zealous Protestant.[14]

Even Ohio, which two successive bishops, Chase and McIlvaine, both men of powerful personality and strong Evangelical views, had made almost as pronounced a center of Evangelicalism as Virginia, showed signs of restlessness. In 1843, the Rev. John Hall, rector of St. Peter's, Ashtabula, whom we have noted as one of those persons, not infrequent at this time, who arrived independently at most of the conclusions of the Tractarian writers, made the following note in his parish register:

He has determined (God willing) henceforward to observe

---

[14]Most of my information about this society is taken from a very amusing little anonymous pamphlet, entitled *Puseyite Developments*, in which the author frequently has the best of the over-zealous ecclesiologists.

in the Church all the appointed Festivals and Fasts of the Church and to administer the H. Communion every Lord's day and to receive no more pew rents.[15]

In 1846, St. Paul's, Columbus, under the rectorship of the Rev. Henry L. Richards, a friend of Walworth and Wadhams, had just completed its structure, Gothic in style, and built with an eye to enriched ceremonial. Bishop McIlvaine, ever on the watch for Romeward leanings, refused to consecrate the church until the stone altar had been replaced by "an honest table with legs." In his diocesan convention that same year the bishop explained his position in his address. He had no objection, he stated, to stone altars as a mere matter of architectural preference. But the recent perversion of many members of the Episcopal Church to Rome showed that such things could no longer be considered matters of indifference. It was being widely taught in the Church that

> "the Lord's Supper is not a mere memory of a sacrifice, but a real propitiatory sacrifice for sin. This is Popery in the essence ... Now where this doctrine exists, it must have a literal altar in the communion ... And it must get rid of a literal table; because that declares the very truth concerning the Sacrament, as simply a commemorative feast upon a sacrifice, once offered upon the cross."

The bishop's position was clear, reasonable—on his premises—and infuriating to the few High Churchmen in the diocese. The Rev. John Hall commented on his address as an "arbitrary popish assumption of authority." But in general the diocese seems to have backed the bishop.[16]

EFFECTS OF EARLY RITUALISM

The marks of this early ritualism were few, and to one accustomed to modern trends in ceremonial, extremely simple. The con-

---

[15]*Hall MSS.*, p. 66. For biographical sketch, see Francis J. Hall, "Life of the Rev. John Hall (1788-1869)," *Historical Magazine of the Episcopal Church*, Vol. IV (1935), 308-313.

[16]Smythe, G. F., *History of the Diocese of Ohio*, pp. 238-52.

THE BEGINNINGS OF RITUALISM

gregation of a modern "advanced" parish, if it could be transported back three-quarters of a century to be present at a communion service in such a notorious hotbed of ritualism as the Church of the Advent, would certainly be shocked—but at the Protestant bareness of the service. Free pews, daily matins and vespers, a weekly Eucharist, the observance of saints' days, stone altars with colored frontals, candles, and a cross, priests vested in surplice and colored stole —these were the outward and visible signs of ritualism in 1850. In addition, one might occasionally find a choral service, and in at least one church, St. Paul's, Baltimore, the sacrament reserved for the communion of the sick. But simple as these things were, they were the indications of an inner revolution.

All these innovations were, of course, but the logical carrying out of the principles of the early High Churchmen, who had advocated daily services, who had emphasized the Eucharist, without, however, doing much about either. The wiser men of the Hobartian school saw this; Doane, for example, thoroughly sympathized with all that the early ritualists were attempting. But, in many quarters, ritualism did undoubtedly help to widen the breach already opened between the Tractarians and the old High Churchmen. Beyond this, it set up a new division within the High Church party. Many priests and bishops, who had been whole-hearted in their acceptance of Tractarian doctrine, were equally whole-hearted in their opposition to ritualistic practices. Chief among these was Whittingham. In 1843, we find him warning Kerfoot, then rector of St. James' Hall, the school for boys established by the bishop, against all attempts at an enriched ceremonial:

> Pray be very cautious about your externals. Do not give in to the desire for symbolism. I have heard from many quarters about the "popish doings" at St. James' . . . Beware of the oratory which I had to pull down with my own episcopal hands.[17]

Similarly, Bishop Cobbs, who as a priest in the diocese of Virginia had been regarded with great suspicion by Bishop Meade for his

[17] Brand, W. F., *Life of Bishop Whittingham*, Vol. I, p. 298.

Tractarian leanings, refused to consecrate a church in his diocese of Alabama in which the altar bore cross and candlesticks. So sharp was this separation in the High Church forces that much of the opposition to ritualism in later years came, not from Evangelicals, but from men strongly High Church in doctrine.

To balance this very real evil done to High Churchmanship by the division of its forces, we must set down much good done by ritualism. The definitely ritualistic churches became more and more the true strongholds of High Church teaching. They were marked by a zeal for the Church, a depth of piety, and, above all, by an intensity of worship that had been too often lacking in the cold and correct orthodoxy of the older High Churchmen. Furthermore, ritualism was capable of reaching many people to whom such abstractions as the apostolic succession made little or no appeal. In this country, as in England, the ritualistic churches were outstanding in their activity in carrying religion to the unchurched masses. Thus they did much to break down that unfortunate alliance, so prevalent especially in the large cities of the East, between the Episcopal Church and wealthy respectability. In such parishes as the Advent and the Transfiguration, the Episcopal Church stood for something more than good form in religion.

In some sense the final test of any innovation, or seeming innovation in religion, is its ultimate acceptance by the Church at large. The Vincentian Canon is as workable now as in the fifth century, and applies to liturgy as well as to dogma.[18] Tried by this test, the ritualism of the Forties was in the long run completely successful. Practically all the points we have noted as characterizing early ritualism—the daily service only excepted—have become universal practices. Opposition to them, so strenuous at first, eventually died out, and the slow permeation, which we noted in regard to High Church doctrine before 1840, extended itself to High Church practice. To-

---

[18] Vincent of Lerins, in his *Commonitorium*, writtin in 434 A.D., states: "Moreover, in the Catholic Church itself all possible care should be taken that we hold that faith which has been believed everywhere, always, and by all *(Quod ubique, quod semper, quod ab omnibus)."*

day, the parish which does not maintain, as a matter of course, the major part of the shocking innovations for which the clergy of the Church of the Advent were so severely censured in 1845, would be held so abnormally Low Church as hardly to deserve the name of Episcopalian.

BIBLIOGRAPHY

ADVENT, CHURCH OF THE, *A Sketch of the History of the Parish of the Advent in the City of Boston* (Boston, 1894).

ANONYMOUS, *Puseyite Developments* (New York, 1850).

AYRES, ANNE, *The Life and Work of William Augustus Muhlenberg* (New York, 1881).

CROSWELL, H., *A Memoir of the Life of the Late Rev. William Croswell* (New York, 1853).

HALL, J., *Annals of the Parish of St. Peter's, Ashtabula, Ohio* (MSS. in General Theological Seminary Library, New York City).

KNAUFF, C. W., *Doctor Tucker, Priest-Musician* (New York, 1897).

SHINN, G. W., *King's Handbook of Notable Episcopal Churches* (Boston, 1889). [Valuable for information in regard to the early days of High Church parishes.]

SMYTHE, G. F., *History of the Diocese of Ohio until the year 1918* (Cleveland, 1931).

UPJOHN, EVERARD M., *Richard Upjohn, Architect and Churchman* (New York, 1939).

WHITE, G., *An Apostle of the Western Church* [Kemper] (New York, 1900).

— *A Saint of the Southern Church* [Cobbs] (New York, 1897).
[Two excellent little volumes.]

CHAPTER FIVE

THE FIFTIES—THE STORM SUBSIDES

THE conflict which the *Tracts* had evoked continued on into the Fifties. There was, it is true, no further attempt to obtain an official condemnation of Catholic doctrine—the convention of 1844 had settled that—but the politicians of the Low Church party thought they had secured in the Onderdonk cases a method of procedure that would serve to deprive their opponents of their chief men. Immediately after the trial of Bishop Onderdonk of New York, Dr. Henry Anthon wrote to Bishop Hopkins, whom the Low Churchmen were eagerly welcoming as an ally, "What about Maryland and New Jersey? Shall not thorns and thistles spring up in their paths?"[1]

THE ATTEMPT THAT FAILED

The next victim selected as the object of the Low Church vendetta was Bishop Doane, the political leader of the High Church party. He had indeed laid himself wide open to attack. In his anxiety to found diocesan schools, he had repeated his error of 1832, overextended his operations, and found himself forced into bankruptcy. Some of his enemies in the diocese of New Jersey, probably egged on by larger men from outside, charged him with misapplication of funds, and in 1849 introduced a resolution in the diocesan convention calling for a committee to investigate the bishop's conduct. This resolution was unanimously and ignominiously defeated. A second attempt was more successful. A thorough investigation was held, it was discovered that the bishop had juggled funds about in a manner worthy of a modern financial wizard, and he confessed a misuse of

[1] J. H. Hopkins, *Life of Bishop Hopkins*, p. 233.

THE FIFTIES—THE STORM SUBSIDES

money, though denying, rightly, any criminal intent. The convention, therefore, refused to take any action against him.

But in spite of this, Bishops Meade, McIlvaine, and Burgess, acting under the canon of 1844 that had proved the doom of Bishop Onderdonk, decided that here was opportunity for action, and, accordingly, in 1852 presented Bishop Doane for trial before the House of Bishops. In this case, as in that, the actuating cause of the presentation was clearly party feeling. The attitude of Meade and McIlvaine toward all things smacking of Tractarianism has already been made plain; Burgess, though quieter, was equally Low Church. It was a partisan move, pure and simple.

But Bishop Doane, although actually more vulnerable, was too shrewd a publicist and politician to fall into mistakes like those which had made easy the conviction of the bishop of New York. Having secured an acquittal of criminal intent from his diocesan convention, thus clearing his honor in the eyes of the general public, he deliberately set out to "make the trial of a bishop hard." Acting as his own lawyer, and so preventing the presenters from appearing by counsel, he shrewdly contrived to block every move of his opponents. Twice the court met, and twice it broke up without ever proceeding to trial. When at length the whole matter had begun to assume a comic aspect, the presenters gave up, and the charges were dropped.[2] This fiasco put an end to the attempt to remove theologically objectionable bishops by judicial proceedings. "Onderdonking" went out of fashion.

THE SECESSION OF BISHOP IVES

Every movement has its lunatic fringe—its enthusiasts who are unable to distinguish between what is essential and what is not; who delight in seizing on the most disputable points in the platform of their party and making them their chief aim; who carry logic to its unreasonable extreme; to whom the cut of a chasuble or the proper number of "double swings" is more important than the teachings

[2] J. H. Hopkins, *Life of Bishop Hopkins*, pp. 250-67.

of the Gospel. The High Church movement has always suffered from such adherents. There are the men who cannot say their prayers without a rosary, or Mass without numberless interpolations; who gleefully ape the tawdriest features of Romanism—often features which the more intelligent Roman Catholics are busily rooting out. Such men had been notably lacking among the older High Churchmen of the Hobartian school, but they began to make their appearance within the party soon after the publication of the *Tracts*. Some of their antics at the General Seminary we have noted two chapters back. Fortunately for the Church, most of them took part in the exodus of the Forties to Rome.

But during the Fifties, when most of the secessions had stopped, a churchman of much greater eminence than Walworth or Wadhams or Breck or Forbes was bitten by the Romanizing bug. The second bishop of North Carolina, Levi Silliman Ives, had long been one of the most eminent High Church leaders. A pupil and son-in-law of Hobart, he had, after a brilliant career as a priest in New York City, succeeded Ravenscroft in the principal High Church see of the South. For nearly twenty years, he was an able and successful bishop, teaching strong churchmanship, founding schools, and preaching the Gospel to the Negroes. He had been one of the chief advocates of the *Tracts,* one of the bishops on whom the younger enthusiasts of the movement depended. But there was in his character a certain hysterical emotionalism, combined with a fatal lack of intellectual power, that was to have unpleasant results. After his conversion, Archbishop Hughes of New York summed him up as a person of "generous, impulsive, somewhat erratic temperament."

About 1849, his friends began to notice a strange mutation in his theological views and practices. In 1844, he had founded at Valle Crucis an institution somewhat resembling Nashotah—a combined mission center, seminary, and monastery. Toward the end of the decade, whispers began to fly about that strange doings were taking place there. The priests stationed at Valle Crucis were said to have taken the three vows of poverty, chastity, and obedience. The Blessed Sacrament was reserved and adored. Prayers were addressd to the Virgin and to the saints. Systematic auricular confession was practiced. As a result of these rumors, the condition of the mission was brought before the diocesan convention of 1849, but the commission appointed to investigate the matter reported that nothing illegal was being done at Valle Crucis. This report was in all probability more lenient than the facts warranted, but one of the striking characteristics of the churchmanship of the period was the loyalty of each diocese to its diocesan in times of stress.

The bishop's own attitude at this time was far from straightforward. Unable on account of illness to attend the convention, he addressed to it a letter repudiating the practice of private confession. But less than a year later, in a pastoral letter, he faced about and strongly advocated auricular confession, prayers for the dead, and the invocation of the saints.[8] This was the most extreme position that had, until then, been taken by any churchman of standing in the American Church. Inevitably, the pastoral revived again the subsiding gales of controversy. Of the answers called forth by its appearance, the most notable was a pamphlet by Bishop Hopkins, in which that ecclesiastic, who was beginning to break away from his anti-Tractarian allies of the previous decade, took the normal Anglican stand that, while private confession was undoubtedly allowed and even encouraged by the Church, routine private confession, such as Ives was recommending, was absolutely foreign to her mind. This storm was too much for the unsteady temperament of Bishop Ives. When the diocesan convention of 1850 met, prepared now for battle against its bishop, he again retreated and retracted. In his address he asserted that he did not hold the doctrine of "private confession in the Romish sense," that he was opposed to reservation, and that he considered prayers to the Virgin and to the saints "clearly derogatory to Christ." This was received as a satisfactory explanation by the con-

[8] L. S. Ives, *The Priestly Office*, passim.

vention. But, by all these shiftings and doublings, Bishop Ives had quite lost the confidence both of the diocese and of his own intimate followers.

Various explanations were offered for his strange conduct, the most common being that illness had deranged his mind. The truth appears to be that, during all this period, he was a man torn by internal strife, in somewhat the mental condition of Newman when he retired to Littlemore, but without Newman's strength of mind and character. His inconsistency was not the inconsistency of a trickster, but of a man who honestly does not know from day to day where he stands. No one was greatly surprised when, in 1852, having obtained leave of absence from his diocese, he went to Rome, and there made his submission to the pope.[4] So great had been his loss of credit that his defection was not felt to be a serious blow to the Church, and not one of his priests, even of those who had lived in the monastery at Valle Crucis, followed him. His later career as a layman in the Roman Church was one of honorable and useful service.

At the General Convention of 1853, he was solemnly deposed from his office—the first deposition of a bishop in the history of the American Church. Bishop Whittingham's note of this deposition in his journal is interesting—for the light it sheds on Whittingham: "Joined in the solemn act of deposition of the late Rt. Rev. Levi Silliman Ives, an absconding and apostate delinquent."[5]

Meanwhile a minor storm was raging in that ancient crater of ecclesiastical storms, Boston. Early in the Fifties, Bishop Eastburn again attacked the Church of the Advent, but on new grounds. The Rev. Oliver S. Prescott, one of the assistant clergy, whom we last saw at Valle Crucis, was brought to trial for hearing confessions and giving absolution. Defended by Dana, he was acquitted, there being no evidence that he had exceeded the authority of the Book of Com-

---

[4]Perry, W. S., *History of the American Episcopal Church*, Vol. 55, pp. 285-89. For the most complete biography of Ives and the story of his episcopate thus far written, see Marshall DeLancey Haywood, *Lives of the Bishops of North Carolina*, (Raleigh, 1910) pp. 91-139.
[5]Brand, W. F., *Life of Bishop Whittingham*, Vol. I, p. 450.

THE FIFTIES—THE STORM SUBSIDES

mon Prayer; but the bishop compelled him to promise to give up the practice. As a result, he left the diocese and took refuge with Whittingham in Maryland, the sanctuary in the nineteenth century, as in the seventeenth, of persecuted Catholics.[6]

A NEW SET OF LEADERS

This decade, with its many changes, saw the appearance of a new set of High Church leaders. The older men, who had borne the strain and stress of battle in the Forties, were gradually disappearing from the scene. Doane, the political leader of the party, died in 1859. Whittingham's anti-ritualism drove him more and more into a position of antagonism to the younger generation of High Churchmen, whom he nevertheless went on receiving and protecting. Hopkins alone of the older group came more to the foreground during this and the following decade. But the places made vacant by death, secession, and old age, were well filled.

Chief among the younger leaders was James De Koven, who has been called, with our national passion for analogies of this kind, the Pusey of the American Church. After studying at the General Seminary, he was ordained deacon in 1854, and was at once offered a place on the faculty of Nashotah, the stronghold of High Churchmanship in the West. In 1859, he became warden of Racine College, a Church institution in Wisconsin, to the upbuilding of which he devoted the rest of his life. Intense in his convictions, without a spark of personal ambition, accepting the Catholic position to the full, and admitting of no compromise in his statement of it, he was from the first a marked man in the Church. The leader of the High Church forces in the lower house of two General Conventions, his courage and honesty kept him from the episcopal chair.

It is probably correct to say that De Koven came nearer to being a bishop, without ever becoming one, than any other man in the American Church. In 1866, he was nominated as coadjutor to Bishop

[6]Grafton, C. C., *A Journey Godward*, p. 77.

Kemper of Wisconsin, and failed of election because of the opposition of the older section of the High Church party. It is difficult to believe, but in 1872 he barely missed election as bishop of Massachusetts.[7] In 1875, he was elected by the clerical members of the diocesan convention as bishop of Fond du Lac, but the laity failed to concur. And in the same year he was elected bishop of Illinois, under circumstances that will be related hereafter, but on this occasion the standing committees refused to confirm his election.

But this was no misfortune to him, though it was perhaps a loss to the Church. His lack of ambition is well attested by the positions he declined: the rectorship of the Church of the Advent, Boston; the rectorship of St. Mark's, Philadelphia; and a curacy at Trinity, New York. He preferred to give his life to his chosen work of Christian education at Racine. A reading of his single volume of published sermons, with their intense mystical note, their warmth of personal devotion to our Lord and to the sacrament of the altar, shows plainly how far this generation had advanced from the sometimes pedantic dogmatism of some of the older school of High Churchmen.

It will be remembered that Hobart was suspicious of the term sacrifice as applied to the Eucharist. The passage from one of De Koven's sermons, quoted below, will serve to show how Eucharistic theology had developed in America under Tractarian influence:

> The Priesthood of Christ, being perpetual, yet employing but a single sacrificial act, must consist in a constant reference to that sacrifice . . . What is the Sacrament of the Altar but the self-same act, done in His earthly kingdom. And, if this be so, must not His blessed human nature . . . be on every altar, as well as in the midst of the throne? There locally, here spiritually; there after the manner of a body, here after the manner of a Spirit; yet, in both, really, truly, certainly, the one and self-same Humanity, the same blessed Person, Sacrifice, and Priest; and a call for men on earth, and angels in heaven, and

[7] "Journal of the Rev. Dr. De Koven," *Historical Magazine of the Episcopal Church*, Vol. II, 205-210.

the redeemed in paradise, to worship and adore the Lamb as it had been slain.[8]

Scarcely less important was Morgan Dix, whose whole ecclesiastical career, from 1855 to 1908, was connected with Trinity Church, New York. Becoming rector after the rather high-and-dry Berrian, he restored Trinity to her place as a rock of Catholic churchmanship. The immense resources of Trinity, which enable it to sustain dozens of churches outside its own wide boundaries, make the rector of Trinity a far more important and influential figure in the Church than many bishops. Dix used his position consistently to strengthen the High Church cause, to aid weak parishes, to help persecuted priests. Himself a person of strong common sense and sane judgment, he was to a large extent the balance-wheel of the party.

At about the same time that Dix became rector of Trinity, there assembled in New York a group of High Church leaders, working in close agreement, sure of themselves and their position, advanced in doctrine and ritual, skilled controversialists and brilliant publicists. This group was composed of John Henry Hobart (son of the bishop), Milo Mahan, George Franklin Seymour, and the younger John Henry Hopkins. Hobart, the eldest of the group, was the least important, but he was an interesting link between them and the group of an earlier day which had gathered about Breck, and he lent them the prestige of a great ecclesiastical name.

Much more significant was Milo Mahan. Like so many of the leading High Churchmen of the mid-century, he had been a pupil at Muhlenberg's Flushing Institute. A Virginian by birth, Mahan became teacher of Greek at the Episcopal High School, located in Alexandria, the very heart of Evangelicalism. Here he worked under the direct supervision of Bishop Meade. From this environment Mahan emerged, amazingly, a firm Tractarian. Ordained in 1845, he was elected, after six years of successful parochial work, professor of ecclesiastical history at the General Seminary, thus carrying on the

---

[8]De Koven, James, *Sermons Preached on Various Occasions* (New York, 1880) p. 223.

tradition of High Church leadership in that important position. Here he soon made himself felt. His position gave him leisure to develop to the full a scholarship second only to that of Whittingham, and to express that scholarship in effective writing. The most solid fruit of his studies was his *Church History of the First Three Centuries,* but his numerous reviews and periodical articles, learned, sensible, acute, often witty, were perhaps more serviceable to the cause than his heavier tomes.

It was the opinion of Bishop William Croswell Doane that Mahan was "certainly the foremost priest in the American Church, her ablest theologian, her soundest and best furnished mind, the wisest counsellor I ever knew."[*]

Mahan's attitude toward the Church of Rome is noteworthy. The older High Church leaders, Hobart and the Hobartians, had been, without exception, bitter anti-Romanists, so much so that their deep-rooted suspicion of anything resembling incipient Romanism often made them shrink from the advanced tendencies of the younger men in doctrine and ceremonial. During the Forties, as we have noticed, there was a definite Romanizing group, most of whom had left the Church after 1845. But Mahan was one of the first, certainly the first leader of importance, who united a complete loyalty to the Anglican Church with an open-minded willingness to borrow from Rome, when Rome seemed to him to have something worth borrowing. That he was no Romanizer, no slavish ape of Roman terms and Roman millinery, is amply proved by such a work as *The Comedy of Canonization,* in which he uproariously ridiculed the Vatican Council. But he was willing to acknowledge excellence in the Roman system, and to adopt whatever he found valuable there.

It was the wish of Bishop Doane, expressed on his deathbed, that Mahan should succeed him as bishop of New Jersey; but, when the diocesan convention met for election, this was represented as an attempt of the old bishop to will away the diocese. So prolonged and

[*]*Albany Convention Journal,* 1870, p. 117.

THE FIFTIES—THE STORM SUBSIDES

bitter was the opposition that Mahan withdrew his name, and William Henry Odenheimer, the moderate High Church rector of St. Peter's, Philadelphia, was elected. In 1864, Mahan became rector of the famous old High Church parish of St. Paul's, Baltimore, which he made a shining example of excellence in ceremonial, introducing altar lights and the linen chasuble, and bringing the music to a pitch of perfection never found before in the American Church.

George Franklin Seymour was the only one of the group to attain the episcopate. In 1854, he founded St. Stephen's College at Annandale, New York. In 1864, he was called to the General Seminary to succeed Mahan as professor of ecclesiastical history, retaining High Church control of that strategic position. In 1872, he became dean of the seminary. His later career—his rejection as bishop of Illinois by the House of Bishops, and his election in 1878 as first bishop of Springfield, will be considered in a future chapter.

But the most attractive figure in the group, and their real leader, was John Henry Hopkins, Jr. Unlike Mahan, Hopkins inherited High Churchmanship. The eldest son of the bishop of Vermont, he inherited his father's musical and artistic abilities, and his independence of character. To these qualities he added a sureness of taste and a judgment all his own. His carol, *We Three Kings of Orient Are*, has actually been printed by careless publishers as a specimen of mediaeval work; his magnificent minor tune to *The Royal Banners Forward Go*, has the breadth and steadiness of the old German chorales. Precocious without being a little prig, Hopkins early learned from his father all that his father had to teach of Catholic doctrine and practice—learned and bettered the instruction. In 1847, he became a student at the General Seminary, and, despite his youth, he at once sprang into notice among the High Churchmen of New York. In 1848, we find him among the members of the New York Ecclesiological Society—a group of pioneers in the study of liturgical art in America. But Hopkins was no mere ecclesiastical milliner. The night before his ordination to the diaconate he passed kneeling in front of the altar of Trinity Church—an act typical of his complete devotion.

Recognizing in himself a special talent, he had already marked out his intended course in the Church—a course which left no place for personal ambition. He was to remain in deacon's orders, and to devote himself to ecclesiastical journalism. In accordance with this plan, he founded in 1853, with the assistance of Mahan and the younger Hobart, *The Church Journal,* which became for three decades the organ of the militant High Churchmen, filling the place previously occupied by Seabury's *Churchman.*[10] For this work Hopkins was superbly fitted. He was a brilliant writer, one of the keenest of reasoners on paper, with a most pointed sense of humor and a notable gift of ridicule. These qualities were absolutely at the service of the advanced wing of the High Church party—for Hopkins, unlike his father, was a partisan on principle. Believing, with Mahan, that the Church had, through the dry centuries following the Reformation, lost many things of value, he deliberately set out to restore to the Church everything useful that she had lost or neglected.

Such qualities and such a program were not calculated to endear Hopkins to the Low Churchmen, nor even to the vast body of slow-moving, conservative moderates, and for years he was, with the possible exception of De Koven, the most hated man in the Church. In his impatience with mere do-nothing conservatism, he was even found at times writing that the greatest enemy of true Catholicism in the American Church was not the Evangelical party, but the old High Church faction. But in spite of the enmity he aroused, no man of his day exercised greater influence, and he has even been compared, as a leader of his party, with Bishop Hobart. Certain it is that the vast majority of the reforms he so strenuously advocated—the cathedral system, the division of dioceses, the provin-

[10] In 1855 Hopkins became instructor in music at the General Seminary. He at once began to introduce the use of the Georgian chant, which so incensed the conservative Dr. Turner that on the nights when that professor officiated, he forbade their use. Hopkins would not play Anglicans, and so a student organist was called in for the night.

THE FIFTIES—THE STORM SUBSIDES

cial system, the revival of missionary monastic orders—have become actualities in the Church today."[11]

In addition to all this, Hopkins was also an excellent practical missionary. Having demonstrated his skill as a politician in the campaign for the election of William Croswell Doane as first bishop of Albany, he enlisted under the banner of that vigorous prelate, and worked for a number of years in the difficult Adirondack field. Bishop Doane testified that

> "his power of work, the extent of its ranges; his unreserved pursuit of difficult and remote places, his absolute self-denial in all matters of aesthetic performance; his simple adaptation to places and people; his faithful pastoral searching after the scattered sheep; his earnest preaching, his untiring labors, are beyond any praise of mine."[12]

THE TEACHING OF FERDINAND C. EWER

Allied with these men, though not actually of the group, was Ferdinand Cartwright Ewer. Ewer was one of those who have found the faith by way of scepticism. Brought up a Unitarian, while a student at Harvard he read theology of all sorts, passed through a semi-agnostic stage, and at length entered the Church. He was confirmed under Pollard at Nantucket, and became naturally a thorough-going Tractarian. After an interlude of journalism in California, he was ordained priest. Coming to New York in 1860, he rapidly became known as one of the great pulpit orators of the day, and soon rose to the rectorship of Christ Church, then one of the fashionable parishes of the metropolis. Here for seven years he preached sermon after sermon, setting forth in the strongest terms the Catholic nature of the Church and the doctrine of the Real Presence. These sermons reached their climax in the series preached in 1868 entitled, *The*

---

[11] See John Henry Hopkins, III, "The Rev. John Henry Hopkins, Jr.," in *Historical Magazine of the Protestant Episcopal Church*, Vol. IV, pp. 267-80. Also, C. F. Sweet, *A Champion of the Cross*, (New York, 1894), being the life of John Henry Hopkins, Jr., including extracts and selections from his writings, 374 pp.
[12] *Albany Convention Journal*, 1877.

Failure of Protestantism. What happened next is best told in his own words:

> For the seven years there was no objection to my teachings: but the moment a change was begun in the ritual to make it harmonize ... with the doctrines that had been taught for seven years, there was an earthquake in a part of the congregation.
>
> I was then more convinced than ever of the usefulness of the ritual.

As a result of the storm which arose from this endeavor to apply abstractions to life, Ewer resigned in 1871. Followed by three of the vestry and a fair number of the congregation, he immediately founded St. Ignatius' Church, which he gradually built into a strong Catholic parish.[13]

In 1879, Ewer published a little volume, long forgotten, but well worth our attention today, with the title: *Catholicity, Protestantism and Romanism.*[14] This is, in essence, an *apologia* for Anglo-Catholicism which, after the passage of seven decades, is far from outmoded. Although the book does not use the phrase, its basic conception is that the Church is the extension of the Incarnation, and that all of Catholic faith and practice are to be derived from that one central idea. Thus the Church—the whole Catholic Church—is infallible as God is infallible, because the Church is a present Incarnation. The sacraments have objective validity because they are "the perpetual Incarnation of God on earth, wrought by the marvellous miracles of Font and Altar." And, as we shall have occasion to explain more fully when we come to the story of Liberal Catholicism, Ewer, in this volume, was the first of American Anglo-Catholics to come to grips with the profound problems presented by the growth of Biblical criticism.[15]

---

[13]Dix, Morgan, "Ferdinand C. Ewer," in the *American Church Review*, Vol. 42, 511-529.

[14]The exact title on the title page: *Catholicity in its Relationship to Protestantism and Romanism, being Six Conferences delivered at Newark, N. J., at the request of Leading Laymen of that City,* (New York, 1879) pp. 296. They had been delivered in May and June, 1878.

[15]*Ibid.*, p. 102.

THE FIFTIES—THE STORM SUBSIDES

Since Ewer was the best theologian the High Church party in America had thus far developed, it is important to see just what his theological position was. In 1883, in answer to Bishop Huntington's question, "What do the Anglo-Catholics want?", he drew up the following concise platform, which summarizes well the views of the advanced section of the High Church party in the Seventies and early Eighties:

> They [the Anglo-Catholics] repudiate the idolatrous cultus of images and the idolatrous cultus of the Blessed Mother of God, that are prevalent in Rome; they are shocked at the extravagant phrases that are used in her worship; they reject Rome's unity without diversity; they utterly and with a sad indignation repudiate the modern claims of the papacy . . . They do not even admit that the primacy of Rome is of divine right . . . They repudiate the Roman definition of transubstantiation; denial of the cup to all but the celebrant; some of the principles of the Roman system of casuistry; the Roman view of purgatory; compulsory confession; compulsory celibacy of the clergy; and the saying of offices in other than the vernacular.
>
> They accept the truth that the souls of the faithful are not ready at death to enter heaven . . . therefore they believe those happy souls can become more happy, and can be helped by our prayers; they accept the Real Objective Presence;[16] they believe the Prayer Book intends that we shall make the Holy Eucharist, and not the Morning Prayer, the main service of the Church; and that the plain English rubric provides that the Eucharist shall be surrounded with its respectful and fitting and expressive adjuncts of vestments, lights, incense, songs, adoration . . . They claim the right of worshipping Jesus Christ by outward acts

---

[16] In *Catholicity, Protestantism and Romanism* (pp. 63-64), Ewer had said five years before:
"So a man separated from Christ's Body Mystical—a man considered merely in himself alone—is the very type of powerlessness. But when set in a socket of Christ's Mystical Body as a Priest or a Bishop, the God within that Body, using the poor frame of clay as His own arm and hand, performs with it His divine and mighty deeds among us, pardons in the Sacrament of Penance, *transforms bread and wine at the Altar*, blesses, regenerates in Baptism, anoints with the Holy Ghost in Confirmation, makes of twain one flesh, confers the grace of Orders through His touch, and either raises the sick from death or sends the soul healed into eternity. The Sacraments and the Ministry are His limbs with which He touches us . . ."

wherever he is . . . They claim that the Prayer Book teaches . . . that the Eucharist is a commemorative sacrifice . . . They claim the right to develop the religious orders in the Church; to hold retreats and missions; to make and hear voluntary confessions.

GROWTH FOLLOWING THE STORM

One layman must be added to the number of High Church leaders of this period—Hugh Davey Evans. An eminent Baltimore lawyer, he edited from 1844 to 1868 a periodical entitled *The True Catholic,* the influence of which was second only to that of Hopkins' *Church Journal.* In addition to his work for this paper, Evans published volumes on such subjects as Anglican ordination, the episcopate in the United States, and the Catholic doctrine of marriage. The fact that he was a layman gave additional weight to his views, and tended to free the movement from the common suspicion of ultra-clericalism.[17]

It is a notable fact that while nearly all of the earlier High Church leaders became bishops, of this group only Seymour was consecrated to the episcopate, and he after much difficulty. This was due in part to the increased violence of party warfare between 1845 and 1855, and still more to the division between the older High Churchmen, the men who claimed to be the true followers of Hobart, and the younger group, influenced by the *Tracts,* and practitioners of ceremonial innovations. As usual, the episcopal elections during the decade are highly significant. In 1851, John Williams, a High Churchman of the specialized Connecticut type, became bishop coadjutor of Connecticut. Henry John Whitehouse, intellectual and Hobartian, began (1851) the succession of High Church bishops in the diocese of Illinois. In 1852, Wainwright, whose defense of High Church principles during the height of the storm we have previously noted, was elected provisional bishop of New York. In 1853, William Ingraham Kip went as missionary bishop to California. In 1859, Oden-

[17]Packard, A. A., *Pretractarianism in America,* p. 14.

THE FIFTIES—THE STORM SUBSIDES

heimer succeeded Doane in New Jersey. Both were moderate High Churchmen. But the taboo against more advanced men was not broken until the election of William Croswell Doane in 1868 as first bishop of Albany.

After 1853, secessions to Rome practically ceased.[18] The last person of note to go over was the eldest son of Bishop Doane, George Hobart Doane, M. D., deacon, in 1855. This cessation of conversions was symptomatic of the general quieting down during the latter part of this decade. The Church, with her vast power of accommodation, had accustomed herself to the Tractarian changes. The ritual innovations of the Forties had in many places become normal practice. New views of the Reformation, a new attitude toward the Middle Ages, a desire for the recovery of lost ground, a new tone of devotion—all these had won tolerance for themselves within the American Church. The wilder extremists had left for other climes. And, above all, the energies of the country were becoming more and more absorbed by the political struggle. The shadow of impending civil war lay over the land.

The attempt at legislative condemnation of the High Church movement, which had failed so signally in 1844, was not renewed in this decade. Indeed, the conventions of this period were by comparison rather tame and colorless, except for one striking episode. The Memorial Movement does not strictly belong to the history of the High Church movement in America, but its aims represent such an unusual fusion of the best of Catholicism and of Evangelicalism that it deserves passing mention.

The Memorial Movement was an attempt to accomplish two things: to stir up again the missionary spirit of the Church, and to make it a center for Christian reunion. The leader of the movement was Muhlenberg,[19] whose views combined so much of the best of High and Low Church. Joined with him were such diversely-minded men as Bishop Potter of Pennsylvania, a great Evangelical, Arthur

---

[18]*See* Appendix at the end of this chapter.
[19]On Muhlenberg, *see above*, Chapter IV.

Cleveland Coxe, who had reacted from his original Tractarianism into a bitterly anti-ritualistic attitude, and John Henry Hobart, Jr., representing the advanced churchmen.

Among the propositions advocated by the Memorialists were the conferring of orders on men outside the limits of the Protestant Episcopal Church, the greater use of itinerant missionaries, the formation of a permanent commission on Church unity, and a greater liberty in the use of the Prayer Book. The growing cleavage between the older and younger schools of High Churchmen is made beautifully apparent by their attitude toward the last of these propositions. The older men, well represented by Bishop Upfold of Indiana, stuck to their traditional ground, and would hear of nothing but strict observance of the unchanged rubrics. The younger men, looking forward to a more advanced ceremonial, welcomed the proposal as a means of attaining the liberty to do what they wanted in a legal fashion.

Notable among the Memorial papers is that of John Freeman Young, then an assistant at Trinity, New York, later bishop of Florida. This document, with its many references to the Sarum Breviary and Missal, its recommendations of greater variability to mark more clearly the seasons of the Church Year, its advocacy of introits and the Agnus Dei, is indicative of the manner in which High Churchmen were beginning to study liturgics historically, and to move steadily in the direction of ritual and ceremonial enrichment.

The combined opposition of high-and-dries and do-nothing conservatives defeated the larger ends of the movement, but something was obtained when the General Convention of 1856 officially stated that Morning Prayer, the Litany, and the Holy Communion were separate offices, and need not be lumped together to make one long and disunified service. This was sound sense, and a slight preparation for ritualistic advance.

Throughout this decade, the formation of High Church parishes went on. In 1853, Christ Church, Elizabeth, New Jersey, was founded

THE FIFTIES—THE STORM SUBSIDES

by the Rev. Eugene A. Hoffman, later to be known as the great dean and rebuilder of the General Theological Seminary. Late in the period, St. Clement's, Philadelphia, a storm center of the Seventies, was begun. In Chicago, St. James', under the strong rectorship of Robert Harper Clarkson, became so decidedly High Church that disgruntled parishioners seceded and formed a new parish. It is one of the pleasant little ironies of history that the parish thus formed, the Church of the Ascension, later became perhaps the most extreme Anglo-Catholic body in the city.

The history of Grace Church, Newark, is, in little, an epitome of ritualistic advance.[20] It was founded in 1837 under the Rev. George T. Chapman, who was profoundly affected by Tractarianism. Under him, it became one of the earliest parishes to have the daily offices and a weekly Eucharist. These innovations, one of Dr. Chapman's successors, during a brief period of reaction, denounced as "of popish origin and tendency." But the reaction wore itself out. In 1866, a vested choir was started; in 1871, there were altar lights; in 1879, a daily Eucharist and regular confessions; in the Nineties, Benediction of the Blessed Sacrament.

In England, the events of 1845 blocked the appointment of any High Churchman to the episcopate for a considerable time. This did not hold true in America. In 1844, when the war was at its fiercest, Nicholas Hamner Cobbs, whom Bishop Meade had forced out of Virginia, was elected first bishop of Alabama, and Horatio Southgate was sent to Constantinople as missionary bishop. In 1849, George Upfold became bishop of Indiana and, in 1851, as already noted, Henry John Whitehouse succeeded Chase in Illinois—a complete reversal. In 1853, William Ingraham Kip, a highly intelligent Hobartian, became first bishop of California. In spite, then, of battles and treasons, throughout this decade the movement grew and prospered.

[20]*See* Edward F. Bataille, *Grace Church in Newark: The First Hundred Years, 1837-1937* (Newark, 1937) pp. 140.

APPENDIX
SECESSIONS TO ROME, 1817-1858

This is, as far as I can determine, a complete list of all clergy who seceded to Rome between 1817 and 1858. The number is not great, but the quality was high. Bayley became archbishop of Baltimore; Wadhams, bishop of Ogdensburg; Forbes, Hewitt, Baker, Preston and Doane were priests of distinction within the Roman Communion. Edward Ives, Connolly, Forbes, and Bakewell, returned to the Episcopal Church.

	Ordained to the Episcopal Church	*Deposed*
Daniel Barber	1786	1818
Virgil Barber	1805	1817
Edward J. Ives	1823	1851
Pierce Connolly	1826	1835
John M. Forbes	1830	1850
George Allen	1834	1847
Henry Major	1838	1846
Frederick W. J. Pollard	1839	1852
James R. Bayley	1839	1842
Jedediah Huntington	1841	1850
Homer Wheaton	1841	1855
Henry L. Richards	1842	1852
Edgar P. Wadhams	1843	1851
Nathaniel A. Hewitt	1843	1846
William J. Bakewell	1844	1850
Norman C. Stoughton	1844	1852
Dwight E. Lyman	1844	1853
Levi S. Ives	1822	1853
William Everett	1844	1853
Benjamin W. Whitcher	1844	1855
Francis A. Baker	1845	1853
Peter S. Burchan	1845	1852
Gardiner Jones	1846	1850
J. Ambler Weed	1846	1858
Thomas S. Preston	1846	1850
Cornelius D. McLeod	1846	1850

THE FIFTIES—THE STORM SUBSIDES

	Ordained to the Episcopal Church	Deposed
George C. Foote	1848	1857
George L. Roberts	1849	1850
William Markoe	1849	1855
George H. Doane	1855	1855

Of the above, the following are represented with sketches in the *Dictionary of American Biography*: Allen, Bayley, Connolly, Hewitt, Huntington, Ives, L. S., Preston. Whitcher's wife, Frances Miriam Berry, was more famous than he and her biography is given (XX, 82). Whitcher did not secede until after her death.

BIBLIOGRAPHY

BATAILLE, EDWARD F., *Grace Church in Newark: The First Hundred Years, 1837-1937* (Newark, 1937) pp. 140.

DEKOVEN, J., Extracts from his Journal, in *Historical Magazine of the Protestant Episcopal Church*, Vol. II, pp. 205-10.
— *Sermons Preached on Various Occasions*, with biographical introduction by Morgan Dix (New York, 1880).

DIX, MORGAN, "Ferdinand C. Ewer," in *American Church Review*, Vol. 42, pp. 511-529.

EWER, F. C., *Sermons on the Failure of Protestantism* (New York, 1868).
— *Catholicity, Protestantism and Romanism* (New York, 1879).

GRAFTON, C. C., *A Journey Godward* (Milwaukee, 1910). [Autobiography, especially valuable for chapters VII and VIII.]

HAYWOOD, M. DEL., *Lives of the Bishops of North Carolina* (Raleigh, 1910.) [For Bishop Ives, see pp. 91-139.]

HOPKINS, J. H., JR., (editor) *The Collected Works of the Late Milo Mahan*, (New York, 1875). [Biographical sketch by the editor.]

HOPKINS, J. H., 3RD, "The Rev. John Henry Hopkins, Jr.," in *Historical Magazine of the Protestant Episcopal Church*, Vol. IV, pp. 267-80.

PACKARD, A. A., *Pretractarianism in America*. MSS. dissertation in library of G. T. S. [Not dependable.]

POTTER, ALONZO, (editor) *The Memorial Papers* (Philadelphia, 1857).

SWEET, C. F., *A Champion of the Cross* (New York, 1894). [Life of J. H. Hopkins, Jr.]

CHAPTER SIX

THE SECOND RITUALISTIC WAR

THE Civil War put an end for the time being to the controversies within the Church, but no sooner had the reunion of the Northern and Southern branches of the Church been accomplished than the struggle broke out again with renewed vigor, and raged furiously up until 1875. This later stage of the strife of High and Low was basically a war over ritual, though necessarily complicated by at least two distinct doctrinal disputes.

CEREMONIAL INNOVATIONS OF THE SIXTIES

The ceremonial innovations of the Forties had become by now commonplaces. Stone altars with crosses had no longer any definite High Church significance, though if candles were added, the church was ritualistic. But there was, as we have noted in the last chapter, a very gradual tendency to proceed to a richer ceremonial than that practiced by such men as Croswell and Whittingham, just as Croswell and Whittingham, in their turn, were advanced ritualists beside Hobart and Seabury. During the Sixties, eucharistic vestments of linen were gradually coming in. The first mention of their use I have found is in the diocese of Western New York in 1860. They are stated to have been introduced there from Vermont. They were worn, without, as far as can be discovered, causing any particular comment, by Bishop DeLancey at his last diocesan convention in 1865.[1] Nor did their introduction by Mahan in St. Paul's, Baltimore, seem to have stirred up any particular difficulty.

Only exceedingly well-informed churchmen of the present day

[1] Hayes, C., *Diocese of Western New York*, p. 234

have ever heard the name of St. Alban's Church, New York. But there was a time, in the late Sixties, when it was probably the most noted—or notorious—parish in the country. In 1860, a group of laymen of Calvary Church organized the Chapel of St. James the Less, to undertake mission work among the poor. As the Church of the Intercessor, it was admitted into union with the convention of the diocese as a parish. In 1863, the dedication was significantly changed to St. Alban, the name coming from the most famous of Anglo-Catholic parishes in London. Shortly after, the Rev. Charles William Morrill became rector, and a building was erected in 1865 on East 47th Street, where the Grand Central Palace now stands. Father Morrill deliberately set out to make his parish, untrammelled as it was by tradition, a center of Catholic life and worship. Among the innovations at St. Alban's were colored eucharistic vestments, the use of incense and the sacring bell, lay servers, and the processional cross. The usages of St. Alban's were in large part adopted by Ewer at Christ Church. There is a very interesting description in a Chicago Church periodical of Low Mass at Christ Church. The writer mentions, almost with bated breath, the dim church, the altar with its red velvet frontal, its prayer cards, cross and candles, the entrance of the priest in crimson chasuble, accompanied by a deacon in alb, stole, and maniple, and goes on to picture what would be the normal ceremonial in hundreds of American churches today.[2]

Few parishes followed St. Alban's and Christ Church in all their ceremonial practices, but ritual advance was in the air. In 1867, the Rev. Colin Tate of St. Paul's, Columbus, Ohio, was attacked by Bishop McIlvaine for introducing a vested choir and a choral processional. The bishop took the extreme ground that these things were contrary to the laws and usages of the Church, and that if Tate continued in them, he was subject to deposition for breach of his ordination vows. Tate was presented by the standing committee for trial, but as in the Doane case, the process was blocked by techni-

[2]*The American Churchman*, Vol. IX, p. 243. In spite of its apparent success, St. Alban's fell into financial difficulties, its location was found to be bad, and in 1880 it was closed.

calities. It is interesting to note that such High Church warriors as Seabury and Hopkins held that, while Tate was legally in the right, as a matter of Catholic discipline he should have submitted to his bishop.[3]

In 1870, Thomas McKee Brown, who, as assistant first to Seabury at the Church of the Annunciation and later to Ewer at Christ Church, was linked to two generations of strong Catholics, founded the Church of St. Mary the Virgin, New York, probably the most famous ritualistic church in America.

In the same year, a furious quarrel broke out in St. Clement's Church, Philadelphia, where the vestry attempted to dismiss the rector, the Rev. Hermon G. Batterson, for various practices—the use of colored stoles, hymns in procession, altar candles, the mixed chalice, standing at the presentation of the collection, bowing to the altar, and teaching auricular confession and the validity of prayers for the dead. In this they were supported by the bishop of the diocese, William Bacon Stevens, who thus delivered himself upon the major charges:

> The American Church recognizes no inherent right in the minister to hear confession and grant absolution, outside of the forms and ways specially provided; and by her legislation, direct and indirect, has protested against the private confessional and absolution . . . The history of the Confessional is one of the foulest pages in the annals of the Church of Rome.
>
> There is not a single passage of Canonical Scripture, nor a sentence in the Book of Common Prayer of the Protestant Episcopal Church, that warrants or countenances, by any fair and honest interpretation, Prayers for the Dead.[4]

As had happened in the Forties, the General Seminary again became a focus of trouble. In 1867 there were reports about that the seminary was not truly "general," and a committee of the faculty felt impelled to report that the teaching of the institution was of "the plain, straightforward Bishop Hobart school." But if the teaching

[3] Smyth, G. E., *History of Diocese of Ohio*, pp. 327-30.
[4] *The Batterson Case, passim.*

was old-fashioned High Churchmanship, many of the students, as might have been expected, were moving beyond this point. In 1870, a senior, Calbraith Perry, of whom we shall hear more later, wrote a sermon on the Eucharist, in which he said:

> "And then he deigns . . . to be upon our altars and to be handled by sinful man. As when in helpless infancy He submitted to be wrapped in swaddling clothes, and to be treated by men as they would, whether with respect or disrespect, so now in the Blessed Sacrament, wrapped in the fine linen of the Church . . . He puts Himself in the power of men."

Eventually, this sermon was submitted to the faculty for judgment, censured by Dean Forbes, and defended by Professor Seymour.[5]

Similar controversies raged in the dioceses of Maryland, Pittsburgh, and Indiana.

BISHOP HOPKINS AND "THE LAW OF RITUALISM"

As a result of the agitations arising from these disturbing novelties, a number of priests, including Morgan Dix, Tucker, Young, and William Croswell Doane, addressed themselves to Bishop Hopkins, now presiding bishop of the Church, asking for his advice as to the legality and advisability of these ceremonial practices.[6] We have seen Hopkins in 1844 and 1845 decidedly aligning himself with the anti-Tractarians. But the lapse of twenty years had stilled his alarms, and both his natural bent and the influence of his brilliant son had gradually brought him back to his normal position as a strong High Churchman. He was now generally recognized as the one of the old High Church bishops most in sympathy with ceremonial advance. So well was his position understood, even in England, that when Walker in 1866 wrote the well-known little treatise, *The Ritual Reason Why*, he dedicated it to Bishop Hopkins as "an episcopal defender of ceremonial." Hopkins, ever ready with his pen, answered the request of

---

[5] William W. Manross, "Growth and Progress since 1860," *The General Theological Seminary Number*, *Historical Magazine*, Vol. V, 210-211.
[6] Hopkins, J. H. Jr., *Life of Bishop Hopkins*, p. 378.

his younger clerical brethren for guidance by publishing in 1866 a small volume entitled, *The Law of Ritualism.*

In this ingenious and intelligent little tract, the bishop first makes clear his own position. In his practice, he had never gone beyond the very moderate ceremonial innovations of the Forties, nor did he intend to, rather pathetically maintaining that he was now too old a man to accustom himself to any further change. After having thus cleared the ground, he goes on to consider the legality of the more advanced ceremonial now causing such a furore. He bases his argument first of all on Scripture, thus cleverly meeting the Low Churchmen on their own favorite ground. In the Scriptures, he finds warrant and example for stone altars, candles, incense, and chrism. He notes with considerable keenness, and directly in the face of most of the Low Church bishops, that the English Reformation was directed primarily, not against ceremonial, but against doctrinal corruptions, and that ceremonial, *per se,* is not only primitive, but in the highest degree scriptural. From this he proceeds to a consideration of the Ornaments Rubric, which he frankly admits to have no binding force in the American Church, but which he nevertheless considers a valuable permissive guide to practice. He concludes that the use of Mass vestments, copes, and mitres is perfectly legal.[7]

Finally, he treats of the advisability of such matters. Refusing, on the one hand, to accept the position of the straitest sect among the newer ceremonialists, that there is only one correct way in ceremonial, and, on the other hand, parting company with the older High Churchmen with their itch for uniformity, he admits, with his usual independent common sense, that there is no great harm in a wide diversity of usage. He plainly declares his sympathy with all intelligent attempts to enrich the services of the Church, and even ventures to predict that ceremonialism, including all the practices he had declared to be legal, was bound to spread until it became the normal custom of the American Church.[8] In this, of course, he was either

[7] Hopkins, J. H., *The Law of Ritualism,* p. 75.
[8] *Ibid.,* pp. 77-85.

THE SECOND RITUALISTIC WAR

over-sanguine or else taking a very long view indeed. The sanity, tolerance, sound learning, and persuasive aestheticism of this little treatise make it pleasant and valuable reading even today after half a century of volumes on ceremonial.

The welcome this book received was not such as its common sense moderation of tone might lead one to expect. For an obscure little church like St. Alban's to indulge in Romish antics was one thing, but for the presiding bishop of the Church to maintain their legality and to predict their spread was quite another. When, therefore, a special meeting of the House of Bishops was held in New York in 1866, the bishop of Vermont's little volume was one of the chief subjects of discussion. No formal action on it was taken, but, during the months following, a *Declaration* was prepared and signed by twenty-eight bishops, condemning in round terms altar candles, incense, reverences to the altar or to the elements, and eucharistic vestments. The secretary of the group who prepared the *Declaration* was Bishop Coxe of Western New York. One would expect to find among its signers the names of McIlvaine, Bedell, Johns, Eastburn, and Cummins. More surprising is the inclusion of Upfold, Williams, Kip, Kemper, Clarkson, Kerfoot, and Armitage, all High Churchmen in a greater or lesser degree.[9] This *Declaration* was sharply ridiculed by the younger Hopkins, in his *Church Journal,* as a "blank cartridge."

THE GENERAL CONVENTION OF 1868

In 1867, Bishop Hopkins died. On October 7, 1868, the General Convention met in New York City. By one of fate's little ironies most of the meetings of the House of Deputies were held in the Church of the Transfiguration—a church noted from its foundation for its Catholic belief and worship. On the fifth day of the convention, Judge Conyngham of Pennsylvania announced that in response to numerous memorials from members of the laity,[10] he was introducing

[9]*The Churchman,* Vol. XXIII, p. 67.
[10]It was clearly proved that these memorials had been circulated from some central source, presumably in New York City.

[113]

in the House of Deputies a Canon of the Manner of Conducting Divine Worship. By the provisions of this canon, the only vestments allowed were surplice, stole,[11] bands, and gown; candles and crucifixes on the altar were prohibited, and likewise bowing except in the creeds, signing with the cross except in baptism, the elevation of the Host, the use of incense and processions.[12] This canon was referred to the committee on Canons, which reported after a long delay that in their opinion a canon on ritual was at present inexpedient. A minority report was presented by the Rev. M. A. DeWolfe Howe, of Pennsylvania, which condemned by name the ceremonial practices attacked. The debate was strangely mild and good-tempered, the precedent of 1844 in favor of toleration being significantly adduced. The only speech which really went to the root of the matter was that of Mahan, who frankly stated that the practices under discussion were not mere trimmings, but symptoms of a world-wide return to greater Catholicity in doctrine and devotion.[13] Eventually, the only action taken was the appointment of a committee of the House of Bishops, consisting of Bishops Lee, Williams, Odenheimer, Clark, and Kerfoot, to consider the whole question and report to the next General Convention.[14]

The pastoral letter of the House of Bishops, while not directly referring to ritualism, betrayed a very keen anxiety about the doctrinal developments involved in ceremonial practice. It included a sharp attack on the "unscriptural and uncatholic pretentions of the Bishop of Rome," and a defence of the Anglican Reformation. Finally, it dealt with eucharistic doctrine in these terms:

> Especially do we condemn any doctrine of the Holy Eucharist which implies that, after consecration, the proper nature of the

---

[11] The inclusion of the stole is interesting. It was first introduced as an ice-breaker for the full Mass vestments. Becoming confused with the scarf, it was widely adopted as an office vestment, and so lost all party significance. Ironically enough, today a priest who wears a stole at Morning Prayer labels himself Low Churchman; a moderate High Churchman wears a tippet; an extreme High Churchman, neither.

[12] *The Churchman*, New Series, Vol. II, p. 334.

[13] *The Churchman*, New Series, Vol. II, pp. 367-68.

[14] Dr. Adams of Nashotah, a good representative of conservative High Churchmanship, proposed the setting up of a permanent congregation of rites.

elements of bread and wine does not remain; which localizes in them the bodily presence of our Lord; which allows any adoration other than that of our Blessed Lord Himself: ... which, in any way, asserts that his sacrifice upon the cross was not a full, perfect, and sufficient sacrifice, oblation, and satisfaction for the sins of the whole world; and which would add to our Liturgy ceremonies and rites designed to teach all or any of these things.[15]

THE GENERAL CONVENTION OF 1871

That the question had not been settled was recognized by both parties, and both accordingly prepared for the struggle to come. The Convention that met in Baltimore on October 2, 1871, was the stormiest since that of 1844. It was, like that earlier Convention, a notable body. Of the leaders of 1844, two only survived: Bishop McIlvaine of Ohio, still perhaps the strongest man on the Low Church side; and Bishop Whittingham of Maryland, whom we have seen metamorphosed from one of the most hated of High Churchmen into one of the chief opponents of ritualism. The Low Churchmen were led by Bishops Lee, Johns and Eastburn in the upper house, and by William Cooper Mead, M. A. DeWolfe Howe and Daniel C. Goodwin in the lower. None of the bishops, except William Croswell Doane, belonged to the newer ritualists, but the lower house showed a noble array of advanced High Church leaders—Breck, Tucker, Waterman, and De Koven. Between the extremes stood, somewhat bewildered by it all, the large mass of old High Churchmen, numbering such bishops as Upfold, Williams, Odenheimer, Coxe, and Kerfoot, and priests like Beardsley, Haight, and Cady. Of the younger bishops two deserve especial mention: William Croswell Doane, first bishop of Albany, a true son of a notable father; and Frederick Dan Huntington, who, after a brilliant career as a Unitarian minister, had entered the Church and become first bishop of Central New York.

[15]*The Churchman*, N. S., Vol II, p. 361.

Bishop Doane had already been the center of one of the minor skirmishes of the war. Coming to Albany in 1867 as rector of St. Peter's, he was soon in conflict with his vestry. Immediately on arrival in the parish, he instituted the daily offices and the weekly Eucharist, which he celebrated in the "eastward position." This might have passed, but when he attempted to reform the music, the majority of the vestry rose in arms. In 1868, there was a bitterly disputed vestry election, in which Doane was accused of sharp practice. Meanwhile, he had signed the address to Bishop Hopkins which brought forth *The Law of Ritualism*. When, therefore, in 1868, the new diocese of Albany was erected, and Doane was put forward as a candidate for the episcopate, the anti-ritualists sharpened their swords. He was elected on the ninth ballot; among his prominent supporters was John Henry Hopkins, Junior. But opposition to Doane did not stop with his election. A determined attempt to block its confirmation was headed by Bishop Coxe of Western New York, seconded by such a staunch old High Churchman as Bishop Kemper of Wisconsin. The attempt of course failed, and Doane became first bishop of Albany.[16]

On the second day of the session, the report of the committee of five—a committee which included three old High Churchmen—was presented to the House of Bishops. This report recommended the prohibition of incense, crucifixes, processional crosses, altar candles, eucharistic vestments, the elevation, the mixed chalice, the ablutions, lay servers, and all reverences to the altar except as provided for in the Prayer Book.[17] That a committee which included Bishops Williams, Odenheimer and Kerfoot should have submitted such a radical set of recommendations as these is positively astounding. It is in large part accounted for by the fact that the ritualistic question had become involved with another of the basic principles of the old High Churchmen. The old High Church party, the party of Hobart and his followers, emphasizing as it did the doctrine of the apostolic succesion, had inculcated and practiced reverence for bishops and re-

---

[16]DeMille, G. E., *History of the Diocese of Albany*, p. 75.
[17]*Journal of the General Convention*, 1871, pp. 263, 598-601.

THE SECOND RITUALISTIC WAR

spect for their authority. But there were some among the men of the ritualistic school who had forgotten that discipline has always been a characteristic of the Catholic Church—who acted as if they thought the best proof of Catholicism was the flouting of a bishop. Both Kerfoot and Whittingham had been much troubled in this way. And thus the opposition of the High Church bishops to the ritualists was something more than mere conservatism. To them, this report was less an attack on ritualism than an attempt to secure authority and order.

The report was referred to a joint committee of the two houses. The episcopal delegation consisted of Bishops Whittingham, Stevens, Bedell, Atkinson, and Coxe. A more anti-ritualistic group of five would have been difficult to find on the whole bench of bishops. The committee from the House of Deputies was a packed body, led by the Rev. Dr. William Cooper Mead, generally considered the ablest politician among the clergy, and one of the arch-opponents of ritualism. The only High Churchmen of any shade on the delegation were Orlando Meads of Albany, and the Rev. Benjamin I. Haight of New York.[18] But in spite of the composition of the committee, a fairly innocuous-seeming canon was reported, containing provisions that the standard of ritual should be the rubrics of the Book of Common Prayer, and the canons of the Church of England *in use* in America before 1789, and stating that all ritual disputes should be settled by the bishop of the diocese.[19] This canon was adopted by the House of Bishops. On the twentieth day of the session an additional canon was offered by Bishop Young of Florida, who had been notable as a priest in New York for his efforts to bring the Church into closer relations with the Eastern Orthodox Churches. This canon, which forbade the elevation, any ceremony not prescribed by the Prayer Book, a celebration without communicants, or the use of unauthorized hymns, prayers, epistles, or gospels, was also adopted by the House of Bishops.[20]

[18] *Journal of the General Convention, 1871*, p. 73.
[19] *Ibid.*, p. 125.
[20] *Ibid.*, p. 367.

Meanwhile, the House of Deputies was engaged in a life and death struggle. The report of the joint commission was presented on the session of the fourteenth day, and the discussion continued intermittently for two days. Then, De Koven having conclusively shown that the second paragraph of the proposed canon—that referring to the canons of the Church of England in use in America before 1789— if it accomplished anything, prohibited the surplice, Mead of Connecticut moved to substitute for the canon reported by the committee another, embodying the much more definite and stringent provisions of the report of the five bishops. The debate now lost all that gentlemanly and conciliatory character that had marked the debates of 1868. From the one side came allusions to "the trumpery of Rome"; statements that "you must regulate ritual by law in some way"; charges that ritualism was corrupting the General Seminary. The counter epithet of the ritualists, who kept their tempers rather better than their opponents, was "Zwinglian." St. Alban's and Dr. Ewer were mentioned by name.

Finally, De Koven came forward, and in a speech which long remained in the memories of men, defended, not only the practices, but the basic doctrine of his party. Part of his speech has often been quoted, but it is worth quoting again:

> I believe in—and this will be printed tomorrow, and I will write it out, if necessary, for anyone who wants to use it—I believe in the Real, Actual Presence of Our Lord under the form of bread and wine upon the altars of our churches. I myself adore, and would, if it were necessary or my duty, teach my people to adore, Christ present in the elements under the form of bread and wine.
>
> And I use these words because they are a bold statement of the doctrine of the Real Presence, but I use them for another reason: they are adjudicated words; they are words which, used by a divine of the Church of England, have been tried in the highest ecclesiastical court of England, and have been decided by

THE SECOND RITUALISTIC WAR

that ecclesiastical court to come within the limits of the truth held in the Church of England."[21]

The effect of these bold and, at the same time, supremely clever words was immense. They killed De Koven's chances of a bishopric, but they also killed the canons on ritual. The stringent canons offered by the Rev. Dr. Mead were first considered, and decisively rejected in both orders. The original canon as reported by the joint committee was then voted on, and though a majority of the House favored its adoption, it was lost for lack of concurrence of both orders. Bishop Young's canon against eucharistic adoration was next considered, and suffered a like fate. Eventually, a pair of harmless resolutions were passed, declaring that the Convention condemned all ceremonies expressing doctrines foreign to the Church.[22] This meaningless statement was the sole tangible result of the anti-ritualistic crusade. Once again, as in 1844, the Church had declared that she stood for the widest possible toleration, even at the risk of anarchy.

But if the legislative action of this Convention was in the upshot mild and tolerant, the pastoral letter of the House of Bishops, like that of 1868, was a distinct attack on De Koven and his followers. In this pastoral, the practice of auricular confession was deplored, the Church was warned against the tendency to extreme veneration of the saints, the new ritualism was condemned, and eucharistic adoration, while not precisely denounced, was treated very coolly and unsympathetically.[23]

Immediately after this Convention, a number of occurrences took place in Maryland, which helped to increase greatly the bitterness of the parties. For a decade, Mount Calvary Church, Baltimore, had been a center of Catholic teaching and of ritualistic practice, though not so pronounced as at St. Alban's. It had made an enviable name for itself by the remarkable work done by its clergy among the poor of the city. Partly as a consequence of the attitude assumed by the

[21] *Debates of the House of Deputies,* p. 506.
[22] *Journal of the General Convention,* 1871, pp. 232-42.
[23] *The Churchman,* N. S., Vol. V, p. 356.

THE CATHOLIC MOVEMENT IN THE EPISCOPAL CHURCH

House of Bishops in the pastoral, the first rector of the parish, the Rev. A. A. Curtis, renounced his ministry and was received into the Church of Rome. He was succeeded by the Rev. Joseph Richey, an advanced High Churchman. Hardly had Richey assumed charge of the parish, when trouble began. Bishop Whittingham, his ancient dislike and suspicion of ritualists strengthened by the defection of Curtis, wrote to Richey, expressing his disapproval of the altar lights, wafer bread, the elevation, the crossings, and the use of the cross in processions. But he confined himself to disapproval, having no legal ground for further action, nor indeed any disposition to become an unlawful persecutor.[24] And in spite of his personal dislike of the practices at Mount Calvary, he steadfastly refused to give any countenance to petty personal attacks on the ritualistic clergy. Thus, in spite of vigorous protest, he ordained the following year the Rev. C. G. Perry, assistant at Mount Calvary, and a zealous ritualist.

Two years later Mount Calvary was again in trouble. The practice of celebrating the Holy Communion at funerals had been gradually gaining ground. Such a celebration had taken place at the funeral of Bishop Hopkins in 1867. Now, at the burial of a priest connected with Mount Calvary, Father Perry used the commendatory prayer from the office for the sick, thus turning it in effect into a direct prayer for the soul of the dead man. This action was so resented by two priests attending the funeral that they presented Perry for trial. The bishop, disapproving the act, though warrant could have been found for it in the teaching of Whittingham's own master, Hobart, attempted to settle the matter by correspondence, and secured from Father Perry what seemed a satisfactory explanation. But the standing committee of the diocese refused to accept this peaceable solution, and proceeded to present the accused priest for trial. This presentment the bishop would not receive, and as a consequence himself narrowly escaped presentment for illegally refusing a trial. Thus there was seen in the Church the distressing but somewhat amusing spectacle of a

[24]Brand, W. F., *Life of Bishop Whittingham*, Vol. II, pp. 211-21.

bishop, the patriarch of the High Church party, who had suffered persecution years before for extreme beliefs, and who now stood forth as one of the chief opponents of ritualism, barely avoiding trial for not consenting to become an anti-ritualist persecutor.[25]

Neither party accepted the solution—or rather the no-solution—of 1871 as final. The books and pamphlets on the subject of ritualism published between 1867 and 1874 indicate how greatly churchmen were exercised over the subject. In 1867 appeared Coxe's *Ritualism*, a lengthly and uncompromising condemnation, and Goodwin's *Shall We Return to Rome?*, the title of which indicates its temper. On the other side, Morgan Dix published *A History of the Past Fifty Years*, a study of the gradual and apparently inevitable ritual advance; Bolles, *An Essay on True Catholic Liberty* and *The Defense of Sound Church Principles;* and Douglas, *The Worship of the Body*, a book of ceremonial for the laity. The Convention of 1871 had, as its aftermath, Wilmer's *Pastoral Letter;* Hoffman's *Ritual Law of the Church*, a lawyer's attack on the application of the Ornaments Rubric to the American Church; and Bedell's *Ritual Uniformity*. The chief reply to these was De Koven's *The Canon on Ritual*. This flood of pamphlets indicated clearly enough what might be expected to happen when General Convention next met.

THE GENERAL CONVENTION OF 1874

The General Convention of 1874 was notable for the personal bitterness imported into the struggle. The long continuance of the fight, the failure in two Conventions to accomplish anything in the way of a canon to bridle the ritualists, and, it must be confessed, the sharp-edged writings of the High Church leaders, brought the Low Churchmen to a pitch of exasperation that recalled the days of the Onderdonk trial. One minor but signficant incident showed the way the wind was blowing. John Henry Hopkins, wielder of the sharpest lance on his side, had been elected as a supplemental deputy from the diocese of Albany. When, therefore, a regular member of the

[25]Brand, W. F., *op.cit.* Vol. II, pp. 222-45.

Albany delegation was given leave of absence, Hopkins attempted to take his seat—and was rejected by the committee on elections, although during the same convention other deputies were seated under similar circumstances.[26] But this was a mere trifle compared with what was to come.

The Very Rev. George F. Seymour, dean of the General Seminary, had been elected bishop of Illinois by the convention of that diocese. He had been mentioned by name in the debates of the previous General Convention as the most dangerous influence in the seminary. He had further made himself obnoxious by becoming chaplain to the Sisters of St. Mary, and by allowing the dreadful Father Grafton access to the student body at the seminary. When, therefore, the committee on the consecration of bishops recommended the confirmation of his election, immediate and intense opposition developed; indeed, the indications are that a large body of deputies came to the Convention pre-determined to block the confirmation. For six days the House of Deputies sat in secret session, holding inquisition into the life and opinions of the bishop-elect.[27] Finally, on the fourteenth day of the session the vote was taken. In the clerical order, the vote stood nineteen for confirmation, ten against, with twelve dioceses divided. Of the laity, thirteen dioceses were for confirmation, eighteen opposed, with nine divided.[28]

[26] *Journal of the General Convention*, 1874, p. 62.

[27] This star-chamber session evoked much indignation among churchmen of all schools. Bishop Doane of Albany, who had himself been a few years before the target of anti-ritualistic attack, was unsparing in his condemnation of the procedure of the Convention. He remarked:

"I think I have the right to say that, in my personal judgment, as a churchman and a man, a grosser misunderstanding of the duties prescribed by Canon has rarely been committed, than the fact and the manner of that deliberation. The closed doors of the House for eight days, demanded and persisted in by the opponents of the confirmation . . . the assumption by that House of the prerogative, not of approving the testimonials of the Bishop-elect, and assenting to his consecration, but of going behind those testimonials, to assume virtually the responsibility of either the electing or the consecrating body, and to pass judicial sentence upon the theological soundness of a man unheard in his defense . . . these matters present so grave questions, that I believe I am bound to call to your attention . . . the tremendous dangers they involve." *Albany Convention Journal*, 1875,p. 111.

[28] *Journal of the General Convention*, 1874, pp. 33, 97-100.

This vote indicates a shift in the center of opposition to High Churchmanship. In 1844, when the fight had been waged entirely over questions of dogma, the opposition to Tractarianism had come mainly from Low Churchmen of the clerical order. But the vote of 1874 indicates how far the laity of the Church, usually indifferent to questions of doctrine, had been aroused and irritated by extreme High Church ceremonial. Here was something they could see, something they could understand, and something a majority of them rather heartily disliked.

Once again the six-year-old battle for a canon of ritual uniformity was renewed. Memorials both for and against restrictive legislation were presented, a number of canons was proposed, and eventually, on the fifteenth day of the session, the committee on canons, still under the strongly anti-ritualistic lead of the Rev. Dr. Mead, presented to the house a canon which prohibited incense, the use of the crucifix, and the elevation or adoration of the elements. But this was far too moderate for the extreme Low Churchmen, who, therefore, proposed a substitute which incorporated all the provisions of the historic report of the five bishops. Even with feelings aroused as they were, this substitute was too extreme to receive much consideration, and it was voted down *viva voce*. De Koven again distinguished himself, opposing all ritual legislation, and ably seconded by the Rev. Samuel S. Harris of Louisiana, the Rev. Dr. Philander K. Cady of New York, Dr. Orlando Meads of Albany, and Dr. George C. Shattuck of Massachusetts, but they were unable to block the passage of the committee's canon.[29]

But still the matter was not settled. The House of Bishops had meanwhile passed a canon on ritual of its own, much more vague in its wording than that of the House of Deputies. The lower house refused to concur, a committee of conference was appointed, and the following canon was finally passed without much opposition, the High Church leaders evidently feeling that this was the most favorable settlement possible at the moment:

[29] *Journal of the General Convention*, 1874, pp. 38, 112

> If any bishop have reason to believe, or if complaint be made to him in writing by two or more of his Presbyters, that within his jurisdiction ceremonies or practices not ordained or authorized in the Book of Common Prayer, and setting forth or symbolizing erroneous or doubtful doctrines, have been introduced by any Minister during the celebration of the Holy Communion, such as
>
>   a. The Elevation of the Elements in the Holy Communion in such manner as to expose them to the view of the people as objects toward which adoration is to be made
>
>   b. Any act of adoration of or toward the Elements in the Holy Communion, such as bowings, prostrations, or genuflections; and
>
>   c. All other like acts not authorized by the Rubrics of the Book of Common Prayer:
>
> It shall be the duty of such Bishop to summon the Standing Committee as his Council of Advice, and with them to investigate the matter.

The canon then goes on to provide for the admonition and eventual trial if necessary of offending priests.[30]

Although High Churchmen attempted to minimize the significance of this canon by asserting that it only prohibited adoration of the *elements,* which they never thought of adoring, and although it was so vague and indefinite as to be practically unenforceable, its passage must be regarded as a victory for the Low Church party, aided, however, by a large body of old High Churchmen.

The Low Churchmen then attempted to improve their victory. The question of Baptismal Regeneration had always troubled the extreme Evangelicals, and, since 1870, there had been a considerable agitation within the Church to water down her teaching on that subject. In 1873, George David Cummins, assistant bishop of Kentucky, accompanied by a small handful of priests, had organized the Reformed Episcopal schism. There were three main reasons for this secession: Cummins and his followers, observing the steady growth

[30] *Ibid.,* pp. 185-88. In the Digest of the Canons, appended to the *Journal of 1874,* it is part of Title I, Canon 22, *Of the Use of the Book of Common Prayer,* Section II.

THE SECOND RITUALISTIC WAR

of ritualism, feared that the Church as a whole was being de-Protestantized; some of them had taken part in a Protestant communion service, and had been roundly rebuked by the old High Churchmen; finally, they had conscientious objections to the Prayer Book teaching on Baptism. Partly in the hope of recalling the schismatics, partly to prevent further secessions, and partly, perhaps, to ease a weight on their own consciences, the Low Church leaders now offered a canon allowing an alternative for the exhortation in the Baptismal office, an alternative which minimized the definiteness of the Church's teaching on that sacrament. At once the alliance of Low Church and old High Church was dissolved, and the canon was overwhelmingly defeated.[31]

Although they had lost a part of the battle in this Convention, the ritualists were far from routed. By its repeated failure to prohibit, the Convention might plausibly be held to have tacitly licensed the use of altar lights, the processional cross, eucharistic vestments, and even incense. Since that time, no important attempt has been made, in General Convention, to legislate against ceremonial advance. It is an excellent comment on the spirit of the American Church, on its natural leaning toward toleration and comprehension, that a Convention, only a small minority of the members of which were themselves ritualists, rejected the various extreme anti-ritualist canons, and by passing only one comparatively innocuous act, left the door open for growth and progress. In 1904, at the general revision of the canons, the canon on Eucharistic Adoration was quietly dropped.

As far as I can discover, but one trial ever took place under this canon. The Rev. Oliver S. Prescott, whom we have seen first at Valle Crucis, later under fire in Boston, joined the Society of St. John the Evangelist, popularly called the "Cowley Fathers," from the name of the place in England where the order was started. He became in the Seventies rector of St. Clement's, Philadelphia. In 1877, he was accused of numerous ritualistic practices, tried under the canon, and admonished by Bishop Stevens. Here the matter ended, accompanied

[31] *Journal of the General Convention*, 1874, p. 205.

by the usual rocket-shower of pamphlets. St. Clement's went on its ritualistic way, despite episcopal admonishment and disapproval.[32] In 1887, the standing committee of the diocese of Ohio investigated the conduct of the Rev. Charles De Garmo at St. John's, Toledo, but nothing came of it. Later attempts to prosecute the Rev. Arthur Ritchie, of St. Ignatius' Church, New York, were defeated by the wise tolerance of Bishop Henry Potter, who likewise in 1903 supported the Church of St. Mary the Virgin, when it was harassed by a visiting English busybody.[33] In 1895, the *New York Sun* could truthfully say:

> "Ritualism in New York as elsewhere has advanced usually by these well-recognized steps: the surplice, unlighted tapers, lighted tapers, plain vestments, colored vestments, high mass, and finally the confessional."[34]

The same paper enumerated four churches in New York supplied with confessionals, and five which used incense. By 1900, the startling practices inaugurated at St. Alban's in 1865 were widespread and rarely noticed.

THE STATE OF THE MOVEMENT IN 1874

Roughly speaking, the year 1874 marks the close of the third phase of the High Church movement in the American Church. During the first phase, that prior to 1840, the great work of the High Churchmen had been to reaffirm the fundamental position of the Church—her Catholicity, the necessity of her orders, and the validity of her sacraments. The polemic of this period was mainly directed against the Protestant sects. During the second phase, from 1840 to 1860, the advanced men of the period were striving to put into

---

[32]*The Prescott Case, passim.*
[33]Hodges, George, *Henry Codman Potter*, pp. 166-179.
[34]This was ritualism in New York; ritualism in Virginia was a very different thing. In 1879, Bishop Whittle of Virginia ruled that while the use of Christmas greens was lawful, flowers at Easter, fruit or vegetables on Thanksgiving, and the decoration of the Lord's Table with cloths of different colors for different occasions, were "a new and strange thing in the Church in Virginia, and ought not to be done or allowed."

practice the logical consequence of the doctrines laid down by their predecessors: to re-emphasize the idea of worship, to surround the services with such accessories as might help the congregation to worship better, to make the Eucharist more central and to increase the frequency of communions, and by the better observance of the Christian Year to help the Church in its teaching office. The third phase, from 1860 on, was characterized by a definite desire for innovation, an attempt to go behind the Reformation, and to restore to the Church some of those features of Catholic life which she had lost, or at least allowed to fall into disuse after the sixteenth century.

Partly corresponding to these three phases were the three sections which now appeared in the High Church party. There were the old High Churchmen— a large and powerful body, probably the largest single group within the American Church. These men held firmly to the principles laid down by Hobart. They believed in the Catholicity of the American Church; they made much of the doctrine of the apostolic succession; they were firm in their attachment to the sacraments; they respected the bishops, and believed in discipline. They had, as a body, accepted the earlier developments in ritual as practiced by such men as Muhlenberg and Croswell. But there they stopped.

The younger group, led by such men as De Koven and Mahan, differed very little from them in fundamental doctrine. Both taught the Real Presence, but the younger men were perhaps a little clearer in mind as to just what they meant by that expression, and much more disposed to show forth the Real Presence by acts of adoration. Furthermore, to the older men the sacrament was instituted solely as a means of communion. High Mass without communicants was to them an abomination. The second group was much more inclined to think of the sacrificial aspect of the Mass, and to use the sacrament as an object of worship. They made use of private confession; they celebrated, though the term was not much in use, requiem masses; they were beginning, particularly in the Mid-Western dioceses, to introduce a richer episcopal ceremonial. While the stress of the older men was laid on the primitive Church, and they were disposed to regard the Reformation as a great blessing, the new generation was decidedly cool toward the reformers, and was frankly desirous of re-introducing practices and beliefs, not primitive, but coming from the Middle Ages.

At the extreme edge of this group, if indeed he does not not fall into the next, was the Rev. Arthur Ritchie. Personally charming, an eloquent preacher and a devoted parish priest who could always count on the support of his congregation, Ritchie was one of those uncompromising Catholics who delight in stating their position in its most extreme terms, to whom any concession is a surrender of the faith, and whose attitude toward ecclesiastical authority is basically Baptist. Ritchie was born in Philadelphia in 1849, trained at the General Seminary, and served his apprenticeship at the Advent, Boston, St. Clement's, Philadelphia, and Mount Calvary, Baltimore. In 1875, he became rector of the Church of the Ascension, Chicago. Chicago, under Whitehouse and McLaren, was far from being a Low Church center, but Ritchie was too High Church even for Chicago. By 1879, he was in hot water with Bishop McLaren over the question of Reservation. At the bishop's request, he temporarily discontinued the practice; but three years later, he was again under episcopal disapproval for celebrating High Mass with only the celebrant communicating, and with all the elements of the service having to do with the communion of the people—Confession, Absolution, Prayer of Humble Access—boldly omitted. The bishop thundered; Ritchie, supported by his congregation, refused to submit, though he offered to arbitrate the dispute, and matters were in this *impasse* when he was called to New York.

The death of Ewer, in 1883, had left St. Ignatius' without a rector. In 1884, Ritchie was called as his successor. Before his call, Dr. Thomas Richey of the General Seminary faculty had assured the vestry that although Ritchie had introduced extreme practices in

Chicago, he had seen the light, and would reform. This promise, made without Ritchie's knowledge, he promptly repudiated, and promptly introduced incense, holy water, confessional boxes, the "shortened" High Mass without communicants, and Benediction of the Blessed Sacrament—this for the first time in the American Church. Some parishioners left, but Ritchie stuck to his guns, and again was in conflict with his bishop. But Henry Codman Potter was a very different person from the somewhat square-toed McLaren. Handling the case with supreme tact, he persuaded Ritchie to give up the disputed usages, and there was peace in the land.

It is important to note, in this connection, that two such war-horses of the Anglo-Catholic party as Bishops Grafton and Seymour were in complete accord with Bishop Potter, and completely at odds with Father Ritchie. Bishop Grafton wrote to Bishop Potter:

> "Pray do not gratify my friend, Arthur Ritchie, by bringing him to trial. . . . Our low church brethren should be very grateful to you for not suppressing him, as he is most successful in hindering the growth of high-churchmanship. . . . For many years I have felt the injury done to real spirituality by excessive ceremonial." [85]

Finally, there was the lunatic fringe, the genuine Romanizers, who were avowedly working for reunion with Rome, who were willing to accept all of Roman doctrine except papal infallibility, who despised manners and customs distinctively Anglican. This group was smaller and less influential than the corresponding group in England, but it was noisy, and by its action often tended to discredit the whole High Church movement in the eyes of many loyal laymen.

Some indication of the strength of the High Church party, when that party was not rent within by factional disturbances, can be arrived at by considering the growth of certain features of Church practice and polity, championed by the party as a whole. By 1874, the three-decker pulpit and the preaching gown had almost disappeared. The use of surplice and scarf—or stole—was universal. Not long

[85] Hodges, G., op. cit., p. 174.

after, a church without an altar of stone or carved wood, vested with colored frontlet, and bearing a cross, was so noticeably "low" as to cause remark. Flowers on the altar, weekly communions, careful observance of the Church's seasons, vested choirs with processions and processional crosses—these were no longer the marks of a High Church parish, but the normal usage of the Church as a whole.

From the days of Hobart, High Churchmen had been insisting that the Church should have smaller dioceses, in which the influence of the bishop would be more immediate and powerful. At the formation of the American Church, the intention had been to make the limits of the diocese coincide with those of the state, but under High Church pressure, backed by plain common sense, there was a steady tendency to break up such unwieldy administrative masses. The first such division was that of New York in 1839. This had resulted in placing Western New York in the hands of the High Church Bishop DeLancey. A second division in 1868 gave the new see of Albany to a pronounced High Churchman, William Croswell Doane; Central New York to Huntington, a High Churchman in doctrine if not in ritual; and Long Island to Littlejohn, a fair representative of the Hobartian school. When, in 1875, Wisconsin was broken up, the first bishop-elect of the new diocese of Fond du Lac was the pet dislike of the Low Churchmen, James De Koven. The standing committees having refused to confirm this election, the see was filled by John H. H. Brown, a strong if not equally well-known High Churchman, and his successor was the dreaded Grafton, under whom Fond du Lac became noted—even notorious—for its ritualism. In 1878, Illinois was divided, and the first bishop of the new diocese of Springfield was Seymour. In 1879, Samuel Smith Harris of Louisiana, one of the chief opponents of ritual legislation in 1871, became bishop of Michigan. Indeed, it is safe to say that, after 1875, the ban on electing High Churchmen, even advanced ritualists, to bishoprics was lifted.

The provincial system, one of the pet projects of the younger Hopkins, became a nominal reality in 1907 and canonically effective in 1913, though it has never justified his high hopes of its effectiveness. Much more important was the introduction, also vigorously advocated by Hopkins, of the cathedral idea. This has been first suggested by the elder Doane in the Thirties. In 1861, the Church of the Atonement, Chicago, was bought and presented to Bishop Whitehouse as his church—the first American pro-cathedral. In 1867, the cornerstone of a cathedral, built as such, was laid at Davenport, Iowa. Nebraska, Minnesota, Utah, Maine, Springfield, Colorado, were among the dioceses that followed suit in rapid succession. But these, though cathedrals in the technical sense, were far from the architectural conception of the cathedral. The first attempt at building a structure that could compare in any way with the great designs of the Middle Ages, was made in Albany under Bishop Doane, a man as magnificent in his plans as his father. Here, in 1884, work was begun on a building which, even in its unfinished state, is a noble expression, in form as in worship, of the Catholicity of the American Church. And, today, the promise of Albany has been grandly fulfilled in the glorious Cathedral of St. John the Divine, New York, and the choir of Washington Cathedral, worthy daughters of Canterbury and Rheims.

BIBLIOGRAPHY

The *Lives* of Bishop Hopkins and of his son, and the *Life* of Bishop Whittingham, are indispensable for the events of this chapter. The debates of the General Convention of 1871 are published in a separate volume; those of 1874 are fully reported in *The Churchman.*

Debates of the House of Deputies of the General Convention of the Protestant Episcopal Church (Hartford, 1871).

HARRISON, H., *Life of the Rt. Rev. John Barrett Kerfoot* (New York, 1886).

HODGES, G., *Henry Codman Potter* (New York, 1915).

HOPKINS, J. H., *The Law of Ritualism* (New York, 1866).

REED, N. F., *The Story of St. Mary's* (New York, 1931).

SUTER, J. W., *Life and Letters of William Reed Huntington* (New York, 1925). [Useful for the General Convention of 1874.]

The American Churchman, [periodical] (Chicago, 1870) Vol. IX.

The Batterson Case (Collection of pamphlets in library of the General Theological Seminary).

The Prescott Case (Collection of pamphlets in library of The General Theological Seminary).

CHAPTER SEVEN

THE COMING OF THE MONKS

IN AMERICA, as in England, it was inevitable that, with the leaders of the High Church movement more and more looking back to the Middle Ages as a mine of materials for Catholic life and worship, there should come a revival of monasticism. On practical grounds alone, there was plainly a great use for a body of unmarried priests, with no hampering domestic ties to prevent their easy mobility, with no financial needs beyond the barest living, with no responsibility save to the Church and its authorities. This was truer in America than in England—America, with its vast expanse of half-settled territory, with its millions of unchurched people.

Long before the Oxford Movement struck this country, the value of clerical celibacy had been recognized by occasional men. Thus in 1820 Muhlenberg, then a pronounced Evangelical, resolved to remain unmarried that he might better serve the Church. After 1840, various projects of community life rapidly made their appearance. Wadhams' attempt was ended by the secession of himself and his associates to Rome; the plan of Hewit and Baker developed into the Paulist order within the Roman Church; Breck's start at Nashotah did result in the founding of a seminary, but the monastic idea connected with it was soon given up; monaticism at Valle Crucis died with the defection of Bishop Ives. These were the false starts; a real one was yet to be made. The deepening of devotion, which was so noticeable a feature of the Catholic movement in the Sixties and Seventies, and which manifested itself clearly in the increasing popularity of retreats, was bound eventually to find its expression in some form of monastic life.

THE CATHOLIC MOVEMENT IN THE EPISCOPAL CHURCH

THE FIRST SISTERHOODS

In America, as in England, the first successful monastic communities springing from the Church revival were sisterhoods.[1] In 1845, Muhlenberg, here once again proving himself a better Catholic than some who were more anxious to claim the title, established at his parish in New York the Sisterhood of the Holy Communion. Anne Ayres, the first sister of the organization, was soon joined by others. At first, the group worked only in the parish from which it was named, but in a few years Muhlenberg founded St. Luke's Hospital, where it found a wider field of effort. The sisterhood, reflecting the strong individuality of the founder, was an extremely loose organization, without perpetual vows, and contemplating no extension of itself beyond the one community. Until 1863 it performed a valuable service; in that year it was suspended. But some of its members still held firmly to the monastic idea.

In 1865, therefore, Harriet Starr Cannon, who had been admitted to the earlier order in 1857, founded, with three others, the Community of St. Mary—the first permanent monastic foundation in the American Church. On the Feast of the Purification, 1865, their professions were received by Bishop Horatio Potter, who assigned to them the care of a home for abandoned girls. In this difficult and delicate task, they were successful, and the community grew steadily in numbers, at the same time constantly extending the field of its work. Miss Cannon naturally became the Mother Superior. In 1872, a convent and novitiate was established at Peekskill, New York, from which center the operations of the order spread until now it maintains two convents and twelve educational and charitable institutions. The progress of the order was not always smooth and easy. During the partisan warfare of the late Sixties and early Seventies, the sisters were often under attack, but the value of their work was so evident that the opposition died away, and in 1880 the General Convention

[1] See Thomas J. Williams, "The Beginnings of Anglican Sisterhoods," *Historical Magazine of the Episcopal Church*, Vol. XVI (1947), 350-372; also, Sister Mary Theodora, C.S.M. "The Foundation of the Sisterhood of St. Mary," *ibid.*, Vol. XIV (1945), 38-52.

just missed giving them official recognition. The example of this pioneer community were soon followed by others: the Sisterhood of St. Margaret in 1873, the Community of St. John Baptist in 1881, the Sisterhood of the Holy Nativity in 1882. At the present time, there are no less than seventeen communities for women in the American Church.

THE COWLEY FATHERS

Monastic institutions for men were later in coming, and encountered much more opposition; perhaps because of that peculiar kink of the popular mind which assumes that chastity is natural for women, unnatural for men. The father of monasticism for men in the American Church was Charles Chapman Grafton. Grafton was a product of the Tractarian phase of the High Church movement. Born in 1832, he received his Church training in the Church of the Advent, Boston, under Croswell. Here he was confirmed in 1851, and here he was imbued with the profound devotion to the sacrament of the altar which had from the beginning been so central a feature in the life of the parish.[2] Eventually, he determined to become a priest. But Boston under Bishop Eastburn was no place for a postulant of Grafton's views. He, therefore, followed Prescott, lately assistant at the Advent, to Maryland, where Bishop Whittingham gave both safe harborage.[3] Here he was ordained priest in 1858. For six years, from 1859 to 1865, he was assistant to Dr. Wyatt at St. Paul's, Baltimore. But his intense nature and flaming devotion longed for a completer self-surrender than that involved in the life of a secular priest. Utterly devoted to the Church, ascetic in the best sense, with a firm belief in authority and discipline, he was perfectly fitted by nature for the work of a monastic founder. After trying himself out by various experiments in asceticism, he resigned his position in 1865, and went to England, where he was introduced by Pusey to the Rev. Richard Meux Benson, an English priest, whose thoughts had for some time

[2] Grafton, C. C., *A Journey Godward*, pp. 6, 26.
[3] *Ibid.*, p. 30.

been turned in the monastic direction. At Cowley, near Oxford, these two, with Simeon Wilberforce O'Neill, made in 1866 their profession as members of the Society of St. John the Evangelist.[4] This order followed strictly the model of no one of the mediaeval orders, but combined in its rule Benedictine and Dominican ideas. A simple habit of a distinctively Anglican pattern was adopted, the daily office was said in choir, the three vows of poverty, chastity, and obedience were taken, and the order prepared to give itself to preaching, conducting retreats, and to missionary work, both in Christian countries and on the frontiers of the Church.

Soon the order found a golden opportunity in America. In 1870 the Church of the Advent was without a rector. The vestry, remembering Father Grafton and mindful of their Catholic tradition, therefore proposed that the Society should take charge of the parish. At Easter, 1872, Grafton, accompanied by Prescott, who had meanwhile become a member of the Society, assumed the rectorship of the parish. At the same time, he was made head of the newly constituted American province of the Society.[5] His work at the Advent was strikingly successful. Magnificent in presence, with a body that seemed to know no fatigue, a born leader of men, authoritative, ascetic, devoted, a sound scholar and a genuine religious thinker, a thorough-going ritualist and an advanced Catholic, yet never in the least a Romanizer, he left his mark on the whole religious life of the city of Boston. Around him assembled an able group of younger men, among them Arthur C. A. Hall, later bishop of Vermont, and Edward W. Osborne, who succeeded Seymour in the see of Springfield. For all his advanced churchmanship, Grafton was both wise and fortunate in his relations with his bishop. Although the Society now proceeded to bring in the full ritualistic service at the Advent—altar lights, chasuble, and incense, with the regular use of the confessional—there was no repetition of the troubles of 1845. Bishop Benjamin Henry Paddock, who succeeded the difficult Eastburn in the same year

[4] Grafton, C. C., *A Journey Godward*, p. 40.
[5] *Ibid.*, p. 48.

that Grafton took over the parish, was at once conciliated by Grafton's action in submittting to him all the details of the services at the Advent, and promising to abide by the bishop's decision in regard to them. As a result of this truly Catholic action and attitude, the ceremonial practice of Grafton—a practice which went far beyond the comparatively mild ceremonies that had caused such trouble in 1845—was carried on with episcopal approval.[*]

The work of the order in America soon spread beyond the confines of the parish of the Advent. A training house for novices was established in Connecticut, and Father Hall, who was placed in charge, soon had eight probationers under him. In 1876, the parish of St. Clement's, Philadelphia, asked the Society to take charge of it. Father Prescott, who became the rector, soon found himself in difficulties with the bishop of the diocese, as we have recorded; but, although he resigned, the work of the Society in the parish was continued—a work made notable a little later by the preaching of Father Maturin.

But the position of the order in America was necessarily unsatisfactory by reason of its ambiguous status. In a body working under American bishops, yet owing allegiance to an English superior, there were bound to be conflicts of obedience. The inevitable trouble arising from this divided responsibility came to a head in Maryland. Bishop Whittingham was heartily in sympathy with the aims of the Society; he had extended his protection to Fathers Grafton and Prescott, and encouraged their joining the order. But Whittingham had too high a notion of the authority of bishop, and too intimate a knowledge, student of ecclesiastical history that he was, of the evils that had arisen in the mediaeval Church when the monastic orders were freed from episcopal control, to allow any avoidable conflict of loyalties within his diocese. He, therefore, prohibited members of the Society from officiating

[*]Grafton, C. C., *A Journey Godward*, p. 49.

in Maryland, and secured from Grafton and Prescott a promise that this order would be obeyed.

When, in spite of the promise, the superior, Father Benson, sent members of the Society into Maryland, both Grafton and Prescott felt their honor was involved, and that the evils of the dual control had become intolerable. They first attempted to obtain independence for the Society in America, this having been promised when there should be twelve professed members in the country. The request was refused. Finally, in 1882, Grafton and Prescott asked and secured a release from their obligations to the Society, and withdrew from it.[7] Grafton remained at the Church of the Advent as rector until 1889, when he was elected second bishop of Fond du Lac.

In 1883, the Society bought from the parish the old church building, which was renamed the Church of St. John the Evangelist, and was placed under Fathers Hall and Osborne, Hall now becoming head of the American province. In a short time, Hall became known as one of the outstanding priests in the American Church, proving remarkably successful in breaking down the still lingering prejudice against the monastic revival. His election, in 1889, as a deputy to the General Convention from the diocese of Massachusetts, marks a turning point in the relations of that diocese to the High Church movement—the dying out of the long and bitter struggle begun in 1832.

But not yet was the Society to have peace. In 1891, Bishop Paddock died. The most notable priest in the diocese was easily Phillips Brooks, one of the greatest preachers and one of the greatest personalities ever known in the American Church. But he was a noted liberal, even suspected by conservative theologians of harboring Arian tendencies. His election, therefore, aroused considerable opposition, and Father Hall, though a close friend of Brooks, voted against him.[8] After he had been elected, some of the High

[7] *Ibid.*, p. 51.
[8] I follow Richardson's account. Fr. Powell, who was a postulant of the Society soon after these events, informs me that the impression of the monastery was that Hall had voted for Brooks.

THE COMING OF THE MONKS

Church leaders made a grave mistake. Forgetting—so quickly are the lessons of history lost—the Low Church opposition to De Koven and Seymour, they made a determined effort to block the confirmation of the election by the standing committees. The leader in this attempt, incredible though it seems, was Seymour himself, seconded by Bishop George deN. Gillespie of Western Michigan. Among the charges brought against Brooks were Pelagianism, Unitarianism, the admission of Unitarians to the Holy Communion, and the invalidity of his own baptism. This was bad strategy; if these charges were true, Brooks should have been presented for trial, and deposed from the priesthood. The more sensible of the High Church leaders, including Doane, Hopkins, and Hall, refused to have anything to do with a proceeding savoring so strongly of partisan rancor, and publicly and vigorously advocated the confirmation of Brooks' election. This stand brought Hall the applause of the Church, but the condemnation of his superior. Father Page, acting partly on the representations of the bishops who had opposed the confirmation, released Hall from his duties as provincial, and ordered him to return to England.[9]

The attack on Brooks had stirred up a great deal of acrimony, and now this apparently arbitrary action of the superior, coming so quickly on the heels of the major controversy, aroused a storm of protest—a protest not confined to Low Churchmen. The bishops of New England addressed a remonstrance to Father Page, in which they were joined by Bishop Doane. The parishioners of the mission church passed indignant resolutions. The Rev. Charles H. Brent, the most promising priest-associate of the American province, withdrew from the Society. So great was the commotion that it seemed for a time as if all that the patient labors of Grafton and Hall had done for the Society in this country, overcoming prejudice and winning confidence, had been lost at one stroke.

Through all this dust and smoke, Father Hall maintained a most exemplary attitude. Manifesting nothing of the soreness he undoubt-

[9] Richardson, G. L., *Arthur C. A. Hall*, pp. 121-33.

edly felt, he remained true to his vows, and returned to England, prepared to do whatever work the superior might give him. A way out of an impossible situation soon presented itself. When, only a little over a year later, Bishop Brooks died, Hall received a considerable number of votes for the vacant bishopric. This came to nothing, but in August, 1893, he was chosen bishop of Vermont. He was, therefore, released from his obligations to the Society, and consecrated in 1894.[10] Already a marked man, both on account of his work in Boston and his stand during the dispute over the consecration of Brooks, he at once took a leading place in the American episcopate. Always one of the foremost High Church leaders, he kept the respect of all parties in the Church until his death in 1930.

The Brooks affair was the last storm the Society had to weather in America. Father Hall was succeeded as American provincial by Father Longridge, under whom the Society quietly went to work to recover the lost ground. Gradually the enterprises of the order increased. In 1901, the Church of St. Augustine and St. Martin, Boston, for colored people, was built, and, at the same time, St. Augustine's Farm at Foxboro, Massachusetts, was established for social work. In 1921, the Society took charge of the Church of the Advent, San Francisco; in 1926, of St. Paul's, Brooklyn. The erection in the same year of St. Francis' House in Cambridge, placed the Society in a strategic position with regard to Harvard University—a position of which it has made excellent use. In 1927, the Society sent out a vigorous new shoot when a Canadian province was established. From its headquarters at Bracebridge, Ontario, this branch has set up a remarkable piece of rural mission work—a field in which the Episcopal Church has been rather backward. The establishment of a province in Japan came several years later.

What appeared to be the second great opportunity of the order in America, came in 1930. The Church of St. Mary the Virgin, New York, the foundation of which we have recorded, was, as it still

[10]Richardson, G. L., *Arthur C. A. Hall*, pp. 134-35.

is, the most famous "ritualistic" parish in the country. In that year the rector, the Rev. Selden P. Delany, seceded to Rome; and the trustees asked the Society to take charge of the parish. But this was a work which could be done quite as effectively by secular priests, whereas the less spectacular operations at Cambridge and at Bracebridge could not, and in 1939 the order wisely withdrew from New York.

The great difficulty the Society had labored under, from its very beginning in this country, was the result of its anomalous position under a foreign superior. The conflict of allegiance had cost the order three of its greatest men—Grafton, Hall, and Brent, all of whom had at one time or other unsuccessfully pleaded for independence of English control. But in spite of the obvious wisdom and eventual necessity of this step, it was long in coming. Finally, in 1914, the American province became autonomous, and in 1921 the American congregation was constituted with the Rev. Frederick C. Powell as its first superior. That this was a great step forward is indicated by the notable progress the American congregation has made since that time.

To estimate the value of the Society's work in America is perhaps impossible as yet. It has remained comparatively small in numbers. But its influence has been out of all proportion to its size. It has demonstrated the possibility of monastic orders for men within the American Church. It has lived down suspicion and prejudice; a Cowley Father is today accepted as a normal feature of American Church life. It has given to the American Church five bishops—a remarkable number when one considers the size of the Society, and an eloquent comment on the type of men it admits to its ranks. And, of these bishops, three—Grafton, Hall, and Brent—have been among the great ecclesiastics of their day.

FATHER HUNTINGTON AND THE ORDER OF THE HOLY CROSS

While the Society of St. John the Evangelist was thus struggling through war to peace, a second order, far different in character and purely American in origin, was springing up—an order which faithfully reflects the personality of its founder. We have had occasion in these pages to sketch the characters of churchmen great and small, churchmen pleasant and unpleasant. James Huntington is harder to sketch, because James Huntington was a saint. There was nothing in him of the strained asceticism one finds in some of the elect. "It is well," says Miss Scudder, "to stress the natural sanity of Father Huntington's life. If anyone could demonstrate a monk's existence is natural, it would be he."[11] The son of the bishop of Central New York, he grew naturally in religion. He seems to have escaped both the storms of adolescence and the internal conflict that marks the beginnings of so many in the religious life. Instinctively unselfish, a lover of nature, with an unfailing cheerfulness, he had certain qualities not usually associated with monasticism. He was convinced "that truth is synthetic, and that progress comes through reconciliation of opposites." He was a passionate believer in liberty, and a passionate worker for social justice.

In 1880, while attending a retreat conducted by Canon Knox-Little of the Church of England at St. Clement's, Philadelphia, Huntington felt a strong impulse to enter the monastic life. With two other young priests similarly minded, Robert Stockton Dod and James G. Cameron, he took over the work of the mission of the Holy Cross in a slum section of New York. The three adopted a habit, and lived in accordance with a rule, but as yet they wisely bound themselves by no vows. The two associates dropped out, but Huntington's monastic vocation proved real. On November 25, 1884, he made his profession as first member of the order of the Holy Cross. Bishop Henry Codman Potter, then assistant bishop of New York, received the profession; Bishops Frederic Dan Huntington (his father) and Charles T. Quintard of Tennessee were present at the service.[12] By this action of Bishop Potter's, episcopal approval

[11]Scudder, V. D., *Father Huntington*, p. 78.
[12]*Historical Magazine of the Protestant Episcopal Church*, Vol. II, p. 39.

was once more expressly given to monasticism in the American Church.

Like every other forward step these pages have chronicled, this act stirred up a tempest—though of minor proportions. Bishop Lee of Delaware, presiding bishop of the Church, wrote to Bishop Potter expressing "the astonishment and distress occasioned by your recent unexampled act, the admission of Mr. Huntington to a so-called religious order, after requiring of him the well-known Romish vows."[13] But Bishop Potter, a true ecclesiastical statesman like all the Potters, stuck to his guns, showing that this was no unexampled act by citing the numerous precedents in which the same vows had been accepted from professed sisters—occurrences which had long ceased to call forth any comment. Other bishops, Stevens of Pennsylvania, Bedell of Ohio, even Littlejohn of Long Island, were but little less emphatic than Lee in their expressions of disapproval. On the other hand, Bishop Whitehead of Pittsburgh expressed the sentiments of the majority of High Churchmen when he thanked Bishop Potter for "being brave enough to put into words what so many of us feel, that the Reformation was not a finality."[14]

While this teapot tempest was raging, Father Huntington was calmly carrying on his work at the mission on the East Side—a work which gave full expression to his passion for social justice. He had read, but not swallowed, *Das Kapital*, and he delighted in teaching the gamins who formed his choir to sing from the *Iron Cross Hymn Book*, "Our Lord he was a carpenter." His reputation as a socially-minded priest soon spread beyond the limits of his mission, and he was greatly in demand as a platform speaker at meetings in aid of one reform or other. He shocked Episcopalian respectability by supporting Henry George and the Single Tax movement. He was one of the founders of the Church Mission of Help. In the summer of 1889, he worked incognito as a farm

---

[13] The first precedent had been set by Bishop Potter's uncle, at the profession in 1865 of Mother Harriet.
[14] Hodges, G., *Henry Codman Potter*, pp. 146-65.

laborer so that he, Brahmin by birth and Harvard graduate, might begin to understand how a workingman really felt.[15] But in spite of the apparent success of these years, Huntington was far from satisfied. The order refused to grow; after ten years only two men had joined him—Fathers Allen and Sargent. He determined, therefore, that the order must be more deeply rooted in the contemplative life before it could bring forth fruit, and rather to the disgust of Bishop Potter withdrew with his associates to Westminster, Maryland, where a small farm had been given them.

The experiment justified itself. Father Hughson, at that time a novice, has written an idyllic account of the brethren walking through the woods, reading their offices and singing their hymns. A rule was developed, superficially like that of the mediaeval orders, but having in fact a character of its own. It was Huntington's definite intention to found a really American order; this intention is reflected in the emphasis the rule puts on cleanliness,[16] and in the founder's remark that "a sense of humor is a necessary element in the religious vocation."[17] Roughly, the Order of the Holy Cross might be said to play the Franciscan to the Dominican of the Society of St. John the Evangelist.

In 1900, the monastery at West Park was built, and there the order made its permanent headquarters. From this as a center, the order soon began to send out branches. St. Faith's House, Tarrytown, had already been established in 1897. St. Andrew's School for mountain boys was begun in Tennessee in 1905, and Kent School, Connecticut, in the following year.[18] But important and valuable as these labors were, the great task of the order was undertaken in 1922. Since 1851, when the Rt. Rev. John Payne was sent out as the first missionary bishop, the Liberian mission in West Africa had been one of the most trying of American mission fields. Bishop

[15]Scudder, V. D., *Father Huntington*, pp. 113-45.
[16]*Ibid.*, pp. 191-208.
[17]*Ibid.*, p. 240.
[18]Huntington wisely refused to take over the Advent, Boston, and the Cathedral in Chicago, both of which were offered him.

had succeeded bishop, killed off or invalided home by that fatal climate; the average tenure of the bishops of Liberia had been thirteen years. When, therefore, the Order of the Holy Cross volunteered to start a new work in the hinterland of this field, the whole Church recognized it as an extraordinary act of devotion. In 1925, the Rev. Robert H. Campbell, O. H. C., was elected by the House of Bishops missionary bishop of Liberia, the first monk in the American Church to become a bishop while still a member of a monastic order.

ST. BARNABAS' BROTHERHOOD AND OTHER ORDERS

The account of the founding of the third of American orders for men can begin in but one way. Once upon a time—in the year 1896, to be exact—there was in New York City a devout layman, who was deeply conscious of a divine call. Every noon, Gouverneur P. Hance used to leave the office where he worked to kneel in Calvary Church, asking what God would have him to do. There being no apparent answer, he finally resigned his job, and appeared at the diocesan office as a willing but vague volunteer. A puzzled archdeacon could find no place for such a man. For a time he worked as a Church Army missioner in western Pennsylvania. Here he learned to endure poverty and to work on a shoestring. Finally, in 1900, he decided what his vocation really was: at Carnegie, on the outskirts of Pittsburgh, he opened a convalescent home for poor men.

> "There were three rooms, consisting of a kitchen, sitting room and a ward. To start this work, I had four beds, a table and some chairs, and no money."

Humanly speaking, it was an impossible venture; but something superhuman was here involved. Slowly the work grew. In 1907, Hance was joined by a second man, Charles Carrington, and the home for convalescents became also a home for incurables. In 1908, the two bought an abandoned hotel in McKeesport, Pennsylvania, and soon its fifty beds were filled.

During all this time, there had been no formal organization, though both men were slowly developing for themselves a type of religious life. Eventually, in 1913, St Barnabas' Brotherhood was finally constituted, and three brothers were professed by the sympathetic bishop of Pittsburgh, Cortlandt Whitehead.[19] Growing as naturally as a tree, the order has made but little noise in the Church or the world. It has engaged in no controversies, broken into no headlines. It has merely demonstrated Christ to the world.

It is perhaps too early to do more than mention other monastic foundations in the American Church. Two attempts at establishing a congregation of Benedictines—the first in Fond du Lac, under the patronage of Bishop Grafton, and a later one in the East— came to nothing. Finally, in 1939, St. Gregory's House at Valparaiso, Indiana, was started as a cell of Nashdom Abbey in England. It is now located in Three Rivers, Michigan.

Earlier, in 1919, a Franciscan friary was set up in Wisconsin. In 1928, this, with its accompanying convent of Poor Clares, was moved to Mount Sinai on Long Island, New York.

OFFICIAL RECOGNITION

Four score years have passed since Father Grafton returned to Boston as a member of a monastic order. During those eighty years, monasticism of the Cowley type has won a definite place for itself in the American Church, and has obtained recognition as a normal part of the varied life of that Church. As early as 1880, Bishop Paddock of Massachusetts introduced into General Convention a canon on sisterhoods; action on this was deferred to the next Convention, which again failed to act. In 1889, Bishop Grafton in turn proposed a canon on monastic orders, with a twofold purpose of approving and regulating them; this canon after having been post-

[19]Hance, G. P., *The History of St. Barnabas Free Home* (pamphlet).

poned, first to 1892, then to 1895, dropped out of sight. Finally, in 1913, a canon "Of Religious Communities" was passed. The provisions of this canon are an interesting reflection of the history and difficulties of such communities in this country. Religious orders are carefully placed under the direction of the diocesan bishops, and it is distinctly stated that in the constitution of such orders: "There shall be a distinct recognition of the Doctrine, Discipline and Worship of this Church as of supreme authority." Another section of the canon provides that "in the administration of the Sacraments, the Book of Common Prayer shall be used without alteration"; attached to this, however, there is the characteristically Anglican proviso, "save as it may be lawfully permitted by lawful authority."

Both the Society of St John the Evangelist and the Order of the Holy Cross have wisely kept their numbers comparatively small; thus they have avoided the cardinal error of the mediaeval orders, which in their zeal for mere size, took in multitudes of people with no genuine monastic vocation. Externally, both orders have amply justified their existence by such works as the Liberian mission and the cultivation of the rural area in Ontario. And both orders, by their nation-wide labors in conducting retreats and parochial misions, have done an immense and immeasurable service in strengthening the inner life and deepening the devotion of American churchmen. Finally, the orders have been most valuable in keeping before the High Church movement the idea of discipline—a basic concept of Catholicism that has been too often forgotten by rugged individualists in the priesthood, who demonstrate the reality of their belief in the apostolic succession by indulging in the sport of bishop-baiting.

BIBLIOGRAPHY

Of works already listed, Ayres' *Muhlenberg* is important for the beginnings of the sisterhoods. Grafton's *Autobiography* is the chief source for the early days of the Cowley Fathers in America. Hodges' *Life of Potter* relates the events accompanying the profession of Fr. Huntington.

Cowley Fathers, The (Cambridge, 1930). [A pamphlet published by the Society of St. John the Evangelist, giving an account of its history and work.]

DIX, M., *Harriet Starr Cannon* (New York, 1896).

HANCE, GOUVERNEUR P., *The History of St. Barnabas Free House* (pamphlet, n. d.).

HARRISON, H., *Loose Him and Let Him Go* (Boston, 1891). [Reprint of a contemporary speech on the Hall-Brooks case.]

HUNTINGTON, A. S., *Memoir and Letters of F. D. Huntington* (Boston, 1906).

HUNTINGTON, J. O. S., "Beginnings of the Religious Life for Men in the American Church," in *Historical Magazine of the Protestant Episcopal Church*, Vol. II, pp. 35-43.

POOR CLARES OF REPARATION AND ADORATION (compiler), *Religious Communities in the American Episcopal Church and in the Anglican Church in Canada* (West Park, N. Y., 1945) pp. 132. [This book lists nine Communities for Men, and fifteen for Women, with a brief historical account of each.]

RICHARDSON, G. L., *Arthur C. A. Hall* (Boston, 1932). [A brilliant piece of biographical writing.].

SCUDDER, V. D., *Father Huntington* (New York, 1940).

SISTER MARY THEODORA, C.S.M., "The Foundation of the Sisterhood of St. Mary," in *Historical Magazine of the Episocpal Church,* Vol. XIV (1945), 38-52.

WARD, M., *Father Maturin—a Memoir* (London, 1920).

WILLIAMS, THOMAS J., "The Beginnings of Anglican Sisterhoods," in *Historical Magazine of the Episcopal Church*, Vol. XVI (1947), 350-372. [The best extant account in 23 pages of the subject.]

CHAPTER EIGHT

THE MOVEMENT IN THE MID-WEST

So FAR our story has been confined largely to the East. This is but natural. The Episcopal Church was strongest on the Atlantic seaboard. There most of the great leaders of the High Church movement had lived and worked; there were most of the famous High Church parishes; there most of the controversies had taken place. But the movement in the Mid-West has a story of its own—a story that has never been told in any detail. High Churchmanship as a definite movement in the Mid-West begins with two events—the consecration of Bishop Kemper in 1835 and the foundation of Nashotah in 1841. Thus, almost simultaneously, the two streams which go to make up American High Churchmanship arrived in this section; Kemper, of course, stands for the old, native, Hobartian school, and Breck for the influence of the *Tracts*.

THE DEVELOPMENT OF NASHOTAH HOUSE

Some notion of the life at Nastotah may be gathered from the account of William Markoe, who was a student there in 1843:

> The fare was generally scant and wretched, partly from poverty and partly on principle. Obedience to rule and unfailing attention to devotions were, with me, points of honor as well as matters of religion. It can readily be understood that this mode of living kept our thought almost constantly on religious subjects. My great ambition was to conform as nearly as possible to the lives of the early Christians. I fasted severely and beyond my strength; even on ordinary Fridays, eating and drinking absolutely nothing till three o'clock in the afternoon

and continuing my work just the same. Some of us had permission to go to communion every day.[1]

Unfortunately, this apostolic sort of life soon ended. Some of the students seceded to Rome, Hobart returned East, Adams married, and Breck pushed on to Minnesota. By 1850, Nashotah had ceased to be in any sense monastic, and had settled down to the life of a small Anglican seminary. Even the Tractarian ideas of the founders had been greatly modified. Particularly after the secession in 1855 of William Markoe, then an instructor in the preparatory department, there was a decided reaction against anything that savored of Romanism. In 1850, Azel D. Cole, a High Churchman of the old school, became president; and Adams, the only one of the founders who remained at Nashtoah, had from the beginning been more conservative than Breck. After the Markoe secession, his suspicion of Roman tendencies became more acute—and more lasting. In 1886, Adams was one of the chief opponents of the election of De Koven as assistant bishop of Wisconsin. De Koven's own time at Nashotah was short, but from the nearby Racine College, where the remainder of his life was spent, he exerted a considerable influence in the direction of a fuller and deeper Catholicism on the students of the seminary. At any rate, the tradition of the place was purely High Church, and its influence spread through the neighboring dioceses. This High Church thrust was strengthened by the nearness of Bishop Kemper, no ritualist but a strong and consistent High Churchman, who, after 1854, made his residence at Nashotah, and who was a steady patron of men who went further than himself on the Catholic road.

During Dr. Cole's long presidency, Nashotah grew slowly but steadily. The plant, at first so primitive, was expanded by new buildings, the student body increased to between fifty and sixty students. Unlike General, from the beginning Nashotah planned to have a preparatory department, so that her sons might have,

---

[1]Quoted in Hawks, Edward, *William McGarvey and the Open Pulpit*, p. 59. This daily Eucharist lasted for a year only.

THE MOVEMENT IN THE MID-WEST

from the start of their college course, definite religious direction. For a time, this department was in the seminary itself; later, the college students were sent to De Koven at Racine. From 1871 on, the department was sporadically maintained within the seminary. Today, the preparatory department operates in conjunction with Carroll College.

THE CHURCH IN ILLINOIS

The influence of Nashotah was soon felt in the diocese of Illinois. Bishop Chase, though violently anti-Tractarian, was, like many of the old Evangelicals, a holder of strong Church doctrine, and he favored as his successor the Rev. Henry J. Whitehouse, the rector of St. Thomas' Church, New York, and a strong Hobartian.[2] Chase's wish, combined with Nashotah sentiment, gave Whitehouse the election in 1851. An intellectual of a rather unsympathetic type, his episcopate was not oversuccessful. But he maintained the old High Church tradition, repressing as far as he could both ritualistic innovations and Evangelical heresies. The city of Chicago was the only place in the section where Low Church views were held; and when the Rev. Charles E. Cheney, rector of a leading parish in that city, omitted the word "regenerate" in the baptismal office, Whitehouse promptly deposed him. This was one of the leading causes of the Reformed Episcopal schism. The withdrawing of the revolting Evangelicals left the High Churchmen in undisputed control of the diocese. The extent of this control is clearly shown in the episcopal election of 1874. Dean Seymour of the General Theological Seminary was elected bishop on the second ballot, in spite of his known connection with the advanced group of High Churchmen. At the same time, a resolution asking the General Convention to forbid the elevation of the Host and other cere-

---

[2] And yet, for causes which I am unable to determine, Whitehouse was one of the leaders in the opposition to Bishop Onderdonk in New York. For an account of his episcopate, *see* Percy V. Norwood, "Bishop Whitehouse and the Church in Illinois," *Historical Magazine*, XVI (1947), 167-180.

monial practices, was decisively turned down, only two out of forty-six clergy voting in favor of it.

The story of Seymour's rejection by the General Convention has already been told. The special convention of the diocese, which met in February, 1875, to elect to the still vacant see, assembled in an angry frame of mind. After protesting against the action of General Convention and affirming their continued confidence in Dr. Seymour, they proceeded to what amounted to a slap in the face of General Convention. De Koven, the floor leader of the ritualists in 1874, was now nominated. On the first ballot, he received 37 clerical votes, his opponent being the Rev. George Leeds of Baltimore, a conservative High Churchman, with 29 votes. The laity having refused to concur, De Koven was twice more elected by the clergy; on the third ballot, the laity agreed to his election. But in the state of feeling in the Church at the time, it was not to be expected that such an action would pass unrebuked. The standing committees refused to confirm the election of De Koven. For the third time, the diocese proceeded to an episcopal election. Even after all that had passed, a large minority of the clergy still voted for De Koven, but his cause was lost. The Rev. William E. McLaren, rector of Trinity Church, Cleveland, a convert from Presbyterianism, was elected and confirmed.[3] McLaren turned out to be a strong High Churchman and a vigorous disciplinarian.

One of the chief measures advocated at this time by the more progressive High Churchmen was the so-called "see principle." As defined by Hopkins, the chief propagandist for it, this meant the seating of a bishop in practically every large city. In 1877, the diocese of Illinois committed itself to this principle by dividing into three. The new dioceses took their names from the three see cities: Chicago, Quincy, and Springfield. Seymour now had his revenge, being elected first bishop of Springfield. Party feeling had by this time so quieted down that the election aroused no particular opposition. He proved a strong and able bishop, who made his diocese a

[3] *Journals of the Diocese of Illinois*, 1875, *passim*,

focus of that type of churchmanship for which he had suffered persecution. The three dioceses now attempted to apply the complementary notion to the see principle—the provincial system. Having secured the permission of the General Convention, they formed themselves into an association, with the characteristically American title, "The Federated Council of the Churches in Illinois." The dioceses persisted in the experiment for a number of years, but it never seems to have accomplished a great deal, and eventually it was allowed to die.

THE DIOCESE OF FOND DU LAC

Meanwhile, the sister diocese of Wisconsin was likewise undergoing division. In 1875, the new diocese of Fond du Lac was erected. The first election of the new diocese was sharply contested. At one time, a majority of the clergy were in favor of De Koven; and only after twelve ballots had been taken did both orders unite on Leighton Coleman. He declined, as did likewise the next bishop-elect, Jacob S. Shipman. Finally, the diocese found its first bishop in John Henry Hobart Brown, a pupil of Muhlenberg, who had made a considerable reputation in the young diocese of Albany. No man with such a name and such antecedents could be anything but a strong High Churchman; and Brown eagerly welcomed the newer tendencies in the High Church movement. He at once made St. Paul's Church, Fond du Lac, his cathedral; and here he founded the order of St. Monica for widows. He was thoroughly in sympathy with monasticism; indeed, he made overtures to Grafton to set up an order for men in the new diocese. He welcomed and made use of the much-persecuted Prescott, and found work for the Rev. Walter Gardner, like Prescott an ex-Cowley Father.

Bishop Brown's natural bent toward ritualism was strengthened by one of the peculiar situations in the diocese. There was within its limits a large Belgian population, which had become estranged from the Roman Church. In them, Brown saw his own Church's opportunity. He, therefore, made plans to foster among them an "Old Catholic" movement. Since such a movement would necessarily use the Latin rite, he was anxious that there should be as little difference as possible between the Old Catholic usage and the diocesan norm; he, therefore, deliberately fostered ritualism. With the object of beginning such a movement, he sent René Joseph Villatte, a leading man among the Belgians, to receive Old Catholic orders in Europe. The project, however, did not turn out well. Villatte turned out to be an ambitious schemer, who, when disappointed in his plan of becoming suffragan in charge of the Old Catholics, broke away from his Episcopal ally, taking with him most of his followers.[4]

The extent to which Fond du Lac had become a homogeneous High Church diocese was shown at Bishop Brown's death in 1888. At his funeral a requiem mass was said. The first choice of the diocese as his successor was the Rev. George McClellan Fiske, of St. Stephen's, Providence, one of the most famous of High Church parishes. When he declined, the diocese then took the step, extraordinary at the time, of electing Father Grafton bishop. A far more dominating personality than Bishop Brown, he at once set out to make Fond du Lac the model of a Catholic diocese. Believing firmly in the teaching value of ceremonial, he encouraged it in all the parishes of the diocese. This was not accomplished without revolts on the part of the laity, but unlike many bishops, Grafton backed his priests through thick and thin. He was the first American bishop to wear cope and mitre as the normal episcopal costume; his example was speedily followed by others. As a result of his efforts, the weekly Eucharist, celebrated with eucharistic vestments and incense, prayers for the dead, the habitual use of the confessional—usages which in most dioceses were the mark of an occasional "extreme" parish, became in Fond du Lac the normal thing. Grafton carried on the work of his predecessor among the Old Catholics. He encouraged the formation of a Polish National Catholic movement, and endeavored, without much success, to secure

[4]Grafton, C. C., *A Journey Godward*, pp. 152-57.

for it official recognition from the General Convention. He was more successful in cultivating good relations with the Eastern Churches.[5]

The homogeneity of these Mid-Western dioceses, the extent to which they had been indoctrinated with High Church principles and practices, was again demonstrated at the election in 1900 of a coadjutor to Bishop Grafton. The only candidates nominated in the convention were Reginald Heber Weller, Father Huntington, President William Walter Webb of Nashotah, and Canon Benjamin T. Rogers of Fond du Lac—about as strong a High Church foursome as could have been assembled. Weller was elected, and his consecration was in some sense the outward and visible sign of Grafton's success. The wearing of copes and mitres by all the officiating bishops, the delivery of the ring and the pastoral staff, the use of chrism, the presence of the Polish National Catholic Bishop Kozlowski and the Russian Bishop Tikhon—all combined to make this the greatest display of episcopal ceremonial that had, until that time, been witnessed in the American Church. The consecration and its attendant ceremonies aroused no particular comment in Fond du Lac itself, but the publication of a picture of the assembled bishops, and the accompanying description in *The Living Church,* brought down on the offending diocese the wrath of the Eastern and Southern Low Church papers. *The Living Church* countered by printing pictures of the mitres worn by Bishops Seabury and Claggett, by pictures of English bishops in cope and mitre, and finally by a reproduction of the letterhead of one of the objecting publications—on which was engraved a mitre.[6]

---

[5] Grafton, C. C., *A Journey Godward,* pp. 158-79.

[6] *The Living Church,* Vol. 24, pp. 91, 146, 278-81. I doubt whether, in all Church history, a picture ever caused so much disturbance. But time marches on. In 1939, the Rev. Spence Burton, superior of the SSJE, was consecrated suffragan of Haiti, with all possible wealth of ceremonial. The consecration took place in Trinity Church, Boston. The consecrator, Presiding Bishop Tucker, had been bishop of Virginia. And no one made a fuss about it all.

Bishop Doane of Albany was an inveterate versifier. He composed some rhymes about the Weller consecration which I cannot forbear quoting in part:

There once was a mad chap named Grafton
Who has dropped his own name, being daft on
The one only marriage he ever did make,
With a lady who called herself Depth of the Lake.

Complacent he sits in a group whose creation
Is all his own work, and from every nation
He draws the lay-figures, Russ, German and Pole
To make up this medley incongruous whole.

THE CATHOLIC MOVEMENT IN THE EPISCOPAL CHURCH

THE RENAISSANCE OF NASHOTAH

Coincident in time with the coming of Grafton to Fond du Lac was the renaissance of Nashotah. Under the long presidency of Azel Cole (1850-1885), the seminary had quietly gone on its way. But Nashotah had always had very little financial resources in back of it, and by the time of Dr. Cole's death the endowment of forty thousand dollars was just about equalled by the accrued debt. When, in 1890, Cole's successor, the Rev. George Carter, retired, Grafton secured the election of Walter Gardner, Grafton's former associate in Boston. He was strongly supported, both by Bishop Grafton and by Bishop Nicholson of Milwaukee. Both these men were widely acquainted with men of wealth in the East, and by their aid the debt was wiped out, and the endowment more than doubled. Gardner at once set about restoring to Nashotah something of its former monastic tradition. A picture of the devotional life of the seminary under Gardner is given by Monsignor Hawks:

> The life was centered in the daily "sacrifice of the mass," which was celebrated in almost exact accordance with the Roman rite. Every student began his day by assisting at one of the celebrations which took place in the chapel, or in one of the numerous oratories which were scattered through the different buildings. There was a daily meditation directed by the professors in turn. The divine office was recited at the canonical hours, the deficiencies of the Book of Common Prayer being supplied by the Roman breviary. Vespers was sung before supper, with incense and cope on the eves of the greater feasts. The Gregorian chant was followed faithfully; in later days the Solemnes *(sic)* method was the norm, the teacher having taken a course of study at the Benedictine monastery in the Isle of Wight. Compline ended the day . . . Liturgical vestments were worn, the altars were adorned with lights and flowers, and incense was used on Sundays and holidays. Before I left, the "Sacrament" was reserved for the purpose of adoration. . . . On Ash Wednesday and Good Friday very few students availed themselves of the morning coffee, and

many took neither food nor drink until noon was passed. The Friday abstinence was a matter of rule.[7]

In all this, there was much that was simply the loyal following of the Book of Common Prayer, much that was wise enrichment, but also the germ of something that was to prove dangerous, if not disastrous.

Gardner was soon succeeded by the Rev. William Walter Webb, a man second only to Grafton in his influence on the Mid-Western phase of the movement around the turn of the century. Short, stout, bald-headed, with twinkling blue eyes, he was an attractive personality and a fascinating teacher of theology. His views may well be gathered from his text-book of moral theology, *The Cure of Souls*. Around Webb gathered a brilliant faculty. Canon St. George, Irish by birth, was a notable student of liturgics and a strong anti-Romanist. In Nashotah, but not quite of it, were two other men of mark, Hughell E. W. Fosbroke, later to become one of the greatest Old Testament scholars in America and dean of the General Theological Seminary, and Burton Scott Easton, equally eminent in the New Testament field. Both men were more than a little suspicious of the extreme tendencies becoming daily more apparent at the seminary.

Closely allied with Nashotah were the bishops of the neighboring dioceses. We have already made mention of Fond du Lac and Chicago.

From the time of Jackson Kemper, the diocese of Wisconsin had been held by bishops of the old High Church school. The episcopate of Edward Randolph Welles (1874-1888), marked a considerable advance.[8] Bishop Welles anticipated Grafton in the occasional use of cope, mitre, and episcopal ring. He was instrumental in the foundation of the Morehouse Publishing Company, a significant step in giving the more advanced High Church group

[7] Hawks, E., *William McGarvey and the Open Pulpit*, pp. 85-86. This quotation, like everything else in Hawks, is to be read *cum grano salis*.
[8] For a biographical essay, see Edward Randolph Welles, II, "Edward Randolph Welles, 1830-1888," in *Historical Magazine*, Vol. IX (1940), 247-256.

means of publicity. In 1886, during his episcopate, the name of the see was changed to Milwaukee. He was followed, after the two-year term of Bishop Cyrus Frederick Knight, by Isaac Lea Nicholson, who was consecrated in 1891. Coming to the Mid-West from the rectorate of St. Mark's, Philadelphia, he was in thorough sympathy with the type of churchmanship advocated by Grafton, Gardner and Webb. His work at Milwaukee was carried on by Webb, who became coadjutor in 1906, and diocesan in the same year.

Another like-minded bishop in the same section was John Hazen White, who became bishop of Indiana in 1895, and in 1899, when the diocese was divided, was translated to Michigan City. Charles Palmerston Anderson, who became coadjutor of Chicago in 1900 and diocesan in 1905, proved an able successor to McLaren. Edward William Osborne, formerly of the Society of St. John the Evangelist, who followed Bishop Seymour in 1906, completes the group.

Under this circle of bishops, with Nashotah prepared to supply them with priests trained for their purposes, the High Churchmanship of the Mid-Western dioceses took on a character quite different in many respects from the older tradition of the Eastern dioceses.

But there was an element of weakness in the Nashotah situation—an element that was to work grave harm to the seminary, and for a time at least to render it suspect to loyal churchmen. A group had developed within the student body, on the faculty of the seminary, and among the priests who looked to it as a center of inspiration, which was rapidly growing less and less attached to the Protestant Episcopal Church. Imitating Roman practices, approaching more and more nearly to Roman beliefs, desiring strongly reunion with Rome, they began to feel themselves aliens within their own Church, and came to value her only as she could be made to approach the Roman standard. We shall tell in the next chapter the story of 1907. The secessions of that year rocked Nashotah on her foundations. Joseph G. H. Barry, who had succeeded Webb as head of the institution, left to become rector of the parish of St. Mary the Virgin, New York. Fosbroke and Easton likewise

THE MOVEMENT IN THE MID-WEST

departed for the East, and under Edward Larrabee, a saint, but neither administrator nor disciplinarian, a period of near-anarchy ensued. Eventually, under the regime of Benjamin F. P. Ivins, Nashotah regained her balance. Again a strong faculty was assembled—Hallock, Stewart, Dunphy, Gavin, Cirlot, among them. Extremists were repressed, loyalty to the Prayer Book was inculcated, the Nashotah tradition of a disciplined life was emphasized, and the seminary resumed its work of sending out into the Church, not scholars, not philosophical dilettantes or eccesiastical milliners, but trained parish priests.

WESTERN THEOLOGICAL SEMINARY

With the opening up of the great Northwest and the building of transcontinental railroads, the city of Chicago began to grow like a giant mushroom. In 1850, it had a population of only 28,000. By 1890, it had passed the million mark. And with the growth of population came a corresponding growth in the Church.

By 1880, it was felt that Chicago, like New York, should have a seminary located in it. At the diocesan convention of 1883, Bishop McLaren recommended strongly the establishment of such an institution. His prayer was shortly granted, when a wealthy layman of the city gave a plot of ground and the beginning of an endowment. In the same year, Western Theological Seminary was incorporated,

> "especially for the education of fit persons in the Catholic faith in its purity and integrity, as taught in the Holy Scriptures, held by the Primitive Church, summed up in the Creeds, and affirmed by the undisputed General Councils."

While the bishops of Fond du Lac, Quincy, Springfield, and Indiana, were members of the board of trustees, from the begining the effective control was held tightly in the hands of Bishop McLaren. An austere and somewhat forbidding person, he was for years dean, the other members of the faculty being little more than tutors under his orders. The Rev. William J. Gold was called from Racine College to do most of the classroom teaching, but in 1885 he was ably seconded by the Rev. Francis J. Hall, just ordained, who then began his great career as theologian and teacher. Bishop Seymour of Springfield came up for frequent lectures in ecclesiastical history. Under such men, there could be no question as to the theological coloring of the new seminary. From the beginning, there was a daily Eucharist, claimed to be the first steady establishment of that custom in any Anglican seminary.

During the Eighties and early Nineties the seminary flourished; additional resident teachers were added, and the faculty took to publication. But late in the decade, things began to go wrong. Bishop McLaren was old and discouraged, and though he resigned as dean in 1898, Dr. Gold becoming warden, the bishop managed to put a wet blanket over plans for improvement. Finances became tight, Dr. Gold died, and Hall, with a single assistant, carried on what was left. In 1904, the school was temporarily closed.

But better days were at hand. Under the energetic leadership of Bishop Anderson of Chicago, funds were raised, the Rev. William C. DeWitt was appointed dean, a new faculty, on which Dr. Hall continued his invaluable services, was organized, and the seminary was reopened on a sound basis.

In 1933, it was united with Breck's foundation at Faribault, Minnesota—Seabury Divinity School—and, as Seabury-Western Theological Seminary, continues to function admirably in Evanston, Illinois.[9]

THE LIVING CHURCH

The story of the movement in the Mid-West would not be complete without some mention of *The Living Church*. Started in 1879, this periodical soon took the place of *The Churchman* and *The*

---

[9] *See* McElwain, F. A., Norwood, P. V., and Grant, F. C., "Seabury-Western Theological Seminary: A History," in *Historical Magazine*, Vol. V (1936), 286-311.

Church Journal as the semi-official organ of the High Church party. Carefully moderate in its tone, but strong in its convictions, it is no exaggeration to say that it has become the most widely circulated and the most influential of weekly Church papers.

CONTRIBUTIONS OF THE MID-WEST

The Mid-West has made two distinct contributions to the Catholic movement in the American Church. It has given us examples of the Catholic diocese: small, homogeneous, untroubled by disputes over varieties of churchmanship, where there are few or no ecclesiastical plums to attract ambitious clerical climbers, where advanced ceremonial is so normal as to be natural, where priests work under the close supervision of their bishop. And it has made a remarkable contribution to the scholarship of the Church. We usually associate scholarship with wealth and an old civilization. And yet from this section, where secular culture appears somewhat raw, where the Church is comparatively new and poor, there has come a surprising number of ripe scholars. The best work on dogmatic theology that the whole Anglican Communion has yet produced is the so-called "Anglican Summa" of Francis J. Hall, long a teacher at Western Theological Seminary. Add to his the names of Gavin, Fosbroke, Easton, Stewart, and one perceives what a very real addition this phase of the movement has made to the thought of the Church.

BIBLIOGRAPHY

The materials for this chapter have been largely drawn from the files of *The Living Church* and from diocesan journals. Grafton's autobiography is useful for the diocese of Fond du Lac. Hawks and Barry, two sharply conflicting acounts of the story of Nashotah, will be noted in the bibliography to Chapter IX.

HALLOCK, D. V., "The Story of Nashotah," in *Historical Magazine,* Vol. XI (1942), 3-17.

THE CATHOLIC MOVEMENT IN THE EPISCOPAL CHURCH

HOPKINS, J. H. 3RD, *The Great Forty Years* (Chicago, 1936). [A history of the Diocese of Chicago, 1893-1934.]

MCELWAIN, F. A., NORWOOD, P. V., AND GRANT, F. C., "Seabury-Western Theological Seminary: A History," in *Historical Magazine,* Vol. V (1936), 286-311.

CHAPTER NINE

THE McGARVEY SECESSION

THE last great crisis the High Church movement in America had to face came in the year 1907. To understand the roots of this, we must go back to Philadelphia in the year 1880. Philadelphia, from 1840 on, had been of all American cities the most generally hostile to High Church developments. From the overthrow of Bishop Henry U. Onderdonk, the see of Philadelphia had been steadily occupied by Low Church bishops—militant Low Churchmen, who had made it their business to attack any advance in churchmanship. The frequent troubles centering around St. Clement's Church are an example of this attitude and of its consequences. These consequences were that, in Philadelphia, High Churchmanship, especially of the ritualistic variety, was a rather self-conscious exotic; that it tended to become a sect within a sect; and that it inevitably assumed an extreme form. Such are the results of persecution.

THE REVEREND HENRY R. PERCIVAL

About 1880, Henry R. Percival, rector of the Church of the Evangelists, began to be known in the city as a leader of the small but extreme High Church group. Percival was a queer, crabbed eccentric, whose churchmanship followed a line all its own. He was a scholar of parts; his work on *The Seven Ecumenical Councils* is still a standard book of reference. He was utterly opposed to all ceremonial elaborations. But his theological position was extreme of the extremes. He was bitter in opposition to anything remotely savoring of liberalism, accepted the whole teaching of the Council of Trent, papal infallibility excepted, and wrote vigorously in defence of the invocation of saints and of late Mass with non-communicating attendance. It has been stated that before his death he had come to regard the Anglican Church as a schismatical body. He was wealthy enough to be able to dispense with the support of the laity. Around him he gathered a group of young priests whom he thoroughly indoctrinated with his peculiar principles. Among these were William McGarvey, William Walter Webb, and Maurice Cowl.[1]

THE COMPANIONS OF THE HOLY SAVIOUR

In 1896, McGarvey became rector of the daughter parish of St. Elizabeth.[2] Here was developed an organization begun at the mother church in 1891, known as the Companions of the Holy Saviour. Its life is thus described by one of its members:

> The Companions promised to rise each day not later than seven o'clock; to say private prayers thrice daily; to recite the Divine Office as contained in the Prayer Book—an obligation by which few American clergymen considered themselves to be bound;[3] to celebrate the Holy Communion at least twice each week; to make a Eucharistic preparation and thanksgiving; to observe complete fast before the Communion; to say table prayers; to make a daily meditation of fifteen minutes; to read each day a passage from a spiritual book; to devote one half-hour each day to sacred study; to make a daily examination of conscience; to approach sacramental confession at least once each month; to observe the days of fasting and abstinence prescribed by the Prayer Book; to cultivate a spirit of poverty; to attend a yearly retreat provided by the Congregation; to recite a daily Collect for the congregation; and finally to confess all breaches of the rule publicly at the monthly conferences.[4]

[1]Hawks, E., *William McGarvey and the Open Pulpit*, pp. 11-23.

[2] "McGarvey's great difficulty was his ignorance. He was a street boy whom Percival picked up and educated in his own image, without sending him to college; he knew nothing at all except the Percivalian theology. And we used to say in Philadelphia that Percival never accepted the Copernican theory; I knew him and I am sure it did not interest him. He had no sense of humor whatever, but was convinced he had; something that made conversation with him trying. He was a valetudinarian and celebrated in an oratory surrounded by plate glass. *And* he used to declare that true Christianity demanded an absolute monarchy."—Letter of Dr. Burton Scott Easton to the author.

[3]A plain misstatement. Insistence on the obligation of the Daily Office had been a High Church trait ever since Hobart.

[4]Hawks, E., *op. cit.*, p. 36.

Apparently nothing could be more thoroughly Anglican. The real difficulty came as a result of two things not set down in the rule, but decidedly lying back of it: the feeling of exclusiveness—the notion that in this small group was contained the real Catholicity of the Episcopal Church; and the determination of the members to practice celibacy.

The outward appearance of St. Elizabeth's Church soon was brought into conformity with the principles of its priests. The high altar carried six candlesticks. Here Mass was said by priests dressed in the full eucharistic vestments, accompanied by crucifix, torch-bearers, banners, and red-robed acolytes. There were side altars dedicated to Our Lady and to St. Joseph. The clergy lived together in the adjoining clergy house. Small wonder that the honest workingman of the neighborhood had difficulty in distinguishing St. Elizabeth's from the Roman church around the corner.

The appointment of Webb as president of Nashotah brought the influence of St. Elizabeth's to bear on the western seminary, and, from 1892 to 1907, the connection between Nashotah and the Companions of the Holy Saviour was constant and intimate. The Rev. Charles Bowles, one of the Companions, became the favorite confessor at Nashotah; another, the Rev. Sigourney Fay, clever, unstable, incompetent as a teacher, succeeded Webb as professor of dogmatic theology. On the other hand, Nashotah men regularly went to St. Elizabeth's as curates.

But in the year 1906 the group began to be conscious of clouds on the horizon. In that year, Webb was elected coadjutor of Milwaukee, and soon drew away from the McGarvey influence. He was succeeded at Nashotah by Joseph G. H. Barry. Barry was a man who had emerged from the "Connecticut Churchmanship" of Berkeley Divinity School with a fully developed High Churchmanship of a rather extreme sort. He had come to Nashotah from the deanship of Fond du Lac Cathedral. But along with his extreme beliefs and practices—clerical celibacy, routine confession, non-communicating attendance, and the like—he managed to retain a deep and genuine loyalty to the

Episcopal Church. Like Grafton, he was bitterly anti-Roman. Friction soon developed between him and the Companion group, which had hoped to dominate Nashotah.[5] This friction, one is forced to conclude, was basically due to the fact that Barry sensed the fundamental disloyalty of his associates, and was, therefore, suspicious of their doings. The situation was complicated by the fact that Liberal Catholicism, stemming from Gore and Tyrrell, was being taken up by a group of the Nashotah faculty—a group which included the best scholars resident there. Against any such tendency, a Percivalite was bound to rebel.[6]

More and more dissatisfied with their position in the Anglican Church, the Companions began to look longingly toward Rome. By the autumn of 1906, their leader, McGarvey, had substantially accepted a queer position. This position was being popularized by a publication called *The Lamp*, edited by Father Paul James Francis, an eccentric genius who had founded a community of Franciscans at Graymoor. Those holding this position believed that the Anglican Church was in schism, and that there must be reunion with Rome. They accepted the decrees, not only of the Council of Trent, but also of the Vatican Council. In fact, they were in the rather egotistic, and hardly logical, position of believing in nothing Anglican except their own priesthood. But they discouraged individual conversions, hoping for the formation of some sort of uniate body under Roman obedi-

---

[5] The following eloquently demonstrates Hawks' animus against Barry:

"From the first the new president showed his complete incompetence. He failed to gain the confidence of the students; he took little or no interest in their difficulties; but his chief defect was an attitude of sarcasm, which was more assumed than real, that made his associates disinclined to discuss matters with him . . . he fraternized with a small group of students, and to a large extent avoided the members of the staff. He was quite incapable of dealing with the troubles that were coming." [Hawks, *op. cit.*, p. 93.]

But Barry, it must be confessed, was not the man to handle an extremely complicated situation. According to Dr. Easton, who was in the midst of all this, "he was essentially unfitted for his position and was unhappy in it. When he came, he relied to an extraordinary degree on Fay, whom he brought with him, and Fay's defection drove him into solitude." [Letter of Dr. Easton to the author.]

[6] The appearance in 1907 of the Papal encyclical *Pascendi* of Pius X was another deciding factor. Condemning the very sort of Biblical scholarship dominant in that decade at Nashotah—a scholarship that made the McGarveyites extremely restless—the encyclical helped to convince them that the dogmatic security they sought was to be found only in Rome.

ence. This view finally bore fruit in the short-lived "Society for Corporate Reunion."[7]

THE OPEN PULPIT CANON

The torch that finally set off this powder magazine seems today a rather trivial matter. At the General Convention, which met in Richmond in October, 1907, the Rev. Cyrus Townsend Brady, whose chief previous title to fame had been his historical novels, introduced the following resolution:

> *Resolved,* the House of Bishops concurring, that Canon 19 be amended by adding, after the words "Lay readers," these words: "or prevent the preaching of sermons or the delivery of addresses by Christian ministers, or men, who may be invited thereto by any priest in charge of any Congregation, or in his absence by the Bishop, who may license them for the purpose."[8]

To the introducer and to those who supported him, this canon was a recognition that Christianity extends outside the limits of the visible Catholic Church, and that Christians outside that body might conceivably have something of importance to say to those within. It was passed by a large majority of the House of Deputies, but not until a number of significant changes had been made. The term "sermons" was cut out, it was specified that the addresses made in accordance with the canon were for special occasions only, and it was finally provided that no such address should be made without the permission of the bishop. With these changes, the canon was passed by the House of Bishops, it is said unanimously. It was certainly supported by such decidedly High Church bishops as Gailor of Tennessee and Doane of Albany.

At first the canon caused very little comment. *The Living Church* seems to have expressed the opinion of the great majority of the High Church party, when it declared the canon innocuous, and by no means

[7] Hawks, *op. cit.*, pp. 90-100, 122.
[8] *The Living Church,* Vol. 27, p. 886.

establishing an "open pulpit."[9] John Henry Hopkins, third of the name, attacked it mildly, as did Westcott, the author of *Catholic Principles*;[10] Fiske of Providence, once bishop-elect of Fond du Lac, was open in support of it.

But to the men of the Percival school, this canon was the last straw. The American Episcopal Church, by thus asserting some degree of fellowship with the Protestant sects, had forfeited whatever claim to Catholicity she might ever have had, and there was but one resort left. In this, as in the somewhat parallel case of the Jerusalem bishopric in England, one more than suspects that the apparent cause was not the real cause. McGarvey and his associates had ceased to have any real loyalty to the Episcopal Church, as they saw it about them; they were more than doubtful of her Catholicity; they were already casting longing glances at Rome. McGarvey is reported to have said a year before this:

> "We are only waiting until Peter beckons. When he does, we will go."

To them the "Open Pulpit" Canon was merely the occasion for a dramatic exit.

The paper attack on the canon was at first led by Father Henry R. Sargent, O.H.C.,[11] but his violence was far exceeded by that of James B. Haslam, curate at St. Elizabeth's, on this occasion the spokesman of the McGarvey group.[12] Alarmed at these strident tones, and still more alarmed by the rumors of dreadful events to come that now began to fly about, some of the High Church bishops began to withdraw their approval of the disputed canon. Both Osborne of Springfield and White of Michigan City announced that they would treat it as a dead letter. But it was too late.

---

[9] *Ibid*, Vol 28, p. 5.
[10] *Ibid*, Vol. 28, pp. 13, 219.
[11] *Ibid.*, p. 220.
[12] *Ibid.*, p. 221. Hawks (*op. cit.*, p. 180) has, without intending it, a very amusing passage about Haslam, who was received into the Roman Church on March 5, 1908:
   "He studied for a time with the Paulists and on their finding him ill-adapted to their life, he returned to the Episcopal Church, and afterward entered the estate of matrimony."

THE McGARVEY SECESSION

THE SECESSIONISTS

In February, 1908, Edward Hawks and James Bourne, priests and teachers in the preparatory department at Nashotah, resigned and sought peace within the Roman fold. Fay, suspected by President Barry, was given indefinite leave of absence. He, too, made his submission to the Pope. These leaders were followed by five students of the seminary. In May, 1908, all but one of the priests working at St. Elizabeth's—McGarvey, Cowl, Hayward, and McClellan—departed in a body. As the parishioners of St. Elizabeth's departed from the last services conducted by the Companions, they were handed McGarvey's valedictory to the Episcopal Church—a tract entitled, *The Future of the Catholic Movement,* in which the author asserts "the emptiness of Protestantism, that Anglicanism is but a house built upon sand, and that the One Church of the Living God is the Catholic and Roman Church."[13] The mother superior of the Sisters of St. Mary, whose chaplain McGarvey had been, followed suit. The members of the monastic community at Graymoor did likewise. In all some twenty priests took part in the exodus.[14] These were serious losses, but still worse were the suspicions engendered by this drastic climax. Rumors flew about of a gigantic conspiracy to lead the whole High Church party into the arms of Rome. More than twenty years after the event, Barry, in his autobiography, still asserted that such a conspiracy had existed, that McGarvey had planned to take with him five hundred priests, and that the impatience of a few, who had gone over too soon, gave away the scheme.[15]

In the face of this apparent danger, the High Church leaders stuck valiantly to their guns. Bishop Grafton, by now the patriarch of the Mid-Western High Churchmen, wrote article after article, urging the

---

[13]Hawks, *op. cit.,* p. 242.
[14]*Ibid.,* pp. 153-80.
[15]"The conspiracy existed chiefly in Fay's vivid imagination; it was he who pictured himself and McGarvey (in that order) leading ten bishops and five hundred priests to Rome, where they would be received not as individuals but as I don't know exactly what, except there was great talk of a concordat to be signed by Fay, McGarvey and Merry del Val. But a 'conspiracy' to form a schism of respectable size certainly existed, and its failure to materialize was a bitter disappointment."—Letter of Dr. Easton to the author.

Catholic clergy to fear nothing and stand fast. At a meeting in New York, he and Bishop Greer appeared on the same platform, and asserted their common Catholicity.[16] *The Living Church* said farewell to the departing brethren in an editorial bearing the bitter title, "And they all forsook him and fled."[17] But the tempest was surprisingly short-lived. It was noted that practically all the secessionists belonged to one group, and that a group whose loyalty to the Anglican Church had for a considerable time been under grave suspicion.[18] The blow was felt most by men like Webb, Grafton, Mortimer; the great majority of churchmen were more inclined to shrug their shoulders and exclaim, "Good riddance."

[16] *The Living Church*, Vol. 28, p. 621.
[17] *Ibid.*, p. 808.
[18] I give what I believe to be a complete list of the converts of 1907-8:

James Bourne, CSSS, Nashotah.
Charles Bowles, CSSS, Ravenswood, Ill.
James Haslam, CSSS, St. Elizabeth's, Philadelphia. (Haslam reverted.)
Maurice Cowl, CSSS, St. Elizabeth's, Philadelphia.
Alvah Doran, CSSS.
John Ewens, CSSS, Manistee, Mich.
Sigourney Fay, CSSS, Nashotah.
Paul James Francis, Graymoor, N. Y.
Otho Gromoll, Pullman, Ill.
Edgar Cowan, CSSS, St. Elizabeth's, Philadelphia.
Edward Hawks, CSSS, Nashotah.
William Hayward, CSSS, St. Elizabeth's, Philadelphia.
William Henkell, Reading, Pa.
William McClellan, CSSS, St. Elizabeth's, Philadelphia.
William McGarvey, CSSS, St. Elizabeth's, Philadelphia.
Francis McFetrick, Philadelphia. [McFetrick had no connection with the others listed here.]
Charles Meyer, CSSS.
James Raker, CSSS.
Louis Small, Secretary to Bishop Webb.
Russell Wilbur, Archdeacon of Fond du Lac.
Henry Yost, Roxborough, Pa.

BIBLIOGRAPHY

Aside from the files of *The Living Church*, there are only two sources at present available for this chapter:

BARRY, J. G. H., *Impressions and Opinions*, (New York, 1931). [An autobiography, which I have found reliable except for the point noted.]

HAWKS, E., *William McGarvey and the Open Pulpit*, (Philadelphia, 1935). [The only complete account in print, but to be used with extreme caution. It is marred by personal animus and theological bias. Nor are its facts always facts. When the first edition of this book appeared, I asked the Rev. Dr. Burton Scott Easton, who was thoroughly informed of the events treated in this chapter, to give me his comments, which are invaluable, and appear in this edition as notes.]

CHAPTER TEN

LIBERAL CATHOLICISM

THE pioneers of the Catholic Movement, both in this country and in England, were, practically without exception, Biblical fundamentalists. One does find hints of a different approach to the Scriptures in the *Remains* of Hurrell Froude, but in this, as in much else, Froude was the unusual. On one side, indeed, Tractarianism was definitely in reaction against the growing influence of German biblical scholarship. To Newman and his followers, Liberalism was the great enemy. In this attitude, Tractarians and old High Churchmen were, in common with all orthodox Christian theologians of their day, the heirs of late mediaeval thought.

But back of this there lay, largely forgotten, an older, more civilized and saner attitude toward the Bible. The Latin and Greek Fathers, to whom High Churchmen were constantly appealing, were often startlingly modernist in their treatment of the Scriptures. And in its constant insistence on the tradition of the Church as a guide to Biblical interpretation, High Church theology contained within itself a liberating principle that was to prove of supreme value when the question of Modernism had to be dealt with seriously.

THE INTELLECTUAL REVOLUTION OF THE 19th CENTURY

Two widely separated currents of thought were eventually to act as dissolvents of the almost universal Fundamentalism that held the field when the *Tracts* were appearing. Nineteenth century science, particularly in the fields of geology and biology, soon found itself at variance with a literal acceptance of Genesis and Jonah. The first reaction of Christian thinkers to Lyell, Darwin, and Huxley, was one of shocked abhorrence. But no sooner had they braced themselves to meet this attack, than orthodox teachers found themselves assailed in the vulnerable rear by a phalanx of Biblical critics, armed with the formidable weapons of disputed authorship, variant readings, et al.

The publication in 1855 of *Essays and Reviews* brought the whole matter to a head. Against this impious volume, Evangelicals and High Churchmen formed one of their transitory alliances. In England, it made such strange bedfellows as Dr. Pusey and the *Church Record*. In this country, Bishop McIlvaine was joined by such divergent bishops as Kemper and Whitehouse, and by clergy of the stamp of the younger Hopkins and Father Grafton, in agreeing that the plenary inspiration, and therefore the literal infallibility of the holy Scriptures, was an essential article of the faith. In 1865, this position was given seemingly official approval when the House of Bishops condemned the teaching of Bishop Colenso, and set its seal on Bishop McIlvaine's pastoral, which unsparingly denounced liberal criticism of the Bible.

The net result of this first battle was the formation of the Broad Church School of Anglican theologians, which for nearly three decades held a practical monopoly of modernistic views in the American Church. In the Seventies, this group gained a foothold in the Philadelphia Divinity School, and practical control of the Episcopal Theological School at Cambridge. In 1874, the Church Congress held its first meeting. This organization was set up as a forum in which questions of theology could be openly and freely debated. Sponsored mainly by Broad Churchmen, this gathering nevertheless included among its members High Churchmen like Bishop Hugh Miller Thompson, Bishop Williams of Connecticut, Professor William Dexter Wilson of Cornell, and even Dr. De Koven.[1] It undoubtedly was of first importance in loosening up thinking in the Church at large, and in the High Church party in particular.

THE INTELLECTUAL LEADERSHIP OF FERDINAND C. EWER

As far as I can discover, the first leader of the Catholic Movement in America to respond fully and favorably to these new influences,

[1] E. C. Chorley, *Men and Movements in the American Episcopal Church* (New York, 1946), pp. 297-314.

and to give them literary expression, was that exceedingly controversial figure of the Seventies and Eighties, Ferdinand Cartwright Ewer. A man of keen and critical intelligence, a born controversialist, in his intellectual pilgrim's progress from the Church to Unitarianism, agnosticism, and back to a full Catholicism, he had become vividly aware of the main currents of thought in the modern world that were affecting theology.

In 1869, Ewer published a provocative little volume entitled *Sermons on the Failure of Protestantism.* Here his standpoint is basically fundamentalist, but he knows what is going on. There have been, he maintains, three great heresies that have sprung up within the Christian Church. The first was Arianism, the second Protestantism, "and the third is modern Criticism, represented by Strauss, Renan, Colenso, and others."[2] Of these three heresies, he holds that the last is "the most intellectual and respectable."[3] This was an important admission. Against this heresy, the only barrier, he is convinced, is the Church. The Bible alone is not enough, because the Bible is not self-attesting:

> "The Catholic knows the Bible is the Word of God, because the infallible Church tells him that it is.... Thus, I have either an infallible Word of God, resting on an infallible Church ... or I have nothing under the sun that I can trust in as a Bible."

This is indeed fundamentalism, but fundamentalism with a significant difference. In the same volume, Ewer cites, with obvious approval, the names of Spencer and Mill and Huxley and Tyndall, and is proud of the fact that these men agree that "their only sympathizers in the religious world are minds that have been trained in the Anglo-Catholic Church."[4] He quotes the assertions of the scientists that the world was not made in six calendar days, that Noah's flood could not have covered the whole earth, and is neither astounded nor shocked by these statements. Already, it is apparent, he had moved a long dis-

[2] Ewer, *Failure of Protestantism*, p. 91.
[3] *Ibid.*, p. 98.
[4] *Ibid.*, p. 146.

tance from the standpoint of the early Tractarians, or from that of his contemporary, Liddon.

In this first volume of Ewer's, there were, then, germs of promise, but it was promise only. Ten years later, the promise was to be in large part fulfilled. In 1878, he published a second volume, called *Catholicity, Protestantism and Romanism,* which is in many respects the most intelligent piece of apologetic the Episcopal Church in America had produced up to that time. In this volume, he comes squarely to grips with the assertions of Biblical criticism, and sums up his conclusions, very different indeed from his conclusions of 1869, in a remarkable paragraph:

"The Bible contains not only a Divine element, but also human elements; the Bible is therefore both infinite and finite, both perfect and imperfect. Parts of It (*sic*) are written in imperfect Greek; Its style is sometimes involved; St. Paul's Epistle to the Laodiceans is gone from It; passages are in It which all agree should be out of It; one half of the Christian world—more than one-half of the Catholic world even—hold that the Epistle to the Hebrews, St. James' Epistle, St. Jude's, the Second and Third of St. John, the Second of St. Peter, the verses from the 9th to the 20th in the XVI chapter of St. Mark, the statement concerning the bloody sweat in St. Luke, and other passages here and there, are not fully canonical.[5] The majority of quotations in the New Testament vary from the Old Testament text. In St. Mark, the Magdalene came to the sepulchre at the rising of the sun; but according to St. John, it was still dark when she came and found the tomb empty. In short, the Bible goes down through the ages bearing the Divine element unharmed within It, but showing at the same time the unsightly bruises and the dark stains of Its human elements with which the Divine is inseparably bound up. The Bible has 925,877 words; and yet while that band of words is organized into the one, perfect, outward body expressive of the infallible message of heaven, each word, in itself considered, is a poor finite word, and each sentence, in itself considered, is liable to imperfections and fallibility."[6]

[5] The agreement on these drastic conclusions was not, of course, as sweeping as Ewer makes out.
[6] Ewer, *Catholicity, Protestantism and Romanism,* pp. 81-82.

One other passage in this lecture catches our attention, since in it Ewer hints at an anticipation of those Christological problems which have became so vital of recent years. He says of our Lord:

> "In His Divine element He was perfect, indefectible and infinite. But in His human element He was finite; He grew in stature and in wisdom; was often wearied, soiled and hungry..."[7]

This, of course, is strictly Chalcedonian Christology, but it is important to remember that the Chalcedonian balance between the human and divine natures of our Lord had often been lost sight of in the intervening centuries, and Christian thinking had often oscillated between Unitarianism and the semi-Monophysitism which frequently passed for orthodoxy. Such a statement as that of Ewer's points, not necessarily to the conclusions of the Kenotic school, but to an awareness of the problems the Kenotic school was facing.

Ewer's whole thesis in this prophetic volume, a thesis foreign to the thought of old High Churchmen and Tractarians alike, is that true Catholicity combines dogmatic certainty in essentials with freedom to think and to develop in the theology which builds upon those essentials. Ewer was, in effect, a Liberal Catholic, far in advance of his time.

THE RECEPTION OF "LUX MUNDI" IN AMERICA

As Ewer was without predecessors in his own party in this country, so he was for a time without successors. And then, in 1889, *Lux Mundi* appeared[8]. This is, in a sense, the primary document of Liberal Catholicism. Here is no radical pronunciamento by starry-eyed Broad Churchmen, but an honest attempt, by a group of scholars and theologians who gloried in the name Catholic, to show that the Catholic faith was a flexible and growing thing, capable of reconciliation with modern thought. It frankly applies the theory of evolution to theological problems, affirms that the revelation of God to

[7]*Ibid.*, p. 81.
[8]Edited by Charles Gore. There were ten other contributors to the volume.

man is a progressive and not a static thing, and accepts with confidence the assured results of Biblical criticism.

Its reception in this country was far different from that accorded to *Essays and Reviews.* In 1890—the early date is significant—Bishop Doane of Albany devoted a considerable part of his convention address to a consideration of this book. Bishop Doane has every claim to be taken as a representative figure in the High Church party. Connected through his father with Hobart and Seabury in this country, and with Keble and Pusey in England, himself a friend and ally of Morgan Dix and the younger Hopkins and Canon Liddon, no man had wider contacts with Anglo-Catholicism in all its manifestations. Furthermore, he was himself a man of powerful mind, wide reading, undoubted orthodoxy, and conservative temperament. All this gives weight and interest to what he had to say.

Doane begins by stating that the attention of theological students is today centered on the Old Testament Scriptures, that the searching study to which the Scriptures have been subjected is largely reverent and real, and that the conclusions of this study must be dealt with, not by angry denunciation, but by intelligent and competent argument.[9] He confesses his own belief that "Moses wrote the Pentateuch, and David the Psalms, and Daniel the Prophecy which bears his name." But he wears his rue with a difference, admitting that there are some Psalms which are plainly not from David, that Moses obviously did not set down the account of his own death and burial, and that, in what he did write, he very likely had recourse to earlier records. The bishop has no difficulty in believing in the vocal cords of Balaam's ass, or that a great fish could have swallowed Jonah.[10] But he is also

> "abundantly sure that no man is qualified today to preach the everlasting Gospel who is not familiar with the best modern writings of men like Lightfoot and Westcott.' "[11]

[9] *Albany Convention Journal,* 1890, pp. 19-20.
[10] *Ibid.,* p. 21.
[11] *Ibid.,* p. 23.

Finally, he rests his faith in the Bible on its acceptance and canonization by the Church, thus reaching back to the past and pointing the way to the future.[12] The valuable thing about this weighty utterance was its total lack of violent denunciation, and its cautious but receptive spirit.

If this deliverance of Bishop Doane's may be taken to stand for the attitude of the more intelligent High Churchmen of the day, Father Ritchie with his entertaining periodical, *The Catholic Champion,* typifies well the position of the extreme Anglo-Catholics. In 1888 and 1889, before *Lux Mundi* appeared, Ritchie was already carrying on a guerilla warfare against the higher critics within the Episcopal Church. Both Heber Newton, a noted New York preacher of the decade, and the faculty of the Episcopal Theological School at Cambridge as a whole, are attacked because they do not accept the literal truth of the Book of Jonah.[13] Naturally, Ritchie had little use for the Revised Version of the Bible. When *Lux Mundi* appeared, *The Catholic Champion* condemned it wholeheartedly in a long article, and returned to the attack again and again.[14] For this, Ritchie was reproved by A. C. A. Hall, whose membership in the Cowley Fathers was almost a guarantee of Catholic orthodoxy. But Ritchie's conclusion was that Hall "was no longer a Catholic Champion, but had become a Church Eclectic."[15] This complete obscurantism of Ritchie's is made more interesting by the fact that Ritchie was the successor of Ewer at St. Ignatius.

THE TEACHING OF FOSBROKE, EASTON AND ROBBINS

By the end of the Eighties, as we have seen, the Higher Criticism had pretty well captured the theological school at Cambridge, and toward the end of the decade it was finding a footing both in the Virginia Seminary and in Western. In 1900, it invaded the stronghold of advanced Anglo-Catholicism, Nashotah House, in the person of

[12] *Albany Convention Journal,* p. 20.
[13] *The Catholic Champion,* Vol II, 40, 73.
[14] *Ibid.,* p. 96.
[15] *Ibid.,* p. 277.

Hughell E. W. Fosbroke, one of the greatest teachers of Old Testament this country has ever seen. A radical textual critic, thoroughly indoctrinated in all the mysteries of J and E and P and D, Fosbroke retained in his masterful teaching no trace of the hesitancies and reserves of such men as Bishop Doane. In his classroom, Balaam's ass and Jonah's great fish were simply laughed out of court. But it was the great merit of Fosbroke as a teacher that he did not stop at mere bleak negations. After all the deductions were made for the mythmaking instinct, after all the doubtful texts were discarded and the work of "later hands" ruled out, there remained to his students a solid residue of positive and invaluable doctrine. One left his classroom with a clear picture, painted as by flashes of lightning, of the great and transcendent Yahweh.

In 1905, Fosbroke found a fit mate at Nashotah when Burton Scott Easton was appointed to the department of New Testament. A man of totally different cast of mind, Easton applied to the New Testament the same searchlight of radical criticism that Fosbroke was turning on the Old. Such advanced teaching could not fail to set up some unfavorable reaction, but fortunately it met with no official opposition. The older High Church bishops who controlled Nashotah were frankly puzzled by these developments, but they were patient and tolerant. Barry, president of the House, was completely in sympathy with the critical methods of Fosbroke and Easton. I think it a fair conclusion to say that, by 1910, radical criticism of the Old Testament, and the results of that radical criticism, had been on the whole assimilated almost painlessly into Anglo-Catholic thinking. The storms that raged in the Protestant denominations were in the Episcopal Church mere passing squalls. This is evidenced by the fact that such a man as Dean Briggs of Union Theological Seminary, driven from the Presbyterian Church as a heretic, found a safe harbor within the Episcopal fold.[16]

[16] Almost the only unfavorable reaction to the ordination of Dean Briggs was the secession to Rome in 1899 of the Rev. Benjamin Franklin DeCosta, a pronounced High Churchman and a historical scholar of considerable weight.

That this new and radical teaching could be thus easily digested by a highly conservative group was due to two facts. As we have pointed out, High Church theologians, from the time of Hobart on, had insisted that the Christian religion was not founded on the Bible, but had been committed by our Lord to his Church, and that the Bible was made and authorized by the Church. What the Church had made, the Church could therefore interpret—and if necessary re-interpret. Furthermore, no basic doctrine of the Catholic faith, no single statement of the Creeds, depended on the Old Testament alone for its verification.

But New Testament criticism trod on more sacred ground. Belief in the Creeds had no necessary relation to the single or multiple authorship of Genesis. On the other hand, the authorship of the Pastoral Epistles and the Fourth Gospel, the authenticity of the end of St. Mark, had a very definite bearing on one's belief in the Apostolic Succession, the Virgin Birth, and the Resurrection; and even the Incarnation itself seemed to need restatement or re-explanation in the light of modern knowledge. This does not mean that a higher critic of the New Testament was inevitably unorthodox on any of these points; it does mean that there was a necessity for a re-examination of these teachings in the light of newly discovered facts.

We can see the operations of both criticism and the reaction against it in the single person of Sigourney Fay, who, in 1906, succeeded Bishop Webb as professor of dogmatic theology at Nashotah. In the beginning, Fay was in complete sympathy with the higher criticism, and was particularly affected by the teaching of such Catholic Modernists as Loisy and Tyrrell. But he was closely associated with the Mc-Garvey group, and as they drew closer to Rome, so did Fay. When, in 1907, Piux X in the encyclical *Pascendi* condemned Modernism and all its works, Fay was convinced that the cause was ended, and his secession was only a matter of time.

In a previous chapter, we have told the story of the departure of the McGarveyites. The result, as far as Nashotah was concerned, was temporarily to deprive her of the intellectual leadership in the Catholic movement, which she had held for nearly a decade. Barry was succeeded as head of the house by Larrabee, a saint, but no scholar, and not even in sympathy with scholarship; under his rule, critical modernism was eliminated from Nashotah. Fosbroke and Easton soon left; Royden Keith Yerkes, then just beginning a great career as a dogmatic theologian, found a more hospitable home in Philadelphia Divinity School; and leadership in the development of Liberal Catholicism passed to other centers of learning.

In 1903, Wilford Lash Robbins went from the Cathedral at Albany to be dean of the General Theological Seminary. With him, Catholic Modernism made its real entrance into the oldest, largest, and most official of the seminaries of the Church. The way had been prepared; Dean Hoffman had strengthened the finances of the seminary so that it was now possible to fill the chairs with genuine professional scholars. Already, in Isbon T. Beckwith, the seminary had a teacher of Old Testament who was aware of modern criticism. Robbins himself was mainly interested in apologetics—a field by its very nature responsive to the currents of modern thought. He brought to the seminary Loren W. Batten, a teacher of Old Testament, Charles Carroll Edmunds, who combined a strong Anglo-Catholic position with a modern approach to the New Testament, and, most important of all, Francis Joseph Hall.

THE WORK OF FRANCIS J. HALL

Hall, who had begun his eminent career as an instructor in Western Theological Seminary in 1885, was by 1913, when he came to General, rapidly becoming the most notable dogmatic theologian our Church in this country has produced. Anglican theology had for a century been conspicuous for its contributions to Church history, but in the field of dogmatics had produced only special monographs. Hall set out to give the Church a comprehensive work covering the whole field of dogmatics. In 1907, the first volume appeared, to be followed at intervals by nine other volumes, the whole constituting the most inclusive and thorough work in that area of scholarship which the Anglican Communion possesses. In no sense an original thinker, Hall was a man of unwearied industry, orthodox temper, and systematic approach. He had read literally everything in his field, from the Fathers to the most modern of modernists. He was not, of course, primarily concerned with Biblical criticism in itself, but he was deeply concerned with the bearings of modern criticism on the dogmatic teaching of the Church.

His doctrine of inspiration may be summarized in five statements:

1. The Bible is the Word of God, having God for its principal author.

2. Holy Scripture *in its inspired purpose* will be found infallible and inerrant. (*Italics mine.*)

3. The authentication of the Word of God pertains to the Spirit-guided Catholic Church.

4. The process of producing the Bible was supernatural, and was absolutely unique in its purpose and result.

5. The method of inspiration was not mechanical; human peculiarities of style and method, and human limitations, appear in Scripture.[17]

At first glance, this looks completely reactionary. But its appearance is a bit deceiving. Hall always uses, by choice, traditional language, but he often gives it a far from traditional meaning. In the italicized words in proposition two, and in the whole of proposition five, the way is made plain for the free play of critical intelligence.

To Hall, Old Testament criticism was not only important in itself. It had a basic relation to the Church's doctrine of creation and of the Fall of Man. In treating these, Hall unhesitatingly, gladly, accepts the theory of evolution. Like John Fiske before him, he sees that "the evolutionary view of the organic world . . . implies a purposeful

[17] *Dogmatic Theology,* Vol. II, P. 216. In stating these propositions, I have used Hall's own words, but condensed by leaving out qualifying expressions. I do not think I have in any respect distorted his meaning.

drama and a goal of development."[18] He then grapples with the apparent contradiction between the Christian view of man as a fallen being, and the evolutionary view of him as a developing being, and concludes that the two views are quite capable of reconciliation. Our primitive parents, he finds, were not perfect beings, but

> "inexperienced children, endowed by nature and grace with sufficient capacity for blameless progress, but with much to learn and with character to develop."[19]

This harmonization is perhaps the most original contribution made by Hall to theological science. The volume in which this synthesis was achieved appeared in 1912. I think it safe to say that, from that date on, Old Testment criticism ceased to be in any way a troubler of the waters of Anglican theology.

As was to be expected, Hall's position in regard to New Testament criticism was much more conservative. Not that he was a blind obscurantist. He accepts the usual solution of the synoptic problem; he admits that the Fourth Gospel contains material not strictly historical, though he holds that, in the main, it is the testimony of an eye witness. But these admissions in his view involve no doctrinal changes. As he points out, attacks on such doctrines as the Incarnation, the Virgin birth, and the bodily Resurrection are usually, though by no means always, based, not on a new exegesis, but on a materialistic philosophy. In his comforting conclusion, no statement in the Creed needs to be modified because of any discoveries of the higher criticism of the New Testament.

I have dwelt at some length on Hall, because he represents so thoroughly the typical Anglo-Catholic attitude, combining a complete willingness to accept the new facts turned up by science and criticism with a whole-hearted certainty that these facts can be fitted into the framework of the Catholic faith. And I think it a fair statement to say that for several decades Hall was the most influential

---

[18]*Dogmatic Theology*, Vol. V, p. 200. "It is no longer possible to defend the opinions concerning the age of the world which have been deduced from the narratives of Genesis." (*Ibid.*, p. 43.)
[19]*Ibid.*, p. 251.

teacher of dogmatic theology in the American Church, and that the effect of his writings on Anglo-Catholic thought has been both deep and lasting.

The last volume of the *Dogmatic Theology* appeared in 1922; for the time being, a synthesis between Catholic theology and modern thought seemed achieved within the American Church. But no such synthesis ever can be called final. Science and scholarship both move on, and no theologian, however eminent, can have more success than King Canute in stopping the advancing waves. The next landmark in the progress of Liberal Catholicism was the appearance, in 1926, of *Essays Catholic and Critical*. This volume was the work of a group of English scholars, all Catholic-minded and progressive in outlook; it was another *Lux Mundi*.

THE POSITION OF "LIBERAL CATHOLICISM AND THE MODERN WORLD"

The term "Liberal Catholicism" seems to have been first used in this country by W. Norman Pittenger. Mr. Pittenger (as he then was) came to the General Seminary by way of Columbia University and Oxford, where he had been in close contact with the teaching of the English Catholic Modernists. An article of his in *The Christian Century*[20] for October 5, 1932, may be considered the American preface to this phase of the Catholic Movement. In this article, Mr. Pittenger defines Liberal Catholicism as that form of Christian thought which

> "stands for the maintenance of the central affirmations of historical Christianity as a religion centering about the person and work of Jesus Christ, while at the same time it welcomes all new knowledge from whatever source it may come and continually seeks to reinterpret the tradition in the light of that knowledge."

He claims as adherents of this school such figures as Bernard Iddings Bell, Paul Elmer More, and Frank Gavin.

[20] It is important to note that this is a non-denominational religious periodical, probably the most influential journal in American Protestantism. Fr. Pittenger has always been aware of Protestantism in a way that some Anglo-Catholics have not.

THE CATHOLIC MOVEMENT IN THE EPISCOPAL CHURCH

On October 21, 1933, *The Living Church* inaugurated a series of articles significantly entitled *Liberal Catholicism and the Modern World*. These articles, Part I of which, on "Belief," was later published in book form, might be called the American counterpart of *Lux Mundi*. To informed readers of the present day, this title may well seem a contradiction in terms, since, in 1949, "Liberal" and "Catholic" have been deformed into antithetic party labels. But the term was chosen with great deliberation. The aim of the theology set forth in the papers composing this volume was

> "to preserve the best of the past in the light of the best of the present so as to build for the best future."[21]

Furthermore, the editors contended that

> "Liberal is a good term. It connotes freedom, adventure, independence, and that dignified quality of the human spirit by which it affirms its hostility to all enslavements, tyrannies, blindnesses, errors, and falsehoods."[22]

Finally, the writers claim that

> "It is our peculiar privilege as Anglicans to set forward and bear witness to a Catholicism that is not imperialistic but free; and to a liberalism that has its living roots in the congenial atmosphere of a vital tradition."[23]

The Rev. Frank Gavin, holder of the historic chair of ecclesiastical history at the General Theological Seminary, the chair of Whittingham, Mahan and Seymour, was the editor of the series; and he was ably seconded, among others, by Cuthbert A. Simpson, Edward R. Hardy, Jr., and Marshall Bowyer Stewart, of the General faculty; by Frederick C. Grant, of Seabury-Western; by William H. Dunphy, formerly of Nashotah; and by Granville Williams, SSJE. The series was also made notable by the inclusion among its contributors of a number of eminent and scholarly laymen—Professors Wilbur M. Urban of Yale, and Jared S. Moore of Western Reserve; Clinton

---
[21] *Liberal Catholicism and the Modern World*, p. vi.
[22] *Ibid.*, p. vii.
[23] *Ibid.*, p. xi.

Rogers Woodruff, Miss Adelaide T. Case and Miss Vida Scudder—who acted as an excellent corrective to the unfortunate tendency of High Churchmanship to become a clerical preserve.

Dr. Simpson's essay on the Old Testament, engagingly entitled "Sources of Our Faith and Our Faith in the Sources," is a masterly piece of condensed statement. Going far beyond Hall in his receptivity to critical results, Simpson here states that not only the Pentateuch, but also the historical, and even the prophetic books, are of composite authorship. But this is to him a gain, not a loss, since the true value of all the books of the Old Testament is their clear witness to the *developing* faith of the Jewish Church as a whole. It is their sanction and acceptance by the corporate body that gives them their authority. Thus, he is applying to the Old Testament what might be called the Hobartian canon, though Hobart was not its originator; we hold, not to Scripture as a thing by itself, but to Scripture interpreted by tradition. Dr. Simpson was, as must be obvious to every careful reader of this chapter, a pupil of Fosbroke, and he here follows Fosbroke in summarizing, in clear-cut terms, the positive and remaining religious value of the Old Testament, after criticism has dealt with the documents in the case. Since Fosbroke rarely committed himself to writing, this essay may perhaps be regarded as the best expression of the Fosbrokian gospel in permanent form. But its lucidity of expression, while partly due to the fact that the writer is here dealing with a synthesis already achieved, owes more to the clear intelligence of Dr. Simpson. His conclusion is:

> "Liberal Catholics in accepting the results of criticism are not assenting to an undermining of the foundations of the Christian faith. Rather they are welcoming a discipline which has delivered the record of God's self-revelation to Israel from the realm of legend, and placed it in the clear light of history, where, examined and tested, it has ceased to be a source of embarassment, while it remains a source of our faith."[24]

By contrast with the cameo-like clearness of Dr. Simpson, Dr. Grant's corresponding essay on the New Testament can only be de-

[24] *Liberal Catholicism*, p. 40.

scribed as disappointing. It contains many excellent things. There is in it a straightforward attack on "biblicism," and a defence of the critical view of the Scriptures as being truly the Catholic view. This is accompanied by a rather lengthy parenthesis, good in itself but hardly relevant, the point of which is that Catholic and Protestant are not truly contrasted and antithetical terms, but rather complementary, and that Protestantism

> "is destined to turn out in the end to be but one episode in the long life of the Catholic Church, partly within it, perhaps partly outside it."[25]

The only direct reference to a critical question occurs when Grant mentions "formgeschichte" as a demonstration that the Gospels are not, strictly speaking, sources for the life of our Lord, but for "the Life and Teaching of the Lord as the Church conceived and believed in Him." The conclusion drawn from this is that "we simply haven't the data for a Life of Jesus in the modern sense of a biography."[26] But the essay as a whole tends to leave the reader floating in the vague. There is no summing up of the assured results of New Testament criticism, and no statement of the crucial questions opened up by that criticism.

Father Dunphy's eloquent chapter on "Christ and the Christian" is a horse of another color. Dunphy welcomes evolutionary thinking, because

> "modern science, illuminated by Revelation, teaches us how one kingdom of life was built upon another, how each lower kingdom ministers to the higher and conditions it, but does not create it."

He takes his stand firmly on the Chalcedonian Christology:

> "If we cannot," he asserts, "in Nestorian fashion, permit naturalistic science and unassisted human reason to dictate to us our faith, no more can we, as unconscious Monophysites, suppress natural knowledge or reason, or seek to alter or manipulate the

[25] *Liberal Catholicism*, p. 48.
[26] *Ibid.*, p. 52.

facts of history or science in the supposed cause of Christian truth."[27]

But Dunphy is well aware that the critical method may be carried to an unhealthy extreme. He is opposed to those who, "with a well-intentioned desire to 'simplify' the Gospel, have really castrated it." He feels that "moderns who would create a gulf between the 'Jesus of history' and the 'glorified Christ' are in the unhappy tradition" of Nestorius and Arius.[28] He accepts unhesitatingly the supernatural birth of Christ and the objective fact of the empty tomb. In definiteness of statement and clean-cut distinction, this paper is one of the gems of the series.

Dr. Stewart's paper on "Freedom and Authority" is a characteristic production of that careful but ingenious theologian. Analyzing authority as it has appeared in Christian history, he reduces it to two cardinal principles—Apostolicity and Catholicity. What these meant in the early Church is at once evident. But, in Dr. Stewart's view, they are enduring factors in Church thinking, and, reduced to modern practice, they become "the authority of the expert over the unlearned," and "the authority of the whole over the part."[29] Now these two have distinct functions, and are often found in conflict:

"Apostolicity discovers, Catholicity reads the papers and weighs and judges of the general bearing of the discoveries. Apostolicity puts forth theses, Catholicity synthesizes. Apostolicity is inspired; Catholicity tries the spirits.."

It is in the struggle between these two that freedom has its chance.

"There is a tension, and always will be until we all have the Beatific Vision, a tension between different kinds of authority (credibility), each of which is deeply, steadily sound and right."[30]

In this state of tension, with its accompanying freedom, Dr. Stewart, like a good Anglican, is content to live.

[27] *Liberal Catholicism*, p. 20.
[28] *Ibid.*, p. 17.
[29] *Ibid.*, p. 129.
[30] *Ibid.*, p. 131.

THE CATHOLIC MOVEMENT IN THE EPISCOPAL CHURCH

These papers began to appear in the fall of 1933, and were published in a collected volume in the following year. The date is significant. In 1929, the crash of the stock market ushered in the great depression. In 1932, Franklin Delano Roosevelt was elected President of the United States, and in 1933 the "New Deal" started on its meteoric and controversial course. The result of these things was that the people of the United States had become conscious as never before of the importance of economics. Capitalism vs. Socialism; *laissez faire* vs. a planned economy—everyone was thinking and talking of these things. Now it is a truism that the Church cannot live forever in a cloister; her theologians do not think in a vacuum; doctrine does affect life. And so it was but right and natural that the leaders of Liberal Catholicism should turn their thinking toward the social order. Therefore, the first series of papers in this manifesto on "Belief" was followed by a second, attempting to show how the Catholic Faith might be applied to modern life. It is unnecessary to give the papers of this second series,[a] which were never republished in book form, the careful examination we have given to the first; but it is important to note that here we find Liberal Catholicism in close alliance with political liberalism.

THE SITUATION TODAY

Unlike both *Essays and Reviews* and *Lux Mundi, Liberal Catholicism and the Modern World* represented, not an attack on an advanced position, but rather the consolidation of lines already won. It caused no conflict, but was received with general acclaim by members of the High Church party. But it will be evident to any reader of these pages that party strife within the Church has its periods of crisis and its eras of comparative calm. Thus, the minor skirmishes of the 1820's, centering largely around the controversial figure of Bishop Hobart, led up to the pitched battle of the Forties. During the two succeeding decades, the fighting gradually died out, until it was

[a]For a list of the essays and authors of this second series, *see* Bibliography at the end of this chapter.

lost in the secular thunder of the Civil War. In 1868, the conflict was renewed, but by 1875 this campaign was over, and except for occasional minor engagements, High Churchmen and Low lived in comparative amity until the McGarvey secessions of 1908. But this never developed into a major crisis, and after it was over, there was again quiet.

Once again, as I write these pages, we live in the midst of alarms. The present battle appears to have been precipitated by the various proposals for union with the Presbyterians; but in times of stress and tension, the battle inevitably spreads from its original field, and there is a general tightening of party lines, a girding for the battle.

This present tension has affected the fortunes of Liberal Catholicism. Much has been accomplished. The battle of the Old Testament is over. High Churchmen, as a whole, have accepted the critical position; I think it fair to say that no High Churchman today would endorse the Biblical views of Liddon or Ritchie.

But criticism of the New Testament has of necessity touched on many sensitive spots in Catholic thinking. The implications of the full humanity of our Lord; the nature of the authority of the Church, and the precise location of that authority; the credibility of New Testament miracles, and especially of the Virgin Birth and the bodily Resurrection; the doctrine of the Atonement; the theology of the Eucharist—Catholic theologians have been forced to re-think all these once more in the light of new facts.

The result has been a new subdivision within the High Church party. Just as Hobartians once battled Tractarians, as Ritualists fought with Tractarians, so now there is a decided variance between conservative and modernist Catholic. What the upshot is to be, the historian of the next generation may record.

BIBLIOGRAPHY

Catholic Champion, The, 1888-1890.

GAVIN, FRANK (ed.), *Liberal Catholicism and the Modern World*, (Milwaukee, 1934), pp. 197. [This is Part I: Belief. Other essayists in this volume, in addition to those mentioned in the text are: Charles L. Street, Alfred Newberry, H. Flanders Dunbar, and F. Hastings Smyth.]

— PART II, *The Living Church*, Vols. 90 and 91 (Feb. 3, 1934-June 2, 1934), pp. 429-949, 9f. The essays and authors in chronological order of publication were as follows:
"Asceticism and the Religious Life," by Rev. Mother Mary Maude, CSM.
"The Life of Prayer," by Rev. Frank L. Vernon.
"The Ministry of the Word," by Fr. Joseph, OSF.
"The Sacrament of Penance," by Rev. John R. Oliver.
"Catholic Sociology," by Rev. C. Rankin Barnes.
"The Anglo-Catholic Movement in the Next Century," by Vida D. Scudder.
"Social Action," by Mary K. Simkhovitch.
"The Oxford Movement and Social Practice," by Clinton R. Woodruff.
"The Economic Order," by Niles Carpenter.
"Human Relations and Adjustments," by Anna S. Allen.
"Reunion," by Rt. Rev. Frank E. Wilson.
"Missions," by Rev. E. L. Souder.
"Liberal Catholicism and the Eastern Churches," by Rev. R. F. Lau.
"Ecumenicity," by Rev. B. I. Bell.
"Revival of Liturgical Music," by Rev. Walter Williams.
"Catholicism and Modern Art," by Chandler R. Post.
"Liberal Catholicism—Its Architectural Expression," by Ralph Adams Cram.

HALL, FRANCIS J., *Dogmatic Theology* (10 vols., New York, 1907-1922).

[I have been greatly helped in preparing this chapter by the Rev. Drs. Burton Scott Easton, M. Bowyer Stewart, and W. Norman Pittenger.]

CHAPTER ELEVEN

THE MOVEMENT AND PRAYER BOOK REVISION

THE weight of any intellectual movement may be measured in two ways. One may determine its importance by its direct influence on those who avowedly subscribe to its principles, who know exactly what they are about, and who have a definite program of changes which they wish to effect. Or one may study its leavening effect on the great mass of mankind, who are more or less unconsciously moved in the general direction taken by the mental current set up by the reforming leaders.

Thus we may estimate the High Church movement by trying to discover what it has done to those who call themselves Anglo-Catholics, or we may attempt to ascertain how it has changed the life and thought of all, or most of, the members of the Episcopal Church in America. Catholicism, being the very opposite of sectarianism, must of necessity aim, not at the cultivation of a few select souls, not at the formation of esoteric cliques, but at the elevation of the Church as a whole. And only by studying its effect on the Church as a whole can we obtain any true judgment of the importance and achievement of the High Church movement.

THE PRAYER BOOK IN AMERICA

Probably the best gauge for measuring this diffused effect of the Catholic revival is the Book of Common Prayer. To outsiders the respect and affection with which Episcopalians regard the Prayer Book seem to approach fetish worship; but those within the Church, knowing full well how profoundly the book affects, and has for centuries affected, the inner life of every churchman, feel quite otherwise about the matter. In practice, the religion of Episcopalians centers far less in the Bible than in the Prayer Book. The Church as a whole, like any other large organization, is a slow-moving body, intensely conservative, extremely reluctant to change its mind or its habits. And the Church has demonstrated her regard for the Prayer Book by making any changes in its pages a complicated and difficult task.

An alteration in the Book of Common Prayer must be proposed in General Convention and passed by both houses. Every diocesan convention is then notified of the action of General Convention. Finally, at the General Convention three years later, after everyone has had opportunity for discussion and consideration, the alterations are again acted upon, and only when passed this second time do they become a part of the Prayer Book. This complicated procedure ensures that no change shall be made hastily, and that any alteration shall represent, not a passing fashion or a successful bit of party strategy, but the sober judgment of the whole Church. When, therefore, we find the Prayer Book being changed, and the changes taking a decided direction, we have good reason for assuming from such evidence that the Church has changed her mind, and that she is moving in the direction which the changes indicate.

The American Church first attempted to revise the Book of Common Prayer in 1785, when the notorious "proposed Book," which we have previously discussed, was brought forth. Fortunately, this book, with its decided smell of heresy, was still-born. The American Prayer Book, as finally adopted in 1789, was a far less radical document. But it differed from its English ancestor in many particulars, and those particulars were signifiicant. True, the canon of the Eucharist was made decidely more Catholic by the insertion of the consecration prayer from the Scottish office; but to balance this gain, the Athanasian Creed and the Ornaments Rubric were omitted, psalms were substituted for the Magnificat and Nunc Dimittis, and only the truncated Benedictus was given. These omissions are indicative of a decidedly non-Catholic trend in the mind of the American Church in 1789. Of similar import was the insertion, in the Ordinal of 1792, of the alternative ordination formula, which significantly omitted all mention of the priestly power to forgive sins.

The first indication in the Prayer Book of the turn of the tide came in 1804, when the Office of Institution of Ministers was added. This office came directly from Connecticut, and well expresses the mind of the old High Churchmen. In it the title, "Eucharist," is used; the priest is authorized to perform "every act of sacerdotal function"; the term "altar" is frequently employed; and the teachings of the Seabury-Hobart school are echoed in the phrases: "Most gracious God, . . . who of thy wise providence has appointed divers Orders in thy Church," "O Holy Jesus, who . . . hast promised to be with the ministers of apostolic succession to the end of the world," and throughout the grand concluding prayer.

After this, for sixty years, the Prayer Book was untouched except for certain trivial alterations of no party significance whatever. The Memorial Movement of 1855 did contemplate radical changes, but the forces of conservatism were too strong, and nothing was then effected. But by the late Seventies, the mind of the American Church had changed, and changed so sharply, that the Prayer Book as it then stood was no longer thoroughly satisfactory.

THE REVISION OF 1892

The first impulse toward revision came, not from the High Church group, but from Broad Churchmen. The term Broad Churchman was used at this time to cover two widely differing sorts of churchmen. There were the so-called Broad Churchmen of the school of the deposed Bishop Cummins, men who were really descendants of the old Low Churchmen, and who carried theological laxity to the point of heresy. Of quite a different color were men like Bishop Henry Potter: sound churchmen themselves, they refused to emphasize points which they considered non-essential; liberals in the best sense, they stood for toleration of Catholic and Protestant alike.

Such a man was the Rev. William Reed Huntington of Worcester, Massachusetts (1862-83), and Grace Church, New York City (1883-

1909). In 1874, he had been a vigorous anti-ritualist, but, like many others, when the scare was over, his views had gradually changed. He called himself a Catholic; he affirmed the necessity of basic dogma; but he believed the Church could profitably abandon an attitude of mere do-nothing conservatism.

In the General Convention of 1877, Huntington introduced a resolution looking toward a modification of the Prayer Book, but this was defeated.[1] But throughout the Church, it was more and more being felt that changes were inevitable; in 1880, therefore, his resolution calling for a joint commission on liturgical enrichment found the Convention in a more receptive mood. He was supported by such decided High Churchmen as Adams of Wisconsin and Shattuck of Massachusetts, and by Phillips Brooks, the leader of the Broad Churchmen. The only opposition came from the old-line Low Churchmen, led by those veterans of many Convention wars, Judge Hugh W. Sheffey of Virginia, and the Rev. Daniel Goodwin of Pennsylvania, who feared that any sort of Prayer Book revision would be an opening of the flood-gates for the ritualists. The resolution was passed and a commission appointed. It was a well-balanced body, in which Bishops Williams, Doane, Young, and F. D. Huntington, and the Rev. Morgan Dix spoke for the various shades of High Churchmen, Bishop Coxe for the anti-ritualists, and Bishop William B. Stevens, the Rev. Dr. Goodwin, and Judge Sheffey for the Low Churchmen. Huntington himself was made secretary of the commission.[2]

Significantly, the commission laid down two basic principles before starting work. Nothing was to be changed which had any doctrinal implications; the door was definitely closed to those who still hoped to get regeneration out of the baptismal office. For a similar reason the Communion Service was not to be touched.[3] The report of the commission was issued in the form of the *Book Annexed*—a specimen Prayer Book incorporating the results of their work. This book repays careful study, revealing as it does the sound liturgical principles

[1] Suter, J. W., *Life and Letters of W. R. Huntington*, pp. 138-41.
[2] *Ibid.*, pp. 142-45.
[3] *Ibid.*, p. 147.

on which the commission generally based its work. It was definitely a return, first to the current English Prayer Book and beyond that to the first Prayer Book of Edward VI. It is, I think, possible to trace the hand of the High Church liturgiologist, Bishop Young, in such matters as the provision of a second set of propers for Christmas, Easter, and Whitsunday; in the new collect for Maundy Thursday; and in the making of the Creed in the Confirmation Office a definite declaration of faith by those about to be confirmed. Both High Churchmen and Broad Churchmen were apparently united in the permissive shortening of the daily offices. And the distinctive Broad Church influence appears in the newly composed offices of the Beatitudes of the Gospel and the short "form of prayer for sundry occasions."[4]

At the General Convention of 1883, most of the *Book Annexed* was accepted; the debates were remarkable for the general absence of party feeling. Two groups only were flatly against revision: the extreme Low Churchmen, who saw in these alterations the beginning of a subtle attempt to overthrow the work of the Reformation, and the extreme High Churchmen, led by Ritchie, who, having no hope of a revision that would satisfy them, preferred no revision at all.[5]

In the Convention of 1886, there was a decided reaction from the pleasant receptivity of 1883, and not until 1892 was the revised Prayer Book finally issued. In the final revision, both High Church and Broad Church gained some, but not all, of what they desired. The daily offices were made somewhat more flexible by the permission to omit the exhortation and the prayers after the third collect. In the Communion Service, the decalogue and the longer exhortations were made variable. But the two newly composed offices were dropped.

More important than these changes in the interest of liberty were the additions. The Feast of the Transfiguration was added to the calen-

[4]See *"Book Annexed," passim.*
[5]Suter, J. W., *Life and Letters of W. R. Huntington*, pp. 158-61. A similar group for similar reasons opposed the English revision of 1928.

dar, with collect, epistle and gospel provided; proper psalms were appointed for more of the great feasts; and, in the daily office, a large number of new introductory sentences, appropriate to the various seasons, was added. The Benedictus was given in its complete form, and the canticles, Magnificat and Nunc Dimittis, were restored to Evening Prayer, as were the versicles and responses from the English Prayer Book. A Penitential Office, drawn largely from the ancient Commination for Ash-Wednesday, was added, and the second set of propers for Christmas and Easter was accepted. It will be perfectly apparent that the general tendency of the revision was toward enrichment, and that most of the changes were really restorations of matter that had appeared in the first Prayer Book of Edward VI, and had later been dropped during periods of Protestant domination. That changes as numerous as these, and of such evident tendency, could be carried through without serious disagreement, is clear proof of the growing good feeling of the era, and of the extent to which the whole Church had moved in the High Church direction. A comparison of the Proposed Book of 1785 with the revised Prayer Book of 1892, gives one a very fair measure of the general diffusion throughout the Church of a more Catholic feeling.

THE INTERVAL BETWEEN REVISIONS

Great as were the advances accomplished by the revision of 1892, no one accepted that revision as final. But in the interval between the completion of this revision and the inception of the next, two allied questions aroused much more controversy than revision itself. As early as 1880 a movement was originated in the Mid-West to alter the name of the American Church in order to get rid of the objectionable term, "Protestant."[8] This, in the form of a proposal to amend the title page of the Prayer Book, nearly side-tracked the whole matter of revision in 1883. The proposal was decisively defeated, but its backers returned to the charge again and again. In 1907, it was one

[8] The first proposal to change the name of the Church, and to insert the term "Catholic," was made in 1844.

of the chief considerations before General Convention, was bitterly debated both in the press and on the Convention floor, and was again defeated. As a result, the wiser leaders of the High Church party were convinced that the time was not yet ripe, and that any immediate attempt at change of name would simply prevent all further revision of the Prayer Book. At the Convention of 1910, therefore, the Rev. William T. Manning, whose position as rector of Trinity Church, New York, gave him a commanding place in the High Church party, proposed that only by a two-thirds vote of both houses should the name of the Church be changed. This wise piece of statemanship had the result of setting at rest the fears of the conservatives.

The second allied question considered in the interval between the two revisions was that of reservation of the Blessed Sacrament. In 1895, the pastoral letter of the House of Bishops had explicitly declared that Reservation was not sanctioned in this Church. However, it was a notorious fact that Reservation, with its accompaniments of Adoration and Benediction, was openly practiced in a considerable number of parishes. The dropping of the canon on Eucharistic Adoration in 1904, while not so intended, seemed to give a sanction to these practices. In 1907, therefore, Bishop Hall, whose Catholicity no one could question, offered a resolution declaring against Reservation for purposes of worship or exposition, and against carrying the Sacrament in procession. But the committee of bishops, to whom the resolution was referred, stated that, since such practices were already clearly against the law of the Church, no new pronouncement on the subject was necessary.

THE REVISION OF 1928

Once again the initial impulse toward revision seems to have come from the Broad Church section. In 1913, the dioceses of Arizona and California presented to General Convention memorials asking for further revision. The actuating spirit in this move was apparently the Rev. Edward L. Parsons of California, who was also one of the leaders in the project on the floor of the House of Deputies. A joint commission was once more appointed, with Bishop Whitehead of Pittsburgh as its chairman, and such excellent students of liturgics as Hart, Parsons, Suter, Gummey, Robinson and St. George among its members.

The report of this commission, which was presented at the Convention of 1916, was in many respects a remarkable document. It re-proposed many of the features of the *Book Annexed* which had failed of passage. But liturgical science had made large advances since 1892, and the results of these advances were largely incorporated in the report. Setting aside the precedent of the previous revision, the commission boldly proceeded to re-examine the Communion Service, and extensive changes were proposed, mainly in the direction of a return to the first Prayer Book of Edward VI.[7]

There is no point in tracing here the necessarily slow process of revision—a process which was completed only in 1928. The Church had obviously changed her mind considerably since 1892. Carried through, like the previous revision, by a coalition of moderate High Churchmen, among whom Bishop Hall was notable, and intelligent Broad Churchmen like the Rev. Dr. Charles Lewis Slattery, the new Prayer Book contained decided changes in more than one direction.

Thus it bears witness to a considerable shift in the Church's avowed attitude toward Holy Scripture. The old Protestant view of the Bible, a view once largely shared by Episcopalians, was a near approach to fetish worship. The Bible, in this view, was all of a piece, all equally inspired and equally valuable, and any attempt to set up distinctions within its covers was damnable heresy. This attitude the Church, in the Prayer Book of 1928, quietly repudiated, accepting as her own the critical view of the Bible, which was one of the great intellectual accomplishments of the nineteenth century. Thus special psalms were provided for every Sunday of the year, so that the more notably un-Christian portions of the psalter could be practically dis-

[7]Parsons, E. L., and Jones, B. H., *The American Prayer Book*, pp. 59-61.

used in public worship. In the lectionary, a much larger use was made of the Apocrypha, once the detestation of all good Protestants. And even in the Epistles and Gospels, there was throughout a decided freedom in the treatment of Scripture, and a large amount of textual correction. This was, of course, a clear reversion to the ancient Catholic tradition of the Fathers, and would have been impossible without the growth of the Liberal Catholicism of Bishop Charles Gore and the Lux Mundi school.

In the daily offices, the tendency toward shortening and flexibility was carried still further than in 1892. It was now made permissible to omit the exhortation on all occasions, and even at most times the whole penitential introduction. This was a direct return to the first Prayer Book of Edward VI. The canticle *Benedictus es, Domine*, rejected in 1892, was adopted as an alternative to the Te Deum. The Breviary form of absolution was given. Another innovation coming direct from the Breviary was the provision of invitatory sentences before the Venite.

But the really important changes were those in the Communion Service. The word "militant" was significantly dropped from the title of the Prayer for the Church, and in the prayer was inserted this petition:

> And we also bless thy holy Name for all thy servants departed this life in thy faith and fear; beseeching thee to grant them continual growth in thy love and service . . .

Well might Bishop Whittingham, who had waged war against the clergy of Mount Calvary Church for using prayers for the dead, have turned in his grave at the sight of the Church thus officially writing into her most sacred office a definite petition for the souls of those departed, where its use would be compulsory every time Mass is said. Nor was this the only evidence of the Church's complete change of mind in regard to intercessions for the dead. In the burial office were inserted equally definite petitions; and a beautiful litany for the dying, breathing the deepest spirit of Catholic piety, was introduced. One of the most significant facts about these changes was their almost unanimous approval by the House of Deputies. Thus, after more than one hundred years, the Church as a whole had accepted the daring teaching of Bishop Hobart, with its inevitable implication of an intermediate state beyond the grave.

Other significant changes in the Communion Service were the permissive shortening of the Ten Commandments, the placing of the Lord's Prayer in its original position at the end of the Canon, and the Prayer of Humble Access immediately before the communion of the priest. In the Collects, Epistles and Gospels, there were three important additions: by providing suitable propers, the Church now licensed requiem Eucharists, nuptial Eucharists, and the commemoration of saints not in the official calendar.

In the baptismal office, a prayer of the eucharistic type for the blessing of the water was provided; in the visitation office, prayers for the unction of the sick; and in the marriage service, a prayer for the benediction of the ring. Finally, an office of instruction was set forth, drawn in part from the old catechism, setting forth in the most explicit terms the Catholicity of the Church, the nature and importance of Holy Orders, and the meaning of the Sacraments.

It is interesting to note some of the proposals for change which were not accepted. That of the Rev. John H. Melish, a rather extreme liberal, for a rubric which would have given each congregation almost complete liberty to use as much or as little of the Prayer Book as it pleased, was overwhelmingly defeated. The old High Church notion of complete uniformity of worship in all parishes had long since disappeared, but the Church was not yet prepared to license utter anarchy. Short shrift was given to the suggestion that the Athanasian Creed be reintroduced. And the recommendations of the joint commission in favor of "The Holy Eucharist" as an alternative title for "The Holy Communion," for the inclusion of the Agnus Dei and the Benedictus Qui Venit, and for the adoption of a rubric specifically permitting Reservation for the communion of the sick, were likewise rejected.

THE MOVEMENT AND PRAYER BOOK REVISION

In general, the book passed through all the long stages of revision with surprisingly little acrimony, and it was joyfully received by the great mass of churchmen. Two groups only manifested any considerable dissatisfaction—the diminishing band of old-style Low Churchmen, who, however, made no very vigorous attack, and the extremists on the opposite side. To this last group, the Prayer Book of 1928, like all its English and American predecessors, was a mere compromise, to be done away with as soon as possible.

"THE AMERICAN MISSAL"

And so the advanced High Churchmen prepared a book of their own, *The American Missal*, ostensibly to supply needed ceremonial directions and private devotions for the priest, but in practice an actual substitute for the Book of Common Prayer. The publication of this volume was the occasion for one of the Church's periodical ritual storms. The attacks were not directed particularly against the minute ceremonial directions, of which the book is full. Manuals for the clergy, containing such directions, had long been in use, and, indeed, in the present state of Prayer Book rubrics, are a necessity. The real gravamen was that the *Missal* interpolated a large amount of matter into and around the canon of the Eucharist, that it provided for the direct invocation of the saints, and, worst of all, that it encouraged that indefinable error called "Mariolatry."

That Low Church bishops should at once have attacked such a volume was to be expected; much more damaging were the condemnations, varying in strength, of such strong churchmen among the bishops as Johnson of Colorado, Fiske of Central New York, Moreland of Sacramento, Manning of New York, and Wilson of Eau Claire. To such men as these, thus to offer the Church a frankly partisan Prayer Book seemed a highly un-Catholic action, tending, indeed, to increase the obvious sectarianism within the Church, which is one of the evils of Anglicanism. The use of the *Missal* was, therefore, forbidden by many distinctly High Church bishops as a breach of Catholic unity.[8]

---

[8] Even *The American Missal*, was not enough for some. We now have *The English Missal*, which is merely the Roman Missal in a rather bad translation, with occasional permitted interpolations from the Book of Common Prayer.

THE CATHOLIC MOVEMENT IN THE EPISCOPAL CHURCH

THE CATHOLIC CONGRESS

The Prayer Book of 1928 measures quite accurately the diffusion of Catholic principles through the Church at large. But as High Churchmanship has broadened its influence, the High Church party, as such, has by no means relaxed its efforts. In 1923, the formation in New York City of the Central Conference of Associated Catholic Priests, with members from the First, Second, and Third Provinces, initiated a nation-wide organization of the High Church wing. It was a distinct attempt to break down the excessive individualism, which has been perhaps the greatest obstacle to the advance of Catholic principles. It was followed in 1924 by a priests' convention in Philadelphia, at which services were held in St. Mark's and St. Clement's, sermons were preached by Bishop Webb and Canon Bell, and addresses were made by many other lights of the movement. Visiting the convention were the presiding bishop, Bishop Talbot, and more surprising, the bishop of Pennsylvania.

In 1925, the first Catholic Congress was held in New Haven, Connecticut. This has been followed, at varying intervals, by similar great gatherings of priests and laity, at which the rites of the Church are performed with all the solemnity and magnificence the Church possesses. But the Catholic Congress has been more than a mere display, however splendid, of ecclesiastical millinery. It has provided a forum from which the leaders of the party, representing all the diverse shades of opinion which the High Church movement includes, could impress fundamental principles on the rank and file.

It is possible that the Congress which met at Philadelphia in 1933 will prove an important landmark in the history of Catholicism within the American Church. In England there has been since 1850 a close alliance between Catholicism and social reform. The famous churches of the English Catholic revival—St. Alban's, Holborn; St. Peter's, London Docks; St. Agatha's, Landport—made their name, not only by the splendor of their ceremonial, but by their apostolic work among the poor. In America, on the contrary, the connection between Catholic teaching and social justice has been less intimate, in spite of the example set by Father Huntington in the Eighties. But at the Congress of 1933, the Rev. Julian D. Hamlin, rector, appropriately, of the Church of the Advent, Boston, in a speech that was the sensation of the gathering, pointed out in these words the way for the next advance of American Catholicism:

> Sacramentalism lives in a world of thought where the machine must be used, not to enslave man, but to free him. It must not be used to exploit him. It must not be used to destroy his spirit or his creative activity. It must belong to God and man; which is only another way of saying that it must belong to Jesus Christ, for He is both. Sacramentalism has too often meant heated arguments about two sacraments or seven; heated metaphysical discussions about the nature of the Real Presence; groups of clergy sitting up all night in heated arguments about where the Gloria in Excelsis should be said, while the world passes on its way, and we with the stupendous gospel have been living with spiritual dynamite in our cupboard, and no thoughtful realization of how it can be applied to the world. We have been living in a world where men were made for machines, where machines have been used to destroy the human spirit, where grain elevators have been full of bread, and men and women have been starving.[9]

As we have seen, Fr. Hamlin's keynote was picked up and echoed by the writers of the second series in *Liberal Catholicism and the Modern World*. A further step in the same direction was the formation, in 1939, of the Society of the Catholic Commonwealth, an organization of priests and laymen which believes in the application of Catholic liturgical analysis to the secular social and economic process. Regardless of the merit of the particular reforms advocated from time to time by those who believe that there is a Catholic sociology, the orientation of the Catholic movement in this direction is a healthy demonstration to the world that ritualists are not mere ecclesistical milliners, nor High Churchmen merely snobs. It is an excellent cor-

[9]*The Living Church*, Vol. 90, p. 10.

rective to the eccentricities of the lunatic fringe—and the lunatic fringe we have always with us.

BIBLIOGRAPHY

HUNTINGTON, W. R., *Short History of the Book of Common Prayer with papers illustrative of Liturgical Revision,* (New York, 1892).

PARSONS, E. L., and JONES, B. H., *The American Prayer Book* (New York, 1937).

PROCTOR, F., and FRERE, W. H., *A New History of the Book of Common Prayer* (London, 1920).

SUTER, J. W., *Life and Letters of William Reed Huntington* (New York, 1925).

The Book Annexed (New York, 1885).

The Book of Common Prayer (New York, 1845). [Version of 1789.]
  Ibid. (New York, 1898). [Revision of 1892.]
  Ibid. (New York, 1929). [Revision of 1928.]

The English Missal for the Laity (London, 1933).

EPILOGUE

A MODERN AMERICAN DIOCESE

 VERY fair notion of the state of churchmanship in the American Church today might be obtained from a survey of the diocese in which this book is written. Organized as a separate diocese in 1868, it stands in one of the older sections of the country, containing some twenty-odd parishes founded before 1800. Like most of the northeastern dioceses, it holds within its limits a mixture of tendencies and traditions, lying thus between both extremes. It has had four bishops, all strong Catholics, but has never been subjected to such a regimentation as Bishop Grafton gave the diocese of Fond du Lac. Its churchmanship is, therefore, the result of a normal growth.

In the see city, from which the diocese takes its name, rises the half-finished structure of the first attempt at a building on the true cathedral scale in the American Church, even in its uncompleted state a noble House of God. Here, notably on Christmas Eve, one may see the Holy Eucharist celebrated with all that there is of dignity and splendor—the procession with thurifer, cross, and candles, winding through the long aisles to the high altar, where the sacred mysteries are performed by the priests, vested in full eucharistic vestments, attended by numerous servers, while the bishop pontificates in cope and mitre. And with all this richness of ceremonial, it is a service in strictest loyalty to the Book of Common Prayer, with no omission of confession and absolution, with no interpolation from alien rites—a Catholic service in the best sense.

Within the diocese are one hundred seventy-six parishes and missions. These may roughly be divided into four groups. There are nine parishes only that can fairly be labeled "Low"—parishes where the services are bare and lacking in reverence, where sacramental teaching and devotion to the sacraments are conspicuous by their absence, where doctrine is lax.

The great majority of the parishes fall into two divisions. Seventy-odd would have been considered High Church, even Romish, one hundred years ago. The routine of their services would probably be considered normal procedure today in the vast majority of churches in America. Vested choir, processional, and altar with cross, colored frontal, and candles, a low celebration every Sunday and holy day, with a late celebration on the first Sunday of the month—these are the external signs of the normal parish. Not quite so numerous—fifty-odd—are those parishes which might be called moderately ritualistic, which have, in addition to the points just enumerated, eucharistic vestments, either white or colored, servers, and more frequent celebrations, including in many cases a sung Mass every Sunday.

Finally, there is a group, eighteen in number, which stand out a bit as definitely "high," and which add to the practices of the last group the use of incense, private confessions, and the Reserved Sacrament. Even within this group I can count only three which are notably "spiky," which plainly ape Roman practices, which follow the Roman calendar, and which give the ordinary churchman the feeling that he has dropped into the wrong place. These are externals, but externals which mean much.

When one compares this state of things with that roughly sketched in the first chapter of this work, when one considers that there are in this comparatively small and poor diocese more parishes, more priests, more communicants than there were in the whole United States at the close of the Revolution, one begins to have some conception of the almost miraculous revival of the American Episcopal Church since that day. In this revival, all parties, all sections of the Church, have had their part. Evangelicals have contributed fire and missionary spirit. Broad Churchmen, by insisting on re-interpretations of the

Church's teaching in the light of modern science and scholarship, have kept the door open for throngs of intelligent people driven out of other bodies by ignorance and obscurantism. But the chief credit belongs, I am firmly convinced, to those far-sighted pioneers who have, through strife and persecution, re-awakened within the Church a consciousness of her Catholicity, who have re-taught the Catholic faith, who have re-lit the fires of Catholic devotion.

In the hope that all churchmen may, through this brief and imperfect survey, come to have a fuller understanding of what Catholicism means, and what it has done for the Episcopal Church in America, this book is written.

CONSOLIDATED BIBLIOGRAPHY

I. Official Publications

Book of Common Prayer (New York, 1845). [Version of 1789.]
— *Ibid.* (New York, 1898). [Version of 1892.]
— *Ibid.* (New York, 1929). [Version of 1928.]

The Book Annexed (New York, 1885).

Proposed Book of Common Prayer (1785).

DIOCESE OF ALBANY,
    Convention Journal, 1870, 1875, 1877, 1890.

DIOCESE OF FOND DU LAC,
    Convention Journal, 1875, 1900.

DIOCESE OF ILLINOIS,
    Convention Journal, 1874, 1875.

DIOCESE OF NEW YORK,
    Convention Journal, 1841, 1845, 1852, 1855.

GENERAL CONVENTION OF THE PROTESTANT EPISCOPAL CHURCH IN THE UNITED STATES OF AMERICA,
    Journal of, 1844, 1853, 1868, 1871, 1874, 1880, 1907.

Proceedings of the Court Convened for the Trial of the Right Rev. Benjamin T. Onderdonk, D.D. (New York, 1845).

The Revision of the Book of Common Prayer (Milwaukee, 1925).

II. General Histories

CHORLEY, E. CLOWES,
    Men and Movements in the American Episcopal Church (New York, 1946).

MCCONNELL, S. D.,
    History of the American Episcopal Church (New York, 1891).

MANROSS, W. W.,
    History of the American Episcopal Church (New York, 1935).

CONSOLIDATED BIBLIOGRAPHY

PERRY, W. S.,
History of the American Episcopal Church (2 vols., Boston, 1885).

III. DIOCESAN AND PARISH HISTORIES

ADVENT, CHURCH OF,
A Sketch of the History of the Parish of the Advent in the City of Boston (Boston, 1894).

BATAILLE, E. F.,
Grace Church in Newark (New York, 1937).

BEARDSLEY, E. E.,
History of the Episcopal Church in Connecticut (2 vols., New York and London, 1868).

DEMILLE, G. E.,
A History of the Diocese of Albany (Philadelphia, 1946).

DIX, M.,
A History of the Parish of Trinity Church in the City of New York (6 vols., New York, 1898ff.)

GRAY, L. H.,
History of the Parish of St. Ignatius (New York, 1946).

HALL, J.,
Annals of the Parish of St. Peter's, Ashtabula, Ohio (MSS. in General Theological Seminary library).

HAYES, C. W.,
The Diocese of Western New York (Rochester, 1904).

HOPKINS, J. H. 3RD,
The Great Forty Years (Chicago, 1936).

REED, N. F.,
The Story of St. Mary's (New York, 1931).

SHINN, G. W.,
King's Handbook of Notable Episcopal Churches (Boston, 1889).

SMYTHE, G. F.,
History of the Diocese of Ohio until the year 1918 (Cleveland, 1931).

TUTTLE, MRS. H. C.,
History of St. Luke's Church, New York (New York, 1926).

WILSON, J. G.,
The Centennial History of the Protestant Episcopal Church in the Diocese of New York (New York, 1886).

IV. BIOGRAPHIES

AYRES, ANNE,
The Life and Work of William Augustus Muhlenberg (New York, 1881).

BARRY, J. G. H.,
Impressions and Opinions (New York, 1931).

BEARDSLEY, E. E.,
Life and Correspondence of the Rt. Rev. Samuel Seabury (Boston, 1881).

BEARDSLEY, E. E.,
Life and Correspondence of Samuel Johnson (Boston, 1887).

BRAND, W. F.,
Life of William Rollinson Whittingham (2 vols., New York, 1886).

BRECK, C.,
Life of the Rev. James Lloyd Breck (New York, 1886).

CROSWELL, H.,
A Memoir of the Life of the Late Rev. William Croswell (New York, 1853).

DIX, M.,
Harriet Starr Cannon (New York, 1896).

DOANE, W. C.,
Memoir of the Life of George Washington Doane (New York and London, 1860).

GRAFTON, C. C.,
A Journey Godward (Milwaukee, 1910).

GREEN, HOWARD,
The Reverend Richard Fish Cadle (Waukesha, 1936.)

HALL, F. J.,
Life of the Rev. John Hall (MSS. in the library of the General Theological Seminary; published in *Historical Magazine of the Protestant Episcopal Church*, Vol. IV, pp. 308-313).

HARRISON, H.,
Life of the Rt. Rev. John Barrett Kerfoot (2 Vols., New York, 1886).

HAYWOOD, M. DEL.,
Lives of the Bishops of North Carolina (Raleigh, 1910). [Especially valuable for the lives of Bishops Ravenscroft and Ives.]

CONSOLIDATED BIBLIOGRAPHY

HENSHAW, J. P. K.,
Memoir of the Life of the Rt. Rev. Richard Channing Moore (Philadelphia, 1842).

HEWIT, A. F.,
Life of the Rev. Francis A. Baker (New York, 1868).

HODGES, G.,
Henry Codman Potter (New York, 1915).

HOLCOMBE, J.,
An Apostle of the Wilderness (New York, 1903). [Concerned with James Lloyd Breck.]

HOPKINS, J. H., JR.,
The Life of Bishop Hopkins (New York, 1873).

HUNTINGTON, A. S.,
Memoir and Letters of F. D. Huntington (Boston, 1906).

JOHNS, J.,
Memoir of the Life of the Rt. Rev. William Meade (Baltimore, 1867).

KNAUFF, C. W.,
Doctor Tucker, Priest-Musician (New York, 1897).

MCVICKAR, J.,
Early Years of the Late Bishop Hobart (New York, 1834).
— *Professional Years of Bishop Hobart* (New York, 1836).

NORTON, J. N.,
The Life of Bishop Ravenscroft (New York, 1859).

PENNINGTON, EDGAR L.,
Apostle of New Jersey, John Talbot, (Philadelphia, 1938).

RICHARDSON, G. L.,
Arthur C. A. Hall (Boston, 1932).

SCHROEDER, J. F.,
Memorial of Bishop Hobart (New York, 1831).

SCUDDER, V. D.,
Father Huntington (New York, 1940).

SEABURY, W. J.,
Memoir of Bishop Seabury (New York and London, 1908).

STONE, J. S.,
Memoir of the Life of the Rt. Rev. Alexander Viets Griswold (Philadelphia, 1844).

STOWE, W. H., and others,
The Life and Letters of Bishop William White (New York and Milwaukee, 1937).

SUTER, J. W.,
Life and Letters of William Reed Huntington (New York, 1925).

SWEET, C. F.,
A Champion of the Cross (New York, 1894). [John Henry Hopkins, II.]

TYNG, C. R.,
Life of Stephen H. Tyng (New York, 1890).

TURNER, S.,
Autobiography (New York, 1863).

UPJOHN, E. M.,
Richard Upjohn, Architect and Churchman (New York, 1939).

WALWORTH, C. A.,
Reminiscences of Edgar P. Wadhams (New York, 1893).

WARD, M.,
Father Maturin—A Memoir (London, 1920).

WHITE, G.,
An Apostle of the Western Church (New York, 1900). [Bishop Kemper.]
—*A Saint of the Southern Church* (New York, 1897). [Bishop Cobbs.]

V. MONOGRAPHS

ANONYMOUS,
Puseyite Developments (New York, 1850).

CLARKE, C. K. L.,
Bishop Hobart and the Oxford Movement (Milwaukee, 1933).

Debates of the House of Deputies of the General Convention of the Protestant Episcopal Church (Hartford, 1871).

DE KOVEN, J.,
Sermons Preached on Various Occasions (New York, 1880).

DOANE, G. W.,
A Brief Examination (Burlington, 1841).

EWER, F. C.,
Sermons on the Failure of Protestantism (New York, 1869).
—*Catholicity, Protestantism and Romanism* (New York, 1878).

CONSOLIDATED BIBLIOGRAPHY

GAVIN, F. (ed.),
    Liberal Catholicism and the Modern World (Milwaukee, 1934).

HARRISON, H.,
    Loose Him and Let Him Go (Boston, 1891).

HAWKS, E.,
    William McGarvey and the Open Pulpit (Philadelphia, 1935).

HOBART, J. H.,
    Apology for Apostolic Order, in *The Churchman Armed* (New York, 1844).
    — *Companion for the Altar* (New York, 1843).
    — *The State of the Departed* (New York, 1825).

HOPKINS, J. H.,
    The Law of Ritualism (New York, 1866).
    — *The Novelties which Disturb our Peace* (Philadelphia, 1844).

HUNTINGTON, W. R.,
    Short History of the Book of Common Prayer with Papers illustrative of Liturgical Revision (New York, 1892).

MCILVAINE, C. P.,
    Oxford Divinity (London, 1841).
    — *Charge to the Clergy of the Diocese of Ohio* (New York, 1843).

PACKARD, A. A.
    Pretractarianism in America (MSS. in the library of the General Theological Seminary).

PARSONS, E. L., AND JONES, B. H.,
    The American Prayer Book (New York, 1937).

POOR CLARES OF REPARATION AND ADORATION, THE (Compiler),
    Religious Communities in the Episcopal Church (West Park, 1945).

POTTER, ALONZO, (editor),
    The Memorial Papers (Philadelphia, 1857).

PROCTOR, F., AND FRERE, W. H.,
    A New History of the Book of Common Prayer (London, 1920).

ST. JOHN THE EVANGELIST, SOCIETY OF,
    The Cowley Fathers (Cambridge, 1930).

The Batterson Case (collection of pamphlets in the library of the General Theological Seminary).

The Prescott Case (collection of pamphlets in the library of the General Theological Seminary).

WALWORTH, C. A.,
The Oxford Movement in America (New York, 1895).

WILLIAMS, N. P., (editor),
Northern Catholicism (London and New York, 1933).

VI. PERIODICALS

American Churchman, The, 1870.

Catholic Champion, The, 1888-90.

Church Journal, 1853-75.

Churchman, The, 1804-80.

Historical Magazine of the Protestant Episcopal Church, 1932-1949.

Living Church, The, 1878-1933.

[The dates indicated are those of the years for which I have used these periodicals.]

GENERAL INDEX

A

Adams, Rev. William, 43, 45, 150, 194.
Albany, Diocese of, 99, 116, 205-6.
Anthon, Rev. Henry, 56, 88.
Apostolic Succession, Doctrine of, 11, 12, 15, 18, 30, 36, 52, 78.
Architecture, Church, 28, 37, 75-6, 78-9, 84.
Ayres, Anne, 134.

B

Baker, Rev. Francis A., 67, 79, 106.
Baptismal Regeneration, Controversies over, 13, 36, 124, 151.
Barry, Rev. J. G. H., 158, 165, 166n.
Batterson, Rev. Hermon, 110.
Bayley, Most Rev. James R., 67, 106, 107.
Bibliography, 8, 38, 72, 87, 107, 131, 147, 161, 170, 190, 204.
— Consolidated, 208-14.
Book Annexed, The, 194.
Bowles, Rev. Charles, 165.
Breck, Rev. James L., 43, 45, 77, 115.
Brent, Rt. Rev. Charles H., 139.
Broad Church Party, 172, 193.
Brooks, Rt. Rev. Phillips, 80, 138, 194.
Brotherhood of St. Barnabas, 145-6.
Brown, Rt. Rev. John H. H., 130, 153.
Brown, Rev. Thomas M., 110.
Brownell, Rt. Rev. Thomas C., 35, 51, 64.
Burgess, Rt. Rev. George, 89.

C

Cadle, Rev. Richard, 45n.
Campbell, Rt. Rev. Robert H., 145.
Carey, Rev. Arthur, 43, 55-8.
Cathedrals in the American Church, 131, 205.
Catholic Congress, 202-4.
Cannon, Harriet Starr, 134.

Chandler, Rev. Thomas B., 10, 18.
Chapman, Rev. George T., 105.
Chase, Rt. Rev. Philander, 32n, 35, 57, 58, 64, 151.
Cheney, Rev. Charles E., 151.
Christ Church, New York, 99, 109.
Church Journal, The, 98.
Churchman, The, 26, 27, 36, 37, 41, 52.
Church of the Advent, Boston, 79-82, 92, 94, 128, 136.
Church of the Ascension, Chicago, 105, 128.
Church of the Evangelists, Philadelphia, 163.
Church of the Holy Communion, New York, 78, 82.
Church of the Holy Cross, Troy, N. Y., 78.
Church of St. Mary the Virgin, New York, 110, 126, 140.
Church of the Transfiguration, New York, 82, 113.
Claggett, Rt. Rev. Thomas J., 27n, 33.
Cobbs, Rt. Rev. Nicholas H., 50, 85, 105.
Cole, Rev. Azel D., 150, 156.
Common Prayer, Book of, 6, 14, 191-201.
Community of St. Mary, 122, 134, 169.
Companions of the Holy Saviour, 164.
Confession, Auricular, 21, 35, 91, 119, 127.
Congress, Catholic, 202-04.
Connecticut Converts, 4, 5, 10, 11.
Cowley Fathers, *see under* Society of St. John the Evangelist.
Coxe, Rt. Rev. Arthur C., 43, 77, 104, 113, 115, 116, 117, 121, 194.
Croswell, Rev. William, 80, 81.
Cummins, Rt. Rev. George D., 113, 124.
Curtis, Rt. Rev. A.A., 120.

[215]

GENERAL INDEX

D

Daily Offices, 9, 25, 35, 52, 68, 80, 83, 116, 164, 195.
Dana, Richard Henry, 80, 92.
Dashiell, Rev. George, 33.
Dead, Prayers for the, 21, 57, 110, 120, 199.
Dehon, Rt. Rev. Theodore, 31.
De Koven, Rev. James, 93-5, 115, 118, 121, 123, 130, 150, 152, 153, 172.
DeLancey, Rt. Rev. William H., 35, 52, 63, 64, 108.
Delany, Rev. Seldon P., 141.
Dix, Rev. Morgan, 95, 111, 121, 194.
Doane, Rev. George Hobart, 103, 107.
Doane, Rt. Rev. George W., 24-6, 29, 34, 35, 53, 62, 64, 67, 85, 88-9, 93.
Doane, Rt. Rev. William C., 80, 96, 99, 103, 111, 115, 116, 122n, 131, 139, 155n, 167, 176-7, 194.
Dod, Robert S., 142.
Dunphy, Rev. William H., 186.

E

Eastburn, Rt. Rev. Manton, 64, 80, 92, 113, 115.
Easton, Rev. Burton S., 157, 158, 164n, 166n, 178.
Ecclesiological Society of New York, 83.
Elliott, Rt. Rev. Stephen, 63.
Empie, Rev. Adam, 58.
Eucharist, Doctrine of the, 10, 13, 20, 21, 36, 52, 54, 94, 101, 111, 114-5, 118.
— Frequency of, 10, 25, 31, 35, 45, 47n, 68, 80, 82, 84, 116, 130, 160, 206.
— Reservation of, 83, 85, 91, 128, 197.
Evangelical Movement, 15, 16, 30, 32, 33, 34, 35, 47, 48, 49, 50, 58, 83.
Evans, Hugh Davey, 102.

Ewer, Rev. Ferdinand C., 99-102, 109, 128, 173-5.

F

Fay, Rev. Sigourney, 165, 169, 179.
Fiske, Rev. George M., 154, 168.
Fond du Lac, Diocese of, 130, 138, 153-5.
Forbes, Rev. John M., 67-9, 83, 111.
Fosbroke, Very Rev. H. E. W., 157, 158, 178, 180, 185.
Francis, Rev. Paul J., 166.
French, Rev. William G., 68.

G

Gardner, Rev. Walter, 153, 156.
Gavin, Rev. Frank, 183, 184, 190.
General Convention of 1844, 58-61.
— 1868, 113-15.
— 1871, 115-19.
— 1874, 121-5.
— 1877, 194.
— 1880, 194.
— 1883, 195.
— 1886, 195.
— 1892, 195-6.
— 1895, 197.
— 1904, 197.
— 1907, 197.
— 1910, 197.
— 1913, 197.
— 1928, 198.
General Theological Seminary, 22, 26, 43-4, 55, 61-3, 65-6, 69, 95, 111, 122, 128.
Gold, Rev. William J., 160.
Goodwin, Rev. Daniel C., 115, 121, 194.
Grace Church, Newark, 105.
Grafton, Rt. Rev. Charles C., 122, 129, 130, 135-8, 146, 154-5, 156, 169, 172.
Grant, Rev. Fredrick C., 185.
Griswold, Rt. Rev. Alexander V., 15, 16, 35, 48, 79.

H

Hall, Rt. Rev. A. C. A., 136, 137, 139, 140, 177, 197.
Hall, Rev. Francis J., 35n, 160, 161, 180-3.
Hall, Rev. John, 35, 83, 84.
Hamlin, Rev. Julian D., 203.
Hance, Gouverneur P., 145-6.
Hawks, Rev. Edward, 156, 166n, 169.
Hewit, Rev. Augustine F., 67.
Hobart, Rt. Rev. John H., 11, 15-24, 33, 40, 41, 80.
Hobart, Rev. John H., Jr., 45, 95, 104.
Hoffman, Very Rev. Eugene A., 105.
Holy Cross, Order of, 141-5.
Hopkins, Rt. Rev. John H., 28-9, 35, 37, 53-5, 55, 57, 61, 64, 76, 88, 91, 93, 111-13, 120.
Hopkins, Rev. John H., Jr., 95, 97-8, 99, 110, 113, 116, 121, 131, 152, 172.
Hopkins, Rev. John H., 3rd, 168.
Houghton, Rev. George B., 82.
Howe, Rt. Rev. M. A. DeW., 114, 115.
Huntington, Rt. Rev. Frederic D., 101, 115, 142, 194.
Huntington, Rev. J. O. S., 142-4, 155.
Huntington, Rev. William R., 193, 194.

I

Illinois, Diocese of, 122, 151-3.
Ives, Rt. Rev. Levi S., 35, 62, 63, 64, 68, 83, 90-2.

J

Jarratt, Rev. Devereux, 16, 30.
Jarvis, Rt. Rev. Abraham, 12.
Johns, Rt. Rev. John, 50, 64, 113, 115.
Johnson, Rev. Samuel, 10.

K

Kemp, Rt. Rev. James, 33.
Kemper, Rt. Rev. Jackson, 32, 35, 44, 45, 63, 64, 67, 94, 113, 116, 150, 172.
Kerfoot, Rt. Rev. John B., 77, 85, 113, 114, 115, 116.
Kip, Rt. Rev. William I., 102, 113.

L

Law of Ritualism, The, 112-13.
Lee, Rt. Rev. Alfred, 64, 114, 115, 142.
Liberal Catholicism, 166, 171-89.
Living Church, The, 160, 167, 184.
Low Church Party, 33, 34, 35, 47, 61, 62, 88, 124, 125, 194.
Lux Mundi, 175, 177.

M

Madison, Rt. Rev. James, 7.
Mahan, Rev. Milo, 95, 96, 97.
Markoe, William, 149.
Maryland, Diocese of, 27, 47.
Massachusetts, Diocese of, 25, 29.
McGarvey, Rev. William, 164, 166, 168, 169.
McIlvaine, Rt. Rev. Charles P., 35, 48, 51, 53, 57, 61, 62, 64, 89, 109, 113, 115, 172.
McLaren, Rt. Rev. William E., 128, 152, 159.
McMaster, B. B. J., 55, 56, 56n, 66, 67.
Mead, Rev. William Cooper, 115, 117, 123.
Meade, Rt. Rev. William, 3, 31, 34, 35, 49, 58, 63, 85, 89, 95.
Meads, Orlando, 117, 123.
Memorial Movement, 103-4.
Milwaukee, Diocese of, 157-8.
Missal, The American, 201.
Missions in the West, 23, 32.
— In Liberia, 144-5.
Mitre, Use of, 13, 33, 154, 155, 157.
Monasticism in the American Church, 133-147.
Moore, Rt. Rev. Benjamin, 18.
Moore, Rt. Rev. Richard C., 30, 35, 47.
Morrill, Rev. Charles W., 109.

GENERAL INDEX

Mt. Calvary Church, Baltimore, 119, 120, 128.
Muhlenberg, Rev. William A., 77-8, 103, 133, 134.

N

Nashotah House, 45, 149-51, 156-9, 165, 178, 179, 180.
Newman, John Henry, 20n, 38, 41, 53, 55, 68, 171.
New Jersey, Diocese of, 25, 34, 88, 96.
New York, Diocese of, 7, 64, 65.
Nicholson, Rt. Rev. Isaac L., 156, 158.
North Carolina, Diocese of, 31, 90-1.
Novelties which Disturb our Peace, The, 54.

O

Odenheimer, Rt. Rev. William H., 77, 83, 97, 114, 115, 116.
Ogilby, Rev. J. D., 60, 62.
Ohio, Diocese of, 35, 83.
Onderdonk, Rt. Rev. Benjamin T., 24, 35, 52, 53, 56, 63-5, 79.
Onderdonk, Rt. Rev. Henry U., 33, 35, 61.
Order of the Holy Cross, 141-5.
Osborne, Rt. Rev. Edward W., 136, 158, 168.
Otey, Rt. Rev. James H., 32, 35, 53, 63.
Oxford Divinity, 48.

P

Parsons, Rt. Rev. Edward L., 197.
Pennsylvania, Diocese of, 33, 61, 163.
Percival, Rev. Henry R., 163.
Perry, Rev. Calbraith G., 111, 120.
Pittenger, Rev. W. N., 183.
Pollard, Rev. Frederick, 79, 99.
Potter, Rt. Rev. Alonzo, 103.
Potter, Rt. Rev. Henry C., 126, 129, 142.
Potter, Rt. Rev. Horatio, 70, 134.
Prayer Book Revision, 191-201.

Prescott, Rev. Oliver S., 68, 92, 125, 135, 137, 153.
Preston, Rt. Rev. Thomas S., 68, 83, 106, 107.
Proposed Book of Common Prayer, 6, 14, 192.
Provoost, Rt. Rev. Samuel, 7, 33.
Putnam, Edward, 67.

R

Racine College, 93, 94, 150, 151.
Ravenscroft, Rt. Rev. James, 31, 34.
Real Presence, Doctrine of, *see under* Eucharist.
Reformed Episcopal Church, 124, 151.
Reservation of the Blessed Sacrament, *see under* Eucharist.
Revision of the Book of Common Prayer, 15, 191-201.
Richards, Rev. Henry L., 67, 84.
Richey, Rev. Joseph, 120.
Ritchie, Rev. Arthur, 126, 128-9, 177, 195.
Ritualism, 29, 44, 47n, 74-87, 97, 105, 108-31, 151, 155, 156, 165, 205.
Robbins, Very Rev. Wilford L., 180.
Roman Catholic Church, 55, 67, 68, 96, 106, 120, 158, 166, 179.
— Secessions to, *see under* Secessions.

S

St. Alban's Church, New York, 109.
St. Clement's Church, Philadelphia, 105, 110, 125, 128, 137, 142, 202.
St. Elizabeth's Church, Philadelphia, 164.
St. Ignatius' Church, New York, 100, 126, 128.
St. Mark's Church, Philadelphia, 94, 158, 202.
St. Mary's Church, Burlington, N. J., 9.
St. Paul's Church, Baltimore, 26, 97.
St. Peter's Church, Philadelphia, 83.
St. Stephen's Church, Providence, 82, 154.

GENERAL INDEX

Scripture, Authority of, 51, 171-89.
Seabury, Rt. Rev. Samuel, 7, 11-15.
Seabury, Rev. Samuel, II, 27, 36, 41-2, 52, 57, 110.
Secessions to Rome, 65-69, 103, 106-07, 169-70.
Seymour, Rt. Rev. George F., 95, 97, 111, 122, 129, 130, 139, 151, 152, 160.
Simpson, Rev. Cuthbert A., 185.
Sisterhood of the Holy Communion, 134.
Sisterhoods in the American Church, 134-135.
Smith, Rev. Hugh, 56.
Society of St. John the Evangelist, 125, 135-41.
Southgate, Rt. Rev. Horatio, 65, 82, 105.
Stuart, Rev. John, 11.
Stevens, Rt. Rev. William B., 110, 117, 125, 143, 194.
Stewart, Rev. M. Bowyer, 187.
Surplice, Use of the, 25, 74, 81, 129.

T

Talbot, Rev. John, 9.
Tate, Rev. Colin, 109.
Tracts for the Times, 40-72, 78.
Trinity Church, Boston, 25, 81.
Trinity Church, Nantucket, Mass., 49, 79.
Trinity Church, New York, 17, 64, 76, 83, 94, 95.
True Catholic, The, 102.
Tucker, Rev. John I., 43, 77, 78, 111, 115.
Turner, Rev. Samuel, 44.
Tyng, Rev. Stephen H., 36n, 58, 60.

U

Upfold, Rt. Rev. George, 104, 113, 115.
Upjohn, Richard, 76, 81n, 83.

V

Valle Crucis, Monasticism at, 68, 83, 90-1.
Vermont, Diocese of, 14, 29, 140.
Vestments, Eucharistic, 97, 109, 116.
Villatte, Rene Joseph, 154.
Virginia, Colonial Church in, 1, 2, 3.
Virginia, Diocese of, 2, 50, 126.

W

Wadhams, Rt. Rev. Edgar, 43, 66, 67, 67n, 106.
Wainwright, Rt. Rev. Jonathan M., 43, 65, 102.
Walworth, Rev. Clarence, 43, 66, 67.
Waterman, Rev. Henry, 82, 115.
Webb, Rt. Rev. William W., 155, 157, 164, 165, 202.
Weller, Rt. Rev. Reginald H., 155.
Welles, Rt. Rev. Edward R., 157.
Western Theological Seminary, 159-60.
Whicher, Benjamin, 67, 106, 107.
White, Rt. Rev. William, 4, 12, 17, 33, 35, 78.
Whitehead, Rt. Rev. Cortlandt, 143, 146, 198.
Whitehouse, Rt. Rev. Henry J., 102, 131, 151, 172.
Whittingham, Rt. Rev. William R., 26-7, 35, 44, 47, 52, 64, 67, 74, 85, 92, 93, 115, 117, 120, 137.
Williams, Rt. Rev. John, 65, 102, 113, 114, 115, 116, 172, 194.
Wyatt, Rev. William E., 27n, 47, 47n.

Y

Young, Rt. Rev. John F., 104, 111, 117, 194.

[219]

www.ingramcontent.com/pod-product-compliance
Lightning Source LLC
Chambersburg PA
CBHW070313230426
43663CB00011B/2113